Reel Fulfillment

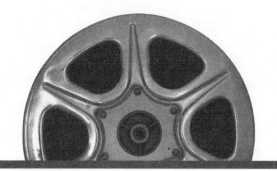

A 12-STEP PLAN FOR TRANSFORMING
YOUR LIFE THROUGH MOVIES

MARIA GRACE, Ph.D.

McGraw·Hill

New York   Chicago   San Francisco   Lisbon   London   Madrid   Mexico City
Milan   New Delhi   San Juan   Seoul   Singapore   Sydney   Toronto

Library of Congress Cataloging-in-Publication Data

Grace, Maria.
    Reel fulfillment : a twelve-step plan for transforming your life through movies / by Maria Grace.
        p.   cm.
    Includes index.
    ISBN 0-07-145907-3 (alk. paper)
    1. Self-actualization (Psychology).   2. Self-defeating behavior.   3. Motion pictures—Psychological aspects.   I. Title.

BF637.S4G732   2005
158'.1—dc22   2005020733

1 2 3 4 5 6 7 8 9 0 FGR/FGR 0 9 8 7 6 5

ISBN 0-07-145907-3

Interior design by Monica Baziuk

McGraw-Hill books are available at special quantity discounts to use as premiums and sales promotions, or for use in corporate training programs. For more information, please write to the Director of Special Sales, Professional Publishing, McGraw-Hill, Two Penn Plaza, New York, NY 10121-2298. Or contact your local bookstore.

This book is printed on acid-free paper.

To the memory of Charlie Chaplin,
and to all of us who dreamed as children
the life we are living as adults

Contents

Acknowledgments

The following people have been part of this book's birth process, from the time it was conceived to the time it was released to the world. You have all enriched my life in amazing ways, and I am deeply grateful to know you.

In New York:

Karen Gantz-Zahler, my outstanding literary agent and a beautiful person, whose role in the birth of this book has been much more valuable than words would ever describe; John Aherne, my wonderful editor at McGraw-Hill, whose secrets of excellence are his amazing talent and true love for what he does; Meg Leder, former editor at McGraw-Hill, who saw the potential of this project and believed in it; Claire Landiss, who offered initial editorial assistance; Liberty Rees, who assisted me throughout the manuscript-writing process with editorial input; and, of course, everyone at McGraw-Hill who contributed to the creation of this book as a published product.

Olivier Bernier, president of the Van Waveren Foundation, who generously supported this project through a monetary award; the staff in the Christine Mann Library and in the New York Society Library, who helped me with my research and writing needs; Trish Marx, author, and Louis

Frumkes, director of the Marymount Manhattan College, who gave expert input and recommendations during the proposal stage.

Dr. Forrest Church and Reverend David Robb, ministers of the Unitarian Church of All Souls, who gave me the opportunity to teach my method to the congregation; Annie Gorycki, the church manager, who always had the best room available for my courses.

Dr. Arthur Caliandro, the minister of Marble Collegiate, and Nina Frost, director of adult education, who supported my seminars with genuine enthusiasm; the congregation of Marble Collegiate, who is one of the warmest, most accepting communities I have known.

Samantha Del Canto, executive vice president of the Learning Annex, who introduced me to New York audiences by including my seminar in the Annex program.

In Austin, Texas:

John Aeilli, the amazing host of KUT Eklektikos, who regularly invited me to speak on his program about my seminars on Reel Fulfillment; the owners of the Alamo Draft House Cinemas, Arbor Theater, Scottish Rite Theater, Hyde Park Theater, and Zilker Hillside Theater, who opened their doors to my seminars.

Fred Johnson, David Psencik, Maggie Fitch, Donna Remmert, Dr. Peter Gonzales, Dr. Pedro Ruggero, and Dr. Don Mannerberg, who believed in my work and encouraged me to take it to the next level.

In Hollywood: Tom Laughlin, the star of *Billy Jack* and a superb connoisseur of Jungian psychology, who generously shared with me his writings and thoughts on movies and the psyche.

Also: the late Dr. Carl Rogers, founder of humanistic psychotherapy and my first mentor, who taught me the power of empathy; all my clients, students, and group and seminar participants, who have been and continue to be my greatest teachers and inspiring forces.

And: My mother, who was my first English tutor. When I was four years old, growing up in Greece, she sat me at our kitchen table and, pointing at the Oxford Dictionary, taught me how to say in English "this is a book." Mother, today I can say "this is *my* book!"

My father, who on Sundays used to take me to a children's matinee; there, the magic of Hollywood classics transported me to places I promised myself that I would see as an adult. Thanks to those Sundays, today I am not dreaming inside a theater in Greece but living my dreams in America, the magical place of my childhood.

Francisco, my other half, creative soul mate and destiny's most precious gift. No words can express his magnificence. I am forever indebted to life for bringing us together.

Introduction

DEAR READER,

The book you are holding was born on a Tuesday afternoon, in my psychotherapy office, a moment before I was about to tell my client Tomas that I could no longer help him resolve his problems. Tomas was young, brilliant, and very troubled. Every week for six months in our sessions, he spoke about how unfulfilled he was: he did not like his work, had no romantic partner, had difficulty connecting with people, and had no motivation to get physically fit. I, being his therapist, was supposed to help him move out of his rut by inspiring him to get interested in himself and excited about going after his own happiness. After six months of trying my very best, I was at the end of my rope. Having exhausted all my professional skill, I began the session on that Tuesday ready to declare defeat. As Tomas entered my office, I looked at him, rehearsing in my mind what I was about to say. "Tomas, I think that we have reached a plateau in our therapeutic process and perhaps we should take a break to reevaluate our goa . . ."

"There is no spoon!" he exclaimed out loud as he sat on the couch. "My God! How come I'd never seen that before, Maria? There is no spoon!"

"Excuse me?" I asked and automatically squinted, trying to "see" what Tomas meant. "Are you here for an ice cream today?"

"No, no, Maria, oh no!" he said animatedly. "This is what it is: when Neo goes to the Oracle to find out if he is the One, he has to wait in the waiting room, right? There's a boy there that bends spoons just by looking at them. Neo thinks that he's some kind of a child guru, with special mental powers and everything, and he gets intimidated. Because Neo has been told that he's the One, like the chosen one, but he doesn't believe it. He doesn't trust himself, right? So, he asks the boy how he does this without even touching the spoon, and the boy goes, 'Can't you see? There is *no* spoon!'"

"Where does all this happen?" I asked him, trying to follow his story.

"In *The Matrix*!" he replied, his eyes shining with hope. "Maria, you must see this movie! It has *all* the answers you've been trying to make me see all this time."

"Such as . . . ?" I asked, honestly curious.

"Such as that there is no spoon!" he said once more. "All the obstacles we see out there are just reflections of our own inner obstacles, you see? Like me—I've been feeling so depressed thinking that my life goes nowhere, but in fact, it's me who's been going nowhere. If I want my life to move on, I'm the one who has to get going! No one's setting me back, only myself! It's all up to me! I'm the One! There is no spoon! I just have to follow the rabbit! Maria, go see *The Matrix*, and you'll see what I mean!"

I did. I saw *The Matrix* and did recognize the profound message it had for Tomas: he had identified with the main hero, Neo, a young man disgruntled with life who discovers that he is the chosen one to save the world. But in order for Neo to achieve his status of a world savior, he goes through a series of initiations that transform him from an irresponsible computer hacker to a spiritually and emotionally mature leader. Tomas, on the other hand, saw that he was not the One to change the world but the only one in the world who could change himself. His discovery that "there was no spoon" was a freeing revelation that his obstacles were created by his own negative patterns. Thanks to his identification with Neo, Tomas was now inspired to correct his patterns, with my guidance, through determination and patience. And so he did. Today, thanks to the revelation *The Matrix* triggered in him back then, Tomas loves himself more than ever: he has bought his own home, works out regularly, and is in a relationship that makes him happy.

I, on the other hand, thanks to Tomas, discovered in the movies the most powerful teaching and therapeutic tool that has ever existed. Movies became my allies in my work with clients. Shortly after I watched *The Matrix* to understand Tomas's transformation, I began watching films with our human problems in mind. And every time, I found that the movies not only had answers to all our problems but also had the power of inspiring and guiding us to take action and improve our lives.

Soon after the incident with Tomas, I began discussing the role of movies in my other clients' lives. More and more clients kept telling me about their "affairs" with the movies that, contrary to real life, offered them all the safety, privacy, and control they needed in order to experience emotions and find answers to problems. Their "affairs" varied from being a weekly ritual of going to the theater to a full obsession with a particular film that forced them to watch it over and over again. That is how I found out that Kelly had seen *Titanic* seventy-three times, each time reliving her own love story with the man she never married; George had seen *Star Wars* thirty-six times, in his effort to reconcile with his estranged father, who abandoned him when he was six; Elena had seen *One Fine Day* forty-eight times, to soothe her pain from a recent breakup, which left her feeling very lonely; and Olga had seen *As Good as It Gets* fifty-eight times, being drawn to the protagonist's extreme outspokenness, which she desperately needed in her own life.

My clients' stories prompted questions I felt compelled to answer: What is it about movies that makes them the most effective tools for teaching us about life, healing our emotions, and inspiring us to take bold steps and do great things? Why is it easier to have such strong feelings for movie characters than for real people? What is it that we get from watching a movie again and again, memorizing lines, replaying scenes in our mind, pretending we are part of the script? And why do many of us allow ourselves to cry freely at the movies, whereas we would never let the public see tears in our eyes?

The more I researched movies, the clearer it became that movies are such powerful teachers, guides, and healers because they provide personal growth experiences that fulfill three essential needs: safety, privacy, and control. We are easily influenced by movies because we feel safe to watch them. The reality presented in a movie may be similar to ours, but, in fact, it is completely separate from us. As spectators, we are invited to be part of that reality, but we are not held responsible for the unfolding events. This gives us the necessary safety to have emotions about the characters of the story and their experiences, as though their experiences were our own. When we feel safe to emote, healing and growth happen. Real life does not give us this luxury very often. Most of the time, we have to stay guarded, making sure that we perform our social role to the best of our ability, in order to receive others' approval. Movies, on the other hand, are unconditional. They happen before us without judging our reactions to them.

Movies give us privacy. Because they are unconditional, they allow us to experience them in our own personal way, feeling free to like or dislike the characters and their actions as we watch them. By giving us privacy, movies let us be intimate with the characters and their lives in ways that are very difficult to be with others in real life. Usually, when we get close to a real person, we run the risk of being invaded by that person's needs, and most often we are. That's why most of us are conflicted by our need for privacy versus our need for intimacy. Movies never create this conflict in us: they give us a private encounter even though we may watch them in a big theater among hundreds of other people. This privacy allows us to have an intimate experience with the characters, as they enter our minds and touch our hearts in ways that real people most often cannot.

Movies give us control. Because they present a reality that is like ours but not exactly ours, we have a safe distance from the events as we watch them unfold. As a result, we are in a position of control with regard to the characters of the story. This enables us to recognize situations in the lives of the characters that we may have difficulty recognizing in our own lives, being immersed in them. For example, due to this sense of control movies afford us, we can recognize negative patterns in the characters that we have a hard time seeing in ourselves. In Tomas's case, his breakthrough happened thanks to his sense of control over Neo's transformation in *The Matrix*. In his own life, Tomas might never have seen that "there was no spoon."

After years of researching ways to help people find fulfillment, I finally arrived at a way that I consider highly effective—a method of life transformation that uses movies as tools of inspiration and guidance. The fruit of my labor is this very book, which I am so happy to know has become your own. It is a guide showing you how to use your favorite films not as escapes from the life you have but as tools to create the life you want. You love movies, don't you? Then just like Tomas, who found in *The Matrix* the tools to break free from his dull existence and enter a realm of fulfilling possibilities, you will learn how to use the power of films to move toward the life you desire to have.

My Own Journey to Fulfillment

Psychotherapy as my vocation chose me in 1974 at a friend's thirteenth birthday party in my hometown in Greece. We were a group of junior high students sitting in a circle, talking about what we wanted to become when we grew up. When my turn came and I was about to speak, Yannis cut me off.

"*You* must study psychology," he told me as I gasped. "It's the profession of the future, and you can help many people. This is what you are made for!"

Yannis was the oldest and wisest in the group. He had traveled abroad, and everyone admired his knowledge. He was also right about me: I *was* made to become a psychotherapist. Since I was a child, people of all ages and their emotional needs fascinated me: I loved to watch human interactions everywhere, listen to distressed friends and relatives, visit orphanages and seniors' homes, bring food, and talk to street beggars. So when Yannis spoke, I took his words to heart and started weaving my dream: my destiny was psychology, and I was going to become a psychotherapist. The problem was that there was not a school of psychology in Greece. My only option was then to surrender to my dream, leave my home country in due time, and study abroad.

In February 1984, ten years after that party, I graduated with a bachelor's degree in classics and philosophy from the University of Athens. A month later, my dream summoned me: I was awarded a Fulbright scholarship for a master's degree in counseling in an American university. That summer I left Greece to begin my long and winding path toward making my dream reality.

That path had many stops: a master's in counseling at the University of California, Santa Barbara; a Ph.D. in counseling at McGill University in Montreal; a number of training programs, such as client-centered therapy, gestalt, family systems, cognitive-behavioral therapy, and Jungian dream analysis; several internships in different mental-health settings and hospitals in Chicago and Montreal; teaching appointments at McGill and the University of San Jose, Costa Rica; and the practice of psychotherapy for more than fifteen years with hundreds of individuals from all walks of life and nationalities.

As an intern and, later on, a licensed psychologist and professional counselor, I worked with recovering addicts, survivors of abuse, people with mental illnesses, immigrants and ethnic minorities, couples and families, college students and artists, homemakers and professionals, hospital staff and members of the police force, schoolteachers and college professors, business managers and financial brokers, successful entrepreneurs and retirees. Every single person I helped as a therapist had a gift for me that added to my learning, enriched my understanding of human nature, and fulfilled my deep desire to be of help to others.

In 1994, ten years after I left Greece, I went through a very painful divorce that triggered my midlife crisis. I had married someone who at first seemed to be everything I needed but soon proved to be alien to my soul. The marriage was short, but my recovery from the divorce seemed to take forever: four years later I was still hurting, feeling ashamed, angry, and guilty. I needed to heal, but neither my academic training nor psychotherapy as I knew it could help me find the comfort I needed. Crucial, deeply human issues had surfaced in my psyche, putting my life on hold and demanding my immediate attention: my severed roots, with which I longed to connect; my relationship with my family, strained from years of absence and lack of communication; my ever-changing identity, which for ten years had been molded by cultures foreign to my origin; personal choices I had made in good conscience, which disappointed me; religious beliefs I had served in good faith, which betrayed me; and values I had always held but had to reassess because they no longer worked.

The time had come to search for a source of inner truth, peace, and forgiveness that could replace all my education and other external sources of guidance I had followed up to that point. I knew that I had to go home to myself and find the peace I so desperately needed. Instinctively, I took a great turn into spirituality. For the next several months, I replaced reading with meditating, allowing stillness and silence to connect me with my inner core; I learned the symbolic language of my dreams and began interpreting them in order to understand the desires of my own psyche; I practiced journaling as a healing activity that allowed me to remember my own voice and hear my own truths. One by one, the layers of a lifetime of external influences peeled away, allowing me to finally reconnect with my true self.

I was never to be the same person again.

The biggest gift of my spiritual quest was realizing that we are born psychologically, spiritually, and emotionally whole. Wholeness is our natural predisposition and inherent purpose. Yet our entry into the human world demands that we learn the rules of the culture that raises us. This culture consists of our family, our schools, our social and religious community, and the world at large. As children, we learn to interact with the human reality, learn its rules, adapt to its limitations, and meet the challenges of our environment. To achieve this, we develop emotional patterns to cope with a reality that we cannot change, and we adopt truths that are not inherently ours. This is how we lose our wholeness. As adults, we yearn to become whole again and create a life we love. To achieve this, we must gain freedom from the emotional patterns we developed through years of simply coping and replace them with healthy, fulfilling ones.

When I realized that by repeating my coping patterns I remained stuck in my past and sabotaged my efforts to fulfill my future, I experienced emotional and spiritual adulthood. Finally, I felt free to let go of truths that were not mine and reclaim my wholeness. As an emotional adult, I was able to recover my natural ability for happiness and turn it into practice. To attain this, I had to take responsibility for my negative patterns and take action to transform them. Seeing that I could be in charge of my life by changing my patterns filled me with confidence and hope. A healing process had begun, and I was excited to follow it all the way.

As I transformed my patterns, the negative emotions that had held me in their grip for so long loosened. Gradually, anger gave way to creativity. I began writing, and in a matter of months, I completed a screenplay, a number of poems, and a novel. Fear gave way to hope, and hurt gave way to forgiveness. I felt lighter about the past and began looking forward to each day's possibilities for new experiences. Shame gave way to belief in my self-worth, and I trusted my ability to live the happiness I deserved. The sadness that had clouded my heart before was now replaced by the growing faith that my former yearning for self-love was no longer a burning wish but a heartwarming, self-validating, *real* experience.

As my own life was changing, I began looking for a way to share with my clients the lessons of my healing journey. I realized that one-on-one psychotherapy took a lot of time and money and addressed only one person at a time. I needed to find a means of teaching the steps of life transformation to large groups of people. And then I discovered the healing power of movies and began using them as teaching tools.

In 1997 I started giving multimedia seminars in Austin, Texas, in which I used films to talk about our spiritual journey to fulfillment. My first seminar was in a small theater of forty sold-out seats. The second one was in an auditorium of two hundred participants. The third one was standing room only, with about fifty people turned away for lack of space. For the next three years, I regularly presented these seminars, using popular films to talk about psychological and spiritual issues. The response was amazing. I began getting numerous requests for a manual outlining my method that people could use on their own or in groups. I received a grant to write a book on my method, and in the fall of 2000, I was invited to present it in a conference on mental health and the media in New York City.

When I arrived in New York for that conference, another dream summoned me: I saw myself living in New York, teaching my seminars and developing the course manual into a published book. The dream was so powerful that it felt natural to follow it. A year later I was living in New York City, and since then I have been teaching this method to groups and individuals. My initial notes grew into a complete method of life transformation. This method is the child of my own healing labor that brought me to a life I love to live. Teaching others how to transform their lives fills me with joy, as I watch them also create a life they love to live.

As I look back at my path of the last twenty years, I can't help but think that it began as a dream at that birthday party in 1974. My friend Yannis was right: helping people was my natural gift and the dream I had to follow. Studying psychology gave me the credentials of a professional helper. But the truth is that I did not fulfill my dream thanks to my degrees and academic achievements. I found fulfillment only when I freed myself from my past and forgave all that I could not change about me, my life, and others.

Forgiving allowed me to feel my own humanity, embrace my own imperfections, and accept my life and others as they are. It opened my heart and enabled me to feel love. Living a life of love was my dream, and thanks to my journey, my dream became reality. Love has filled me with the certainty that, thanks to our ability to feel and show love, our life is indestructible, ongoing, forever blessed.

Now to you, voyager of this journey, I wish that you may also arrive at the joy you dream of and the love you deserve to live.

Overview of the Book

This book takes you through a journey of personal growth, giving you four major gains: inner clarity, emotional health, spiritual fitness, and joy. You achieve each gain as you work through the chapters, which are written as building blocks, in a progressive order. Each separate chapter offers you

- An introduction to the theory and the main concepts involved. The ideas are illustrated with examples from popular movies and the lives of your favorite movie characters.
- A section titled "Movie Time! Watch a Movie for Fun, Learn a Lesson of Life." This unique feature of the method gives you lists of selected films followed by specific assignments. Your homework is to watch a movie and complete the assignments. (More about "Movie Time" later.)
- A section with exercises and activities designed to help you apply the new learning to your life. Completing them is an opportunity to put the theory into action and enjoy great results.
- A list of key points to remember.

The Appendixes at the end of the book offer detailed charts, lists, and grids that you may use as a reference while working on the exercises.

The Promise and the Unique Tools of This Method

The promise of this book is that if you work through the twelve chapters, you will create the life that you dream. Furthermore, you will acquire skills you need in order to experience fulfillment and transform into the person you desire to become. You will learn how to focus on developing successful habits, giving you new meaning and purpose. As you discover yourself, you will notice changes in your relationships and the way you live your life.

The method taught in *Reel Fulfillment* has three unique aspects that are also tools for growth and recovery. They are

- "Movie Time" once a week
- weekly homework
- a two-minute meditation, three times a day

"Movie Time"

This work will change the way you see films and enrich your film-watching experience. "Movie Time" will encourage you to enjoy films not only as entertaining distractions but as valuable experiences of personal growth. We all love films. We lose ourselves in the lives of the characters we watch on the big screen, and in the same characters, we also find ourselves.

Films are magical, powerful, wonderful myths of our modern culture. They are magical because they are collective and yet very private experiences. We may watch films in the anonymity of packed theaters, yet we respond to them in a very personal and strictly individual way. Movies are powerful because their imagery touches our souls. Films make us feel, and feeling emotions makes us know that we are alive. Films are wonderful not only because they fill us with wonder but also because they can create wonders: they can inspire us to take risks and make life changes, they can teach us new ways of being that we had never thought existed, and they can motivate us to take action and become the person we dream to be.

Watching a film every week and completing its corresponding assignment will help you advance your progress. The "Movie Time" activities will give you food for thought. As you assess and process the characters' actions in each story, you will sharpen your self-observation skills and increase your self-awareness. Let the characters of these films become your friends, guides, and companions in your own journey to self-discovery. Use their stories to learn more about you. And share these films with people who can appreciate their healing power as much as you do.

How to Watch the Films Recommended in "Movie Time"

To get the maximum benefit of your movie-watching experience in this method, it is wise to follow these guidelines:

- Watch the movie not as a cinematic plot involving movie stars but as a story involving human characters.
- Try not to evaluate the characters of the movie for their acting qualities; instead, look into how their relationships unfold and how their actions affect one another. Look into each character's inner world; try to connect with their feelings and the motives influencing their choices and reactions to the events that occur in their lives.
- Try to recognize the qualities of the characters, how these qualities manifest themselves through their actions, and how you relate to each character's qualities.

Note on Film Rating

The films chosen for this method are popular to very large audiences worldwide. They cover a wide scope of human issues and portray a variety of characters from all walks of life, ethnic groups, cultures, and socioeconomic backgrounds. Some of them may contain scenes of violence, criminal behavior, partial nudity, sexual references, or profanity.

Note: in order to safeguard your personal sensibilities regarding film rating, I recommend that throughout your work with this book, you choose your films after reading about them. Visit reelfulfillment.com/movie_ratings/ or read the jacket of the respective video or DVD at your local library or video store.

Weekly Homework

No method promising transformation is likely to work unless you apply it through concrete actions. This is why I strongly encourage you to do some homework on a weekly basis by completing all or most of the exercises in each chapter. These exercises are designed to help you ask important questions of yourself in order to identify and pursue your true goals, needs, and desires. Completing them can help you achieve new insights and have transformational experiences with great results. Also, completing the exercises can give you the satisfaction that you are able to monitor your progress and that you are in charge of your own process.

You may read *Reel Fulfillment* just for inspiration—you will take valuable life lessons from your favorite movie characters. But if you do the homework, this book will become your guide to a total life transformation. If this is what you want to achieve, you will need to keep a journal as your valuable companion and personal documentary throughout your work with *Reel Fulfillment*.

The Two-Minute Meditation

One objective of this method is to teach you how to connect with yourself and stay mentally fit amidst your busy, noisy, and oftentimes chaotic life. This practice helps you become attentive to your inner needs and sharpen your focus. Through a simple yet powerful meditation that you repeat three times a day, you learn to use breathing to center in your body and get grounded in the now. Over time, the three short meditations can become your daily rituals of spiritual recharging. I suggest that you do one in the morning before you go to work, one halfway through your workday, and one in the evening, after dinner.

These breathing meditations are meant to be included in your daily schedule as your "spiritual snacks." You should not have to interrupt your life to meditate. On the contrary, you should include short, frequent meditations to keep your mental energy flowing throughout your regular day. This you can do anywhere—at the office sitting in your chair, on the bus, on a park bench during your lunch break, at home, in a public library, in a parking lot inside your car. There is no limit to the spaces available to you. All you need is a place to sit and support your back and a small alarm to count the time.

Two minutes of breathing in silence last a lot longer than you may think and can have a deep nourishing effect on your energy, mood, and emotions. When you repeat this two-minute meditation three times a day, its healing influence multiplies exponentially. Chapter 9 presents detailed instructions on the meditation. If you wish, you may begin your meditations now and include them in your daily routines as you read this book. Go to Chapter 9, read the instructions for the "Two-Minute Meditation for a Busy, Noisy Life," and begin practicing. Enjoy the serenity of the experience and its cumulative effects on your well-being.

Working with This Book

This book has been designed to fit your individual needs, so I encourage you to personalize it. This section offers ideas and suggestions that you may follow or adapt to your unique learning style.

There are three ways to complete *Reel Fulfillment*: alone, in a group, or in a combination of both. Whichever way you may use, the method works. I have been teaching the book in weekend seminars, in ongoing classes, and with groups of various sizes. I have also been using it with individual students in one-on-one sessions, guiding them through the weekly homework and discussing their progress. Whether using the book individually or in groups, the students of this method consistently get results.

Working Alone

You may want to read through the book once, to get an idea of the concepts involved in each chapter. Reading through the book is not the same as applying the method for desired results.

When you are ready to work on the method, I suggest you make a twelve-week commitment and set a weekly schedule. As with any twelve-week course, this one requires completing your assignments and checking on your progress. Here is an example of how a Sunday-to-Saturday schedule might work:

- On Sunday, begin a new chapter and dedicate a week to it. Read the chapter first, and set aside three hours for "Movie Time": watch a movie from the list at the end of the chapter and answer the questions in that section.
- From Monday to Friday, set aside a minimum of an hour each day to complete the exercises in the same chapter. (They build on each other, so it is critical that you complete them in their presented order.) Do not forget the two-minute meditation, three times a day. Use Saturday for rest.
- Start with a new chapter the following Sunday, and use the same format until you finish the book.

Working with a Group

Even though personal growth is a highly individual process, it can be greatly enhanced by the energy and support of a group. Working with a group may have many benefits, such as the following:

- You share your experience with other members and function as each other's mirror in this process.
- You have the support of the group when you hit rough spots.
- Peer pressure may be a great motivator to complete the exercises.
- Discussing the "Movie Time" questions with your group is far more enriching than answering them alone.

If you prefer the group format, you may form your own support group using the book as your text. I suggest that you have a group facilitator, preferably someone who is familiar with the method and has seen benefits from the process.

Note: unless your facilitator is a trained professional authorized to receive payment for teaching this method, she or he should be a volunteer.

For a successful group experience, here are some general guidelines:

- **Regular weekly meetings.** Set a weekly two- to three-hour meeting for twelve consecutive weeks. Block these dates and attend all meetings. During the week, follow the schedule recommended earlier to complete the exercises, and watch a film from the "Movie Time" section.
- **Size and space.** Any number of participants between three and eight (including the facilitator) is acceptable. Having more than eight members creates a group too large for processing. Discussions can become animated and profound, so you must manage time wisely.

  If you choose to hold the meetings in a neutral space, you may rent a church room, a recreation room in your apartment or condominium complex, a school classroom, or a room in a community center. Otherwise, you may use space in your home, provided that your group has privacy there and it does not interrupt the life of those living with you. Another option is to revolve meetings in members' homes.
- **Structure of meetings.** All members must read this book in advance before starting the group meetings. If you do not have a facilitator, opt for revolving leadership, in which members take turns facilitating the meetings. For maximum effectiveness, your group sessions should adhere to the following format:

  1. **Two-minute breathing meditation.** This is a basic tool of *Reel Fulfillment*, discussed in more depth in a separate section. Opening your meeting with this meditation diffuses the concerns of the day and sets a spiritual focus for the group process to unfold.

  2. **Discussing "Movie Time."** Allot thirty minutes to share your answers to the questions about the film you watched the week prior to the meeting. Use the theme of the movie you discuss as a lead to address your own issues. Focus on your experiences from watching those characters' lives unfold and how you relate to them. Discuss the ways in which the film influenced your own process, the new insights it gave you, and the changes it catalyzed in your thoughts, feelings, and behaviors.

3. **Sharing the learning of the week.** As you discuss "Movie Time," you may transition to sharing your experiences with the completed assignments. The facilitator is responsible for giving all members adequate time for sharing and ensuring that they observe the basic group rules, outlined in the following section.

Finally, choose a film to watch from the "Movie Time" section of the next chapter. Even though all members must agree to watch the same film for the next group discussion, you may also individually watch any other film from the list, as your time permits.

Basic Group Rules

Having ground rules gives the group the necessary structure to develop safety, trust, and a healthy process. I recommend that the facilitator mention the following rules in every meeting after the meditation and before the group process begins:

- All discussions and group sharing are to remain confidential among the participants. When a member is sharing, there is no cross-talk or interruption from others. Comments, advice, analysis, and interpretation from the group are discouraged. The facilitator is responsible for keeping this rule in effect.
- Respect other members' time, and keep your sharing within the designated time. Be aware of how self-involved or off-topic you get when you share. The facilitator is responsible for reminding members of the time and moving the process along.
- Keep an attitude of openness, encouragement, and support toward each other. Creating safety in the group allows all members to share difficulties or rough spots with their process. Keeping a facade to hide your struggles is not helpful for the group or your individual progress.
- Members are responsible for completing the weekly assignments, practicing the daily two-minute meditations, and watching the assigned film from "Movie Time."

When you complete your twelve-week group commitment, you may renew it and continue your group meetings once or twice a month. You may keep the same session format. You may also alternate between a sharing session and a "Movie Time" session. In the second session, you watch a film together, which is followed by discussion of the assigned questions.

Another option is to become a volunteer facilitator for a new group. Being a facilitator has tremendous rewards. Besides keeping you on your toes with your own emotional recovery, you are building a network of comrades on a path similar to yours. As your community grows, you share a spirit of abundance and goodwill, enjoy the privilege of growing support, and cheer one another's accomplishments toward creating the life you love to live.

Last Words Before We Start

Like any recovery method, *Reel Fulfillment* is not a linear but a spiral path, occasionally taking you back to places you thought you would never see again. As you go through this book, you may revisit many of your issues and personal challenges, but each time you do, you are likely to be stronger and more capable of moving forward. There is no such thing as linear growth. Nature's patterns are cyclical, ongoing, and ever changing. Recovery is not what you accomplish at the end of this process but the progress you make along the way, as long as you walk on the path one step at a time, one day at a time.

Only you have the power to bring forth your innermost yearnings. *Reel Fulfillment* gives you the tools to achieve this, using films to teach, guide, and inspire you to build the life you dream. Your life is your own movie, in which you are the screenwriter, the director, and the leading character. This is the most important—and maybe the only—movie you will ever have been called on to create. It is up to you to make it the best one you will ever see.

Have faith in yourself and begin action, now.

First Gain: Inner Clarity

▶ YOUR DIRECTION IN life depends on how clear you are about your needs. When you lack inner clarity, you are more likely to feel unfocused, discontented, and powerless. You then tend to run around in circles, craving direction and control.

Being clear about your needs helps you define your goals and what you must do to fulfill them. As a person with inner clarity, you will develop a fresh interest in yourself, a renewed sense of purpose, and the determination to pursue your happiness through real actions.

The next three chapters will help you achieve that. Using movies for inspiration and special activities, you will learn how to:

- Reconnect with your dreams
- Make sense of your fantasies and put them in a realistic context
- Acknowledge your true needs

Wake Up to Your Dream Life

Shirley Valentine is a forty-something wife and mother who lives in Liverpool, England, where the weather is dull, the sky is gray, and the rain never seems to stop. Shirley's children have already flown the family nest, leaving her with an empty home and lots of empty hours to fill. Every day, Shirley goes grocery shopping, comes home to her little kitchen, pours herself a glass of wine, and as she starts dinner for her husband, Joe, begins talking to her best and only friend in life: the kitchen wall.

The wall has become her closest pal. The wall is always there in her dark kitchen, waiting to hear the small, same old news of her day. Even though nothing changes in Shirley's life, her news somehow never seems boring to the wall's ears.

"You know what I'd like to do, Wall?" says Shirley one evening, standing in front of her stove with a glass of wine in her hand. "Drink a glass of wine in a country where the grape is grown, sitting by the sea, just sipping wine, and watching the sun go down."

This time, the wall has heard something different. This is not Shirley's mundane news but her deep, inner desire. It's a desire to live a dream life in a country she has never visited before, in an open space far, far away from the walls of her claustrophobic kitchen. Her dream life exists in a land of rolling, vineyard-covered hills; bright, open skies; and a warm, glowing sun, which, at the end of the day, goes to sleep in a warm, deep blue sea.

Now that Shirley Valentine has finally confessed her secret desire to the wall, her life will never be the same. A series of events will unfold, forcing her to listen to this inner call: unless she takes action, she will never turn her fantasy into reality. Through this process, Shirley will have to learn and change many things about herself, among which is knowing that she deserves to live the happiness of her dreams and only she can make it happen.

Shirley Valentine's victorious journey from a dead-end existence inside a dark kitchen in Liverpool to a sun-filled life on a blue island in Greece is the subject of a movie made in the 1980s. Not a huge Hollywood production, this modest English film is one of the greatest modern stories about transformation and self-discovery leading to fulfillment. We watch the film's heroine go through steps of personal change, take inner risks, and face external challenges, until she rediscovers herself amidst the reality of her dreams. Once she's there, she invites her husband to have a taste of her newly found joy. "Who knows," she thinks to herself, "he may want to stay here for a while."

Shirley's story could be anyone's story. The fact that she is a bored housewife living in the 1980s does not set her apart from the rest of us. She could be today's fed-up manager with the dead-end job, the overworked executive with the nonexistent personal life, the tired couple who need to rediscover the reasons they were initially attracted to one another, the frustrated college graduate who cannot find meaning as she (or he) jumps from job to job and city to city, or the recent retiree who, after decades of participating in society through the workforce, suddenly feels like an outcast and needs a new, fulfilling purpose.

Regardless of individual differences, we are all placed on this planet with one common goal: to make our heart's desires a reality and to live the life we dream. This is not only a goal but also our birthright that is naturally expressed in our aspirations from childhood to old age. Our aspirations appear to spring from a source beyond our control, pulling us toward the life we dream to live. When we are children, we dream of what we'll be when we grow up. When we are in college, we dream of the job we'll land once we get out or of meeting our soul mate and feeling true love. When we meet that special one, we dream of having a family and living happily together. If we have raised children, when they are ready to leave the family nest, we dream of having the time to do all the things we could not do while raising them. And for our golden years, we all dream of having our physical strength and mental faculties sufficiently intact to live to a good old age and spend time enjoying the things we love without the pressures of work and chaotic schedules.

Dreaming of the life we'd love to live seems natural, as these dreams arise within all of us constantly and effortlessly. It is obvious that we are born with the capacity to imagine our life before we live it. Given that simple premise, it should also be natural to know the process by which one can turn that dream life into reality. But why doesn't that happen? Why should we have such an easy time imagining our perfect lives but have such a difficult time creating and sustaining fulfillment in reality? Why is happiness such a hard thing to achieve and one of those things that money can't buy?

Some answers to these age-old questions can be found by closely examining how the heroes of certain movies attain this "true happiness." Using them as your guides—along with your personal support system of a helpful friend, a good advisor, or a trained therapist—may help you take the first step toward turning your inner dreams into a life you would love to live.

The Three Behavioral Habits That Keep You from Living Your Dream Life

As you begin working with this method, you will be prompted to examine three behavioral habits that keep you from pursuing your own happiness. Following the examples of movie heroes and heroines, and with the help of exercises and activities, you will learn how to identify and ultimately change your happiness-resisting behaviors into actions that will transform your dream life into a living reality.

The three behavioral habits that keep you from living your dream life are discussed next.

Expecting to Be Happy Instead of Looking Forward to Life Ahead

Happiness, fulfillment, and inner contentment depend greatly on our attitude and the ability to cooperate with reality and use concrete actions to pursue our dreams. When we *expect* happiness from life, happiness does not come our way. Instead, we set ourselves up for a major disappointment. On the other hand, once we begin to *look forward* to the things that we are willing to do to become happy and the opportunities that will arise, then we are on a solid path to finding happiness. Life works in mysterious and miraculous ways once we become cooperative with it.

In *Shirley Valentine*, Shirley gets unexpectedly invited on a trip to Greece. Hours later, she finds herself watching the sunset by the sea, sipping wine from the glass she's idly holding; even though she's living her fantasy, she's not experiencing fulfillment. On the contrary, she's feeling disappointed and sad, on the way to her realization that expecting to find happiness by simply living out her fantasy is not the way to fulfill her yearnings. She sees now that she has to take action and do different things to get different results that bring her the happiness she wants and deserves. This discovery wakes Shirley up to her dream life, and she wastes no time. As she begins taking specific actions, she looks forward to her own role in her adventures, instead of expecting to be fulfilled by simply showing up in the scene of her fantasy. As her new life begins unfolding, Shirley is living it a day at a time, savoring every moment, handling both the good and the bad with calmness, sincerity, and faith in a newly found self.

When we expect things to happen in our own ideal way, reality will never conform. The truth is that reality does not care what we expect from it. Life happens in spite of our expectations. Try to remember the last time you said, "I expect X to be really good." Perhaps X was a concert, a date, a lecture, a dream house, a perfect job, or even a perfect marriage. You built a whole fantasy around your expectations, and you expected your fantasy to be the real thing. Once you found yourself face-to-face with a much more complex reality, did you feel a little let down? Did you say to yourself or others, "This isn't what I expected"? Didn't you feel disempowered?

On the other hand, looking forward to whatever life will bring you—surprises, twists of fate, and the unexpected curveballs—empowers you from within. When you say, "I look forward to what will be," you make a statement that you are capable, strong, and prepared to face the unknown. You state that you are grounded in reality and not in your expectations. You pronounce that you are flexible enough to enjoy the good moments and also handle the adversities that may come your way and that you are able and willing to revel in the surprises of every moment. Life is a roller coaster—this is what makes it an ongoing miracle and a place for learning. If you tell yourself that life should always be a rose garden because you deserve it, you are robbing yourself of your own strength to face your challenges and grow from them.

The story of Frances, a writer from San Francisco and the heroine of *Under the Tuscan Sun*, is another example of a person who turned expectations of finding happiness into actions to create that happiness. Left by her husband for another woman, Frances suddenly finds herself homeless and without a fulfilling purpose. While touring the Tuscan countryside on a bus, she sees through the bus window an old villa called Bramasole, which means "yearning for the sun." The dwelling mysteriously calls Frances to buy it immediately, to stay in Tuscany, and to turn the decrepit villa into her home. Frances's real journey begins when she becomes the owner of the villa and faces the challenge of restoring it, just as she must restore her broken life, one piece at a time.

As we watch Frances take on the challenges of the restoration process, we see her learn to change her expectations for happiness to come miraculously into actions taken to create opportunities that will give her happiness.

As the story ends, we see that Frances's three wishes have been fulfilled: she wanted to find someone to cook for, she wanted to have a wedding at the villa, and she wanted to watch children grow up there. But none of these things happened according to her expectations or what we thought were her expectations at the time. She cooks for the many friends she has made, she hosts the wedding party of a young couple who are madly in love, and she helps her best friend who moved in with her from San Francisco to raise her baby. Frances has found her lost faith in life, and it is stronger than ever before.

At the end of her journey, Frances has a new, fulfilling life that includes friendship, family, and love. In the process, she had to surrender her expectations, learn to look forward to whatever life brought her, and become stronger and more flexible until her dream life could become reality. All this happened thanks to her ability to cooperate with life and see each experience as a lesson of wisdom and love.

Sunflowers love the sun, so they turn their heads to follow its orbit. When it's windy, they bend their long stems to keep from breaking. They learn to face natural conditions, both pleasant and adverse, and so they thrive. Frances's message to us is that as long as we are Bramasole, as long as we yearn for the sun, we must learn to follow its orbit—to enjoy its warmth and to bend when it's windy so we don't break. Letting go of expectations and looking forward to whatever life hands you is the way to achieve this.

Not Living in the Right Realm or Time Zone

Our life happens primarily in two realms and three time zones. First, there is the realm of reality, the one we experience with our senses and can verify through hard data. This is the physical world that surrounds us, the house in which we live, the people with whom we work and interact, the lifestyle we have, the places we frequent, the things we buy, and so on. Our physical body is a central but often overlooked part of this reality. Keeping our body healthy and fit is the main prerequisite to feeling happy on a day-to-day basis. Even though severe physical illness can be a great teacher to discovering true happiness, it can also be an enormous impediment to fulfilling our dreams. Keeping the body healthy and reasonably fit is essential for anyone who is serious about being happy.

The second realm in which we live is that of fantasy. This is a world with rules of its own. Anything goes in the world of fantasy, which is the world of our dreams, yearnings, imaginings, and aspirations. This world is always with us, popping spontaneously into our awareness, making us long for another, different life. The world of fantasy does not have a specific space or time. When it summons us, we are taken to other places and times, getting lost in our daydreams and desires.

The three time zones we live our life in are the past, present, and future. Of these three zones, we actually experience our life only in the present, as we are living it. The past is a time zone to which we flee when we are reminded of memories or when we are still emotionally attached to powerful experiences. For example, a powerful romantic experience keeps us remembering the person with whom we fell in love, long after our relationship is over. Or the pain of having lost a pet or a person keeps us from being truly present in the here and now. At these times, our mind and thoughts are elsewhere, not in the present.

The future is a time zone to which we flee when we feel dissatisfied with the present or when we feel insecure about the unknown. In other words, we flee into the future when we anticipate an emotionally powerful experience. For example, when we anticipate a wedding, a big purchase, a move, a new job, a trip to a foreign country, the outcome of a trial, and so on, we place our mind beyond the present and invest our thoughts heavily in the future.

The reward we experience by escaping from our present reality in these ways is a sense of control over the life we imagine will soon begin or that we once had. Oftentimes, escaping into the fantasy realm is the easiest way out of the life we are living but do not love; instead of taking action and changing our real life into the life of our dreams, we flee into a dream life and stay inert and perpetually unhappy.

The story of Cecilia in *The Purple Rose of Cairo* beautifully describes the danger of perpetually escaping into a world of fantasy to avoid dealing with reality. Cecilia is a mistreated housewife living in New Jersey during the Depression. Her only happiness is going to the movies, an addiction that she supports through working in a restaurant. Her sad reality suddenly changes when, as she's watching a movie, Tom Baxter, a movie character, walks off the movie screen into her reality world and falls in love with her. Tom Baxter is a romantic, idealistic archaeologist whose words of love brighten up Cecilia's dull life. He symbolizes the fantasy world in which we immerse ourselves instead of actively changing the life we're escaping.

As we watch Cecilia oscillate between fantasy and reality, we can't wait to see how she will resolve her dilemma and which world she will ultimately choose to inhabit. Will she show the strength and determination Shirley and Frances demonstrated to create the lives they dreamed about? Or will her fascination with romantic movies remain her only escape from a miserable reality that will stay forever the same?

Living your dream life does not happen through your fantasies. On the contrary, it is a matter of taking action to bring your dreams into the world of reality. When you are unhappy with the life you have, you must take action to live the life you dream. When you keep the life you dream locked in the world of your fantasies, you also keep yourself a prisoner in a realm that is not real. You then live in a time zone that does not exist— either the past, the future, or the no-time of your daydreams. While you are in this mode, your life continues to pass you by like water running through open, idle fingers.

Not Fulfilling Your Needs or Not Following Your Own Dreams

The opposite of fleeing into fantasy to avoid changing our reality is to entirely ignore our inner needs and aspirations and "try to stay real" at all costs. When we do this, we simply kill our dreams, the one part of us that knows what can make us really happy. Our life then becomes a flat, dull gray zone in which we repeat the same routines day after day, having no sense of their meaning, our purpose, or true joy. We may have become so accustomed to our daily routines that the thought of reconnecting with our dreams brings us panic, so we avoid dreaming altogether. We simply go through life and numb any pain with food, drugs, alcohol, shopping, and the like. Some of us may develop physical symptoms that are hard to diagnose and get frequently labeled by doctors as "psychosomatic." We may suffer from insomnia, have chronic pain, or get panic or anxiety attacks for no apparent reason. The more we ignore our inner yearnings and stick to reality, the more urgently our stifled spirit seeks to call our attention to its needs. Crushing our dreams exacts a much higher price than many of us would imagine.

Movies are filled with characters whose lives hit dead ends because they either gave up on their dreams or stopped following them altogether. They appear to suffer from chronic dissatisfaction and always harbor secret worries about not doing the right thing with their lives. Though their lives may look like they are moving along the right track, underneath the surface, they are wading through a mire of meaningless routines and empty activities.

In *American Beauty*, a complex and fascinating movie about the different paths we take in life and where they lead us, Carolyn Burnham—a real estate agent with very big ambitions and very low self-esteem—lives in an American suburb with her husband, Lester Burnham, and their teenage daughter, Jane. Lester realizes one day that his life is empty of dreams and aspirations and decides to make drastic changes that upset Carolyn's world order. Her need for social approval is so powerful that she has sacrificed her desires for intimacy, spontaneity, and joy in favor of creating an image of being in total control of her life. What she considers joy is having sex in motel rooms with the "king of real estate," a crude man whose motto is "If you appear successful, you are successful."

"Whatever happened to that girl who used to fake seizures at frat parties when she got bored? Who used to run up to the roof of her first apartment building to flash the traffic helicopters? Have you totally forgotten about her?" Lester asks Carolyn one day, desperately trying to rekindle their dead intimacy. But as the story progresses, Carolyn does nothing to change her life. Instead, she tries to stop Lester from changing his. Change is very threatening to people who have given up on their inner yearnings. It reminds them that something is wrong underneath the surface and that they must take great risks to get free from the trap of their reality and create a new life following their heart's desires.

Unlike Carolyn Burnham, whose life takes a tragic turn as she resists change, the character Phil Connors in *Groundhog Day* has a better fate. Phil is a weatherman who travels to Pittsburgh, Pennsylvania, on the second day of each February for the Punxsutawney Phil event known as Groundhog Day. Phil Connors's character is typical of a cynical, career-driven man who uses sarcasm as a weapon against relationships, his humanness, and his feelings. Phil does not have yearnings; he has ambitions. Living not in the present but in the future, he sees his visit to Punxsutawney as a routine to be faced with the same cynicism he uses with everything else. He will cover the day of the "weather-forecasting rat," as he calls Groundhog Phil, and get out of there as soon as possible.

A sudden blizzard traps Phil in Punxsutawney. But even worse, Phil discovers that he will wake up every day to February 2, to a day where everything around him is exactly the same as it was the day before. His clock radio blares out "I Got You Babe," just like the previous morning; the disc jockey announces the exact same news as he did the day before; and when Phil looks out the window, people are getting ready to go to the same celebration. It is Groundhog Day once again. No one else seems to notice; to them, everything seems perfectly normal. Phil Connors alone is trapped in the endless loop of living the same reality over and over again.

Phil's ordeal with reliving Groundhog Day ad infinitum becomes a journey of self-discovery. At first he is baffled; then he decides to exploit this phenomenon for his own gain. Later, as he continues to live the same day again and again, he becomes severely depressed, and at the depths of his depression, as nothing seems to change, he contemplates suicide. As he continues to live inside his endless loop, repeating Groundhog Day again and again, he begins to accept his fate. This acceptance opens him up to self-reflection, and this is when Phil begins to discover his inner essence and turns into a man who cares less about his career and more about being human.

Phil's story of living Groundhog Day over and over again is a metaphor for the kind of life that we have when we disconnect from our inner yearnings and get stuck in what we call reality. We live on autopilot, and every day, we feel more and more frustrated with a life we do not love. Like Phil Connors, we are consumed by agony when we wake up in the morning, only to go through the same day again. The movie's message is clear: unless we change something, we may forever be stuck in this loop. This is the risk that Phil decides to take, and it's the one that saves him. Letting go of his old way of seeing life, he reaches beneath his own superficial surface and reconnects with the things that make him essentially human: truth, honesty, humility, and, most important, love.

You awaken to your dream life when you connect to your inner needs and take proper actions to fulfill them in the real world. This is a courageous and noble decision, to respect and trust the source of your inner desires, which is also the leading guide to your happiness. The more clear you are about your true needs, the more easily you can focus on doing the appropriate things to fulfill them. The knowledge that you are following your heart's desires anchors you within yourself and fills you with the self-confidence and enthusiasm to follow your path. There is no higher, deeper, more lasting satisfaction than that of successfully turning your dream life into your living reality.

Reel Fulfillment in Action

■■■

Movie Time! ▸ *Watch a Movie for Fun, Learn a Lesson of Life*

Now it's time to watch one of the films mentioned in this chapter or another from the following list of movies that portray the primary issues we have explored thus far. Choose a movie, and watch it alone or with your group. As you watch the movie, please keep in mind the questions that follow the list of movies. Use them as a frame of reference to better connect with the lives of the characters. After you watch the movie, spend some time writing your thoughts in your journal before sharing them with the group. This is an important activity that will help you get better results when you complete the exercises at the end of this chapter.

Feel free to repeat the same activity with other films on the list, as time permits.

Movies About Waking Up to Your Dream Life
American Beauty (1999), directed by Sam Mendes
As Good as It Gets (1997), directed by James L. Brooks
Enchanted April (1992), directed by Mike Newell
The Family Man (2000), directed by Brett Ratner
Field of Dreams (1989), directed by Phil Alden Robinson
Groundhog Day (1993), directed by Harold Ramis
The Ice Storm (1997), directed by Ang Lee
Legally Blonde (2001), directed by Robert Luketic
Love Actually (2003), directed by Richard Curtis
Notting Hill (1999), directed by Roger Michell
Peggy Sue Got Married (1986), directed by Francis Ford Coppola
Pleasantville (1998), directed by Gary Ross
The Purple Rose of Cairo (1985), directed by Woody Allen
Rocky (1976), directed by John G. Avildsen
Shirley Valentine (1989), directed by Lewis Gilbert
Something's Gotta Give (2003), directed by Nancy Meyers

13 Going on 30 (2004), directed by Gary Winick
The Truman Show (1998), directed by Peter Weir
Under the Tuscan Sun (2003), directed by Audrey Wells
What Women Want (2000), directed by Nancy Meyers

Questions to Answer

1. What are the main character's unfulfilled needs?
2. What events force the main character to recognize his or her true needs?
3. What changes does the main character make in his or her life to find fulfillment?
4. How does the environment react to the main character's changes? Is it supportive, adverse, indifferent? Who are the people helping the main character the most? Who are the ones sabotaging him or her the most? What are their motives to behave the way they do?
5. What are the main character's biggest gains at the end of the story?
6. How do the main character's changes influence other characters in the story?
7. What, if any, new insights have you gained from watching this movie?

Wake Up to Your Dream Life ▸ Exercises and Activities

The following exercises are designed to help you develop a deeper and stronger connection with your yearnings by empowering you to develop new attitudes and habits.

▸ Your Morning Thoughts: A Check-In

1. What are your first thoughts of the day?
2. Do you notice a certain pattern in your morning thoughts?
3. Are you looking forward to the day, or would you rather not leave your house (or your bed)?
4. What in particular do you look forward to in your day?

Notice how often you begin your day with a negative attitude. This week pay attention to how you embrace your day when you wake up.

▶ What Is Your "Time Zone"?

For each of the following questions, choose the answer that seems appropriate:

Never—1
Occasionally—2
Often—3
Very often—4
Always—5

How often do you

1. Worry about the future?
2. Think about the next thing you have to do?
3. Daydream of living in another country, city, or neighborhood?
4. Space out at work or daydream of being at another job?
5. Long for a person, a time of your life, or a place no longer present?
6. Hear friends or significant others tell you that they can't get through to you because your mind is always somewhere else?
7. Forget important dates or things to do, with serious repercussions in your life?
8. Misplace or lose your keys, wallet, or driver's license?
9. Get finance charges for not paying bills on time or late penalty fees for not returning items (such as books, videos, or DVDs) on time?
10. Have a hard time concentrating on your daily tasks because you are engrossed in fantasizing about something?

Use the following chart to evaluate your scores:

10: A perfect 10 shows no problem whatsoever. You have both feet firmly planted in reality, and you are perfectly capable of living in the here and now. Whether you are a natural at being grounded or you have achieved it through practice, congratulations!

11–20: No need to worry. Your grasp of reality is good, and you know how to stop yourself from living in fantasies. You are human, after all. Just make sure you don't lose your wallet again or lock your car keys in the trunk!

21–30: Pay attention. You are on the verge of causing yourself some big trouble. People at home and work are getting tired of you, and sooner or later you will be confronted with the consequences of escaping the here and now.

31–40: You definitely need to come back to the here and now and face the issues that bother you and fuel your desire to flee reality. You deserve to live the life of your dreams, and you can achieve this only if you stop daydreaming and wake up to reality. Only you can do it.

41–50: You spend most of your time being removed from reality. You may need professional help in order to come back to the here and now and address the areas of your life that need improvement. Use this book as a guide to take concrete steps, and do seriously think about seeking help from a trained therapist or a competent coach.

▶ Having Expectations: A Check-In

For each of the following questions, choose the answer that seems appropriate:

> Never—1
> Occasionally—2
> Often—3
> Very often—4
> Always—5

How often do you

1. Feel let down by the way others treat you?
2. Blame yourself for not being as good as you should be?
3. Correct the behaviors of friends or significant others to fit your expectations of how they should behave?
4. Get moody thinking that life should meet your expectations and that you should have had it a lot better?

5. Give up on a project or a person because they do not meet your expectations?

6. Complain to others about how poorly life treats you even though you deserve so much better?

7. Feel crushed because a friend or relative told you no to a request you made?

8. Throw tantrums at others to show your disappointment but end up alienating them, which causes even bigger disappointment?

9. Speak poorly of the people in your life because they did not behave (or perform) in ways you had expected them to?

10. Hear others tell you that you are too hard to please?

Use the following chart to evaluate your scores:

10: A perfect 10 shows you are absolutely capable of staying away from expectations, because you know that they do not serve your purposes. Instead of demanding things and people to be a certain way, you deal with life as if you are looking forward to what it has in store for you. You are resilient, strong, and wise. Congratulations!

11–20: Make a list of the occasions in which your expectations were not met. Review them carefully. See what you can do to prevent such occurrences from happening again. Remember that the only constant you can control is yourself—that is, the expectations you create and how you react when they are not met.

21–30: Pay attention to your propensity to harbor expectations from life and others and the damage this may be causing in your relationships.

31–40: Life is not a bowl of cherries but a great journey into fields of opportunities and possibilities. Give yourself the chance to discover the good in the life you have, and stop complaining for not having the life you expect. Empower yourself to change what you can and accept what you cannot change. Only then will you find peace.

41–50: If you don't get over your expectations soon, you will be left alone, fooled and defeated, period. Stop expecting others to meet your standards, and begin finding the good in them. Do consider seeking the help of a therapist or coach who is comfortable confronting you and does not tell you only what you would like to hear. This is your opportunity to trust someone and learn how to love the life you have.

▶ Looking Forward: A Check-In

1. Write down five things you look forward to in your life.
2. Write down three feelings you have when you look forward to something.
3. Now think how often you *have expectations* for your future and how often you *look forward* to your future. Notice how different these two attitudes feel.

▶ Replacing *Expecting* with *Looking Forward*

This exercise will help you shift your attitude from having expectations of your future to looking forward to what you can accomplish in your future. Choose three simple things that you can accomplish this week. Begin looking forward to accomplishing them.

This week I look forward to accomplishing the following three things:

1. _____
2. _____
3. _____

I resolve to enjoy the process of accomplishing them, one thing at a time, and avoid having expectations about the outcomes.

▶ Are You Connected with Your Dreams?

This exercise will help you determine (a) if your reactions to past experiences have disconnected you from your dreams and (b) what you can do to change your direction and reconnect with your dreams.

1. In the last few years, what experience shook you up, threw you off your daily routine, or had a big emotional impact on you? _____

_____

(*Hint:* go as far back as five years. If you have had many experiences of this kind, pick the one with the highest impact on your life or the one that started a string of experiences of similar impact.)

2. What impact did your experience have on your emotions, thoughts, and actions? _____

_____

3. Were you pursuing a dream at that time? What was it? _____

_____

4. Did you abandon or stray from your dream as a reaction to your experience? _____

5. If your answer to question 4 is yes, write three things you can do this week to reconnect with your dream: _____,

_____, _____.

Congratulations! The time has come for you to reconnect with your dream and turn your life into a dynamic, forward-moving adventure.

▶ Please Yourself: An Exercise with Results

This week choose one thing that

- Will give you pleasure
- You have wanted to do for a long time
- You have postponed forever

    This thing is _____

Sign the contract and follow through with action:

This week I resolve to _____, which will give me pleasure and is something I have wanted to do for a long time.

▶ Is Your "Yes" a "No"? An Exercise on Self-Honesty

Being honest about your needs helps you stay focused on your dreams. This exercise will help you improve your self-honesty.

This week notice how often you say yes to other people's demands, when in reality you mean no. Keep a log of these occasions.

Choose three instances when you will say no instead of yes to others' demands that you truly do not want to satisfy. Keep a log of these occasions. Congratulations! You are improving your self-honesty!

....

Things to Remember

- You cannot change past experiences or their emotional impact, nor can you change significant life choices you have already made.
- You can change your life's direction now if you get clear about your needs, reconnect with your dreams, and focus your energies on making them reality.
- Your success in living your dream life depends on how committed you are and you remain to the process until you see results. When you have doubts about yourself, watch a movie from the list, and draw strength and inspiration from the lessons it gives you.

[2]

Make Sense of
Your Fantasies

IN ORDER TO FULFILL your inner desires, you must be able to distinguish them from your fantasies; otherwise, you may fall into the trap of chasing impossible visions. Because telling the difference between desires and fantasies is not always easy, we should begin with a clear definition of both. Knowing the difference will empower you to pursue the goals that fulfill your desires and avoid chasing fantasies in vain.

Desires, also called needs, are instincts. These are natural, inner psychic forces that call our conscious attention through pictures that come to mind, intense emotions felt in the body, and physical reactions that follow those emotions. These powerful inner impulses motivate us to take action in order to satisfy them. For example, hunger is the need for food, calling our attention through picturing food, feeling hungry, or having stomach cramps. In order to satisfy our hunger, we seek food until we find it. Love is another need, one that motivates us to seek a romantic partner and create a family. When we have satisfied a certain desire through appropriate actions, we feel happy, satiated, and fulfilled.

Fantasies are pictures that come to mind when a certain desire is calling our conscious attention. Those pictures are always associated with powerful emotions and physical reactions. Most often, their meaning is hidden not in their imagery but in the emotions they stir in us. The actual purpose of fantasies is to motivate us to take action and satisfy the unfulfilled desire they reveal, without us having to replicate their imagery in reality exactly as we see it in our mind's eye. For example, when we work too hard for too long, we begin fantasizing about exotic beaches, which gives us a restful feeling that lasts as long as we have the fantasy. Therefore, our fantasy reveals a desire for rest. But in reality, this rest does not necessarily have to be on an exotic beach (especially if we cannot afford it!). The fantasy is only telling us that we need a vacation. We then must examine our reality to determine how we can take an affordable vacation to satisfy our need for rest.

Because we are beings propelled by desire and with an endless capacity to imagine, we become very vulnerable to our fantasies, especially when we do not understand their symbolic role. This is a problem particularly when our fantasies are inspired by fancy commercials and other popular media messages. This is why it is so important to see the scenarios of our fantasies as pointers, or indicators of unfulfilled desires, rather than as actual scenarios that have to be acted out in real life.

You are always better off pursuing the fulfillment of a neglected desire than the imaginary scenario of a fantasy, given that your fantasy scenarios most often have nothing to do with reality. Springing from a deep part of the unconscious, they flood your conscious mind with images that awaken powerful emotions. These images arise regardless of whether you are able to make them true. Sometimes, you can successfully replicate them in real life. At other times, it becomes a dangerous chase of impossible visions.

A successful, practical example of replicating a fantasy in real life is buying your dream home when you are actually in debt. The fantasy of owning your dream home ignites enthusiasm and excitement that motivate you to take action and make your fantasy a reality. So you implement a savings program, cut expenses, change spending habits, pay off debt, get support from people who want you to succeed, and find a good real estate agent and a mortgage company with whom you find a home that you can afford and that fulfills your desire to own your hearth. There you are—a homeowner! You have transformed your dream into a reality and have a sense of great pride and fulfillment. This is an example of successfully pursuing a fantasy by fulfilling the desire it reveals through appropriate actions.

Occasionally, however, you may be overwhelmed by a fantasy that is impossible to realize, despite your most rigorous efforts. When you realize this early enough, you do not try to make your unrealistic fantasies come true. But in many instances, your fantasy persists, regardless of your conscious attitude; it can take on a life of its own in your mind, leaving you puzzled with its persistence and, occasionally, embarrassed with its content. In order to break free from a persistent yet impractical fantasy of this sort, you must be able to discern its meaning, recognize the neglected, unfulfilled desires it reveals, and address them in another way.

Olga, a client of mine, developed a confusing and persistent fantasy in which she saw herself living with Melvin Udall, a main character of *As Good as It Gets*. Melvin is initially portrayed in the film as a rude misanthrope whose despicable manners make him repulsive to his neighbors. But in Olga's fantasy, Melvin's rudeness was not repelling; on the contrary, she liked fantasizing about his self-involved attitude and outspoken behavior because his personality was the antithesis of hers. Olga, in reality, was a caretaker; she was always concerned about others' needs, to her own detriment. Her fantasy about Melvin began when she let her twenty-five-year-old daughter and her unemployed husband move into her home. This living arrangement was very difficult and produced considerable distress for Olga. She needed the assertiveness to say, "Please move out—I need my home back," but she could not muster up the courage to take a stand. The more she stifled her need to be assertive, the more persistent her fantasy about Melvin became; Olga developed a full-blown obsession with *As Good as It Gets*. When she sought my professional help, she had watched that film fifty-eight times.

Olga did not recognize that the meaning of this fantasy was a hint at her own need for assertiveness. Awareness of this connection was the key to freedom from her obsession with Melvin's character and her addiction to the film. Olga learned how to discern the meaning of her fantasy using the same tools presented in this chapter. These tools will help you to decode the meaning of your fantasies, no matter how impossible they may seem, to recognize your true needs and to tailor your actions toward their fulfillment.

Fantasies Are Inner Scenarios Triggering Powerful Emotions

Fantasies are mental snapshots that are often spontaneous and fill us with powerful emotions. The word *fantasy* comes from the Greek *fantasia* and means "realm of images" or "the ability to see images as they appear." Such images may be memories of lived experiences or possibilities of a reality not yet lived. They include daydreams, longings, and imaginary situations, as well as inner scenarios inspired by external influences, like advertisements, movies, magazines, and other media.

The images of our fantasies spring naturally from a source within and beyond us, independent of our conscious will and awareness. This source is called the mythic dimension. As soon as these images appear in our mind's eye, they trigger powerful emotions that may vary from soothing to inspiring, from motivating to comforting, from pleasant to exciting. A fantasy of living in a mansion with fifty servants gives us a feeling of being important that satisfies a desire for significance and authority. A fantasy about winning the lottery gives us a feeling of relief that satisfies our desire for financial security. As each emotion satisfies an inner craving, it simultaneously provides an imaginary sense of fulfillment and prompts a desire to experience the same fulfillment in reality by re-creating the fantasy as a real scenario. For example, fantasizing about running your own company not only makes you happy at the moment but also motivates you to actually try and build a company from scratch.

Prices We Pay for Interpreting Our Fantasies Literally

The primary effect of fantasies is the satisfaction and fulfillment they produce as you imagine them. But their ultimate purpose is to make you aware of unfulfilled desires and neglected needs and to motivate you to satisfy them in the real world. This revelation of emotional meaning and its potential to catalyze fulfillment-seeking actions is the true value of fantasies. The key is to know how to interpret them and use their emotional meaning to identify and fulfill the desires they reveal. This is how you achieve inner clarity as the foundation of all the goals you create and the actions you take to accomplish them.

It is unfortunate how often we miss opportunities for inner clarity, as we assign a literal meaning to our fantasies without figuring out what they really mean. Here are two of the most common reactions to interpreting fantasies literally:

- We tend to ignore them, labeling them as unrealistic, dumb, or outrageous and not worth our attention. Offended by the seemingly inappropriate nature of their visual content, we may respond to them with embarrassment, shame, or even guilt. As a result, we dismiss one of the most important tools we have for getting in touch with our real inner desires, the fulfillment of which is essential to our happiness. In Chapter 1, we saw the dangers of suppressing our dreams and the prices we pay for doing so.

- We take them literally and try to replicate them in real life as we imagine them in order to reexperience the fulfillment they produced in our imagination. We already saw that fantasies are indicators of neglected needs, not pictures that always have to be copied in reality. For example, many of my clients have complained that when they carried sexual fantasies out as real-life scenarios, they felt disappointed or even hurt.

Quite often, the practice of reenacting fantasy scenarios in reality becomes an addiction; the people who fall into this trap try in vain to experience the fulfillment their fantasies give them in their imagination, ignoring altogether the fact that reality operates under different rules from those of imagination. When we do not consider the complexities of reality as we try to fulfill imaginary scenarios, we set ourselves up for disappointment and, oftentimes, disaster. For example, a former client of mine caused a real tragedy—a fatal car accident that destroyed three families—after pursuing his fantasy to have an affair with his brother's wife. In essence, his need was to be recognized by his own wife for his efforts as a breadwinner. His wife used to compare him with his wealthy brother, which made him feel inferior and unappreciated.

Chasing Fantasies Often Invites Defeat by Reality

When you try to fulfill a fantasy in the real world, the first thing you must ask yourself is what desire you are trying to fulfill as you pursue the fantasy. Only when you have a clear answer to this question can you then take appropriate actions to fulfill your desire, always taking into account the parameters of reality. Otherwise, you may be setting yourself up for real danger, especially if you ignore the reality rules. Here is a common example: let us assume that you fantasize about owning a very expensive car; meanwhile, your financial reality is miserable. This fantasy gives you a sense of accomplishment that reveals your desire for power and success. Next let us assume that instead of taking actions to feel successful by improving your finances, you buy that car on credit. Now, as you drive it on the highway, you realize that the feeling of success is wearing off rather quickly, and you begin worrying about how you will pay for the car. In time, your worry may turn into guilt, anger at yourself, and shame for not being able to control your financial life.

Another common fantasy is marrying a celebrity, which reveals a desire for recognition and social acceptance. People who give in to this fantasy become celebrity stalkers, and they usually end up not in a wedding chapel but in a prison cell.

The big screen is filled with film characters chasing fantasies only to invite defeat by reality. Some of them learn their lesson quickly and suffer less damage than those who are slower to learn. They are great examples from which to learn how to avoid catastrophe by discerning fantasies from your true desires. One such movie character is Allie Fox, who drives himself and his family to destruction as he chases his fantasy about a perfect world in *The Mosquito Coast*. This film is a parable about the tendency to reject reality as uniformly corrupt and evil and seek a fantasy of happiness in exotic worlds, imagined as pure and perfect.

Allie Fox is a brilliant inventor caught in a fantasy he cannot resist: he resents America as a corrupt culture of relentless consumerism and seeks to create a paradise of authentic living with his wife and four children in the jungles of Central America. He does not pause to consider or test the parameters of his new reality. Believing that he brings civilization to the primitives, he masterminds the installation of an ice machine in the middle of a remote part of Central America, ignoring the fact that ice has no value or purpose in the life of the natives, as they know it. The results of his experiment are catastrophic and cause the family to begin a desperate odyssey through the jungle.

The Mosquito Coast is a metaphor of the modern human who is in denial of the reality in which he or she is called to adapt and create happiness. Today the fantasy of seeking a perfect life in an exotic paradise away from our environment is rather common. As traveling to unusual, remote destinations has become trendy and possibilities to own foreign real estate abound, the fantasy that happiness awaits us in a less developed country is exacerbated by advertising campaigns. Only once we are there, faced with the reality of the foreign place, do we realize that our issues remain the same. We then have to accept that in order to create happiness, we must consider the parameters of the existing reality, observe its laws, and adapt to the civilization that informs that reality.

Many films show the dangerous consequences of pursuing sexual fantasies in real life. *Consenting Adults*, *Fatal Attraction*, *The Good Girl*, and *Damage* are among them. In *Consenting Adults* and *Fatal Attraction*, the main characters are happily married men who choose to have an extramarital affair that proves to be fatal. The cost they pay is very high, as they are forced into a horrifying adventure in a cruel reality once the sexual fantasy is over. In *The Good Girl*, the heroine tries to give meaning to her unfulfilled existence through an extramarital affair with a fantasy-ridden young man, only to end up surrendering to the meager reality of her life.

Damage is a family drama and a real tragedy. The movie's hero is Dr. Stephen Fleming, a member of the English Parliament who enjoys status, wealth, and a seemingly perfect family life. He and his wife maintain a superficial and stagnant relationship; they are either too comfortable or too afraid to admit that underneath the calm surface of their marriage, a crisis that will expose their unfulfilled lives is about to erupt. The fatal moment arrives when Dr. Fleming unexpectedly meets his son's fiancée, Anna, for whom he feels an immediate and passionate attraction. It is not too long before the two get immersed in an illicit affair, despite Anna's continued engagement to Fleming's son, Martyn. Unable to control his lust for her, Stephen Fleming insists on keeping the affair active throughout the preparations for his son's wedding. His desire for love is so strong that as he tries to fulfill it with Anna, he defies reality by trying to manipulate it through deceit. The more addicted he grows to his fantasy, the more immersed he becomes in lying.

Unfortunately, as for anyone who chases a fantasy only to end up defeated by reality, Stephen Fleming ends up paying a very high price. The tragic twist of unfolding events reveals a perennial truth about the law of reality: even when we think that we can evade or control reality in order to pursue a fantasy, reality will always defeat our purposes. We can never find fulfillment through deception and manipulation of other people's real love and trust. Eventually, reality itself will prevail and force us to face the consequences of our actions.

Fantasizing as Addiction: Daydreaming and Compulsive Worrying

Daydreaming and compulsive worrying are two forms of addiction to the feelings produced by our fantasies. When we daydream, we enjoy the pleasant emotional effects of our fantasies without any intention to make them true. When we compulsively worry, we seek the exact opposite: as we indulge in catastrophic fantasies that are irrelevant to our reality (for example, fantasizing that our child is going to be kidnapped or contract an air-transmitted, deadly virus), our real intention is to feel distress and stay perpetually troubled and unhappy. On the other hand, daydreaming makes us feel better as long as we use it. So it can become a habit similar to taking addictive painkillers or other mood-altering substances. As it happens in drug withdrawal, the moment we stop daydreaming, reality hits us again and the uncomfortable feelings return.

Daydreaming begins early in life; while growing up, we are unable to change our reality, so we resort to fantasies to make ourselves feel better. Sometimes daydreaming may take an extreme form, as shown in the powerful film *Rosie*. It is the story of a thirteen-year-old Belgian girl raising herself in an unfair and cruel environment. To cope with her craving for love, she develops a powerful fantasy about a boy as her only true and loyal companion. Propelled by his strong imaginary presence within her, Rosie runs away from home. She embarks on an adventure of creating the perfect family with the boy, in which she enjoys the love she never received in reality. Immersed in her fantasy, she ignores the rules of reality and takes actions that make her a danger both to herself and to others. Eventually, reality wins. Rosie is faced with consequences that force her to realize that even though reality is not always fair, daydreaming alone is not an advisable or effective solution.

Like Rosie, almost all of us have occasionally escaped into daydreaming as children or as adolescents, to cope with sadness or disgruntlement. But as adults, if we use daydreaming as the only way to soothe the unpleasant emotions triggered by a difficult reality without taking any real action, we end up prisoners of the reality we wish to escape, which is what happened to Cecilia in *The Purple Rose of Cairo*. Cecilia is a compulsive daydreamer who indulges in fantasies of love and Hollywood glamour. The more she gets absorbed in daydreaming, the more paralyzed she becomes and the more incapable she is of changing her reality. The price she pays is to surrender to the reality that she so much despises. Obviously, her addiction to daydreaming has done nothing to empower her toward taking action to find true happiness.

The same pattern of using fantasies to enjoy a certain emotional effect holds true with compulsive worrying, but the addiction here is to fantasies with a negative emotional effect. Unlike daydreamers, who escape *unhappiness* through fantasies that cause pleasant emotions, compulsive worriers escape *happiness* through fantasies that trigger unpleasant emotions. Compulsive worriers imagine the worst because they are addicted to the unpleasant feelings these thoughts produce. For them, feelings of contentment and happiness are unacceptable. Compulsive worriers are afraid of happiness, period. They are more comfortable with gloominess and depression, just as people living in basements or dark rooms prefer darkness to sunlight. If you know a compulsive worrier, notice how motivated he or she is to imagine the worst even while everything in life is, in fact, going very well. When a compulsive worrier sees a possibility to feel happy, he or she immediately imagines a catastrophe, like a person used to the darkness covers his eyes or runs away to hide from the sun. This is how compulsive worriers avoid happy feelings and maintain their depressed mood, which is familiar, comfortable, and, therefore, easier for them to feel.

An example of a person with these characteristics is Roy Waller, the main character in *Matchstick Men*. Obsessive-compulsive and agoraphobic, Roy is a small-time criminal living in isolation who spends most of his time worrying and feeling miserable. When his idiosyncrasies begin to threaten his criminal productivity, he seeks the help of a psychoanalyst. From that moment on, he embarks on an adventure that will show him how to let go of his addiction to feelings of misery and learn to enjoy the feelings of love and human warmth.

The addiction to daydreaming or compulsive worrying is similar to an addiction to any mood-altering substance; it drains your energy and paralyzes your will to participate in reality. Because our fantasies are boundless with an infinite array of imagery, daydreaming and compulsive worrying can be endless. The more you engage in them, the more powerless you become over your real life. In order to break free from addictive fantasizing, you must stop using fantasies as a mood-altering substance. You must also learn to discern the emotional meaning of fantasies and use these insights as guidance to fulfill your true yearnings in reality.

How to Make Sense of Your Fantasies

Clearly, trying to make unrealistic fantasies come true or even just obsessing over them can do more harm than good. But fantasies do play a very important role—if you analyze them correctly, they can help you find out which of your emotional needs are not being met. In this part, you are given the tools to make sense of your fantasies in three easy steps. The exercises at the end of this chapter will give you the opportunity to practice the steps with your own fantasies to gain inner clarity. The three steps are as follows:

1. **Distinguish fantasies from desires.** To accomplish this, check how applicable your fantasies are in reality. Answer these questions: How feasible are your fantasies, considering *real* parameters? What will be the material, emotional, and moral consequences of pursuing X, Y, and Z fantasies, both for your life and the lives of others? Give specific and honest answers.

2. **Get the emotional meaning of your fantasies by separating them from the feelings they cause.** Remember that fantasies are pictures triggering powerful emotions, so their meaning is not pictorial but emotional. Do not get caught up in the imagery, but focus instead on your emotional reactions. Answer these questions: What do you *feel* when you have X, Y, or Z fantasies? (Name all of your feelings.) What unfulfilled desires do these feelings reveal? (Name those desires.)

3. **Acknowledge your inner desires and develop reality-appropriate scenarios to fulfill them.** Look at your current life and identify the areas where these desires and needs have been overlooked. Look at your actions. How have you been stultifying or neglecting your needs? Reframe your fantasies as desires seeking fulfillment, and then create reality-appropriate scenarios to satisfy them. Choose appropriate actions considering real parameters and limitations. For example, an unrealistic fantasy to fly your own plane may reveal a desire for freedom. Look at your real life. In what areas do you feel stifled, suppressed, or restrained? What can you do to satisfy your need for freedom without hurting yourself or others? Use real data, exercise judgment, and take steps for which you can evaluate results as you achieve your goals.

A former client named Bill, a sixty-five-year-old retired widower, is a good example of someone who discovered a neglected need in the emotional meaning of a persistent fantasy. Bill sought my professional help to break free from a fantasy that had become an obsession. The fantasy came to him spontaneously one day as he was reading the paper. It consisted of Bill, at his current age, being awarded the gold medal for a marathon in an Olympic stadium, amidst thousands of people applauding his victory. Bill had been a runner in his youth and had satisfied his desire for success in sports, so when the fantasy first came to him, he dismissed it as a distorted memory. But the fantasy persisted and each time triggered powerful emotions ranging from a sense of success, victory, and bliss to acceptance and recognition by other people.

In reality, Bill's life lacked relationships. For five years following the loss of his wife in an accident, Bill had become increasingly withdrawn from social interactions. He was becoming a recluse. A healthy and attractive man with a long career as an engineer, Bill responded to his grief by closing himself off from people and human warmth. He remained emotionally numb for a while, until he began having the persistent fantasy of being a gold medalist. The fantasy, filled with powerful emotion, awoke him to his unfulfilled need of being close to people. Once he understood that the purpose of this fantasy was to awaken his emotions, Bill accepted that he had a tremendous need to reconnect with people and exchange love. Once he realized this, his fantasy subsided. As he saw what his fantasy was really trying to tell him, Bill recognized that he had a new goal to accomplish: to pursue human connections that would fulfill his desire for warmth, acceptance, and love.

Bill remembered his interests in dancing, bird-watching, and kayaking. He joined a dance class for people his age, a bird-watchers' group, and a kayakers' club. He began weekly excursions with people, increasingly enjoying his new friendships. He rediscovered interest in others and in himself, and he eventually began dating. Within a year after he "got with the program," he met a woman whom he eventually married. They had a lovely wedding ceremony filled with friends and family who celebrated their union. On that day, Bill remembered how all this began—with his marathon-winning fantasy! Standing among his friends and family, he held his bride's hand with tenderness, feeling the same emotions that his fantasy had awoken: human warmth, acceptance, and love. Bill knew that he had responded to the message of his seemingly unrealistic fantasy by re-creating his life and finding the happiness he deserved.

Reel Fulfillment in Action

Movie Time! ▸ *Watch a Movie for Fun, Learn a Lesson of Life*

Choose a movie from each of the following two lists, and watch it alone or with your group. Pay attention to the characters' lives and relationships as they unfold in the story. Notice where the characters' process leads them and how you relate to them. Observe your reactions. Afterward, think about the questions that follow each list. Write down your thoughts, and share them with others.

Movies About the World of Fantasies

Blue Velvet (1986), directed by David Lynch
Consenting Adults (1992), directed by Alan J. Pakula
Crimes of Passion (1984), directed by Ken Russell
Cruel Intentions (1999), directed by Roger Kumble
Damage (1992), directed by Louis Malle
Dangerous Liaisons (1988), directed by Stephen Frears
Exotica (1994), directed by Atom Egoyan
Fatal Attraction (1987), directed by Adrian Lyne
Felicia's Journey (1999), directed by Atom Egoyan
Fitzcarraldo (1982), directed by Werner Herzog
The Good Girl (2002), directed by Miguel Arteta
Julia and Julia (1987), directed by Peter Del Monte
Matchstick Men (2003), directed by Ridley Scott
Midnight Cowboy (1969), directed by John Schlesinger
Misery (1990), directed by Rob Reiner
The Mosquito Coast (1986), directed by Peter Weir
Passion of Mind (2000), directed by Alain Berliner
The Purple Rose of Cairo (1985), directed by Woody Allen
Rosie (1998), directed by Patrice Toye
Sweet Home Alabama (2002), directed by Andy Tennant
13 Going on 30 (2004), directed by Gary Winick

Questions to Answer

1. In the film, the main character tries to turn a fantasy into reality. How successful are his or her efforts?
2. How does the main character change as he or she tries to turn fantasy into reality?
3. How do the main character's actions to live out a fantasy affect his or her environment and family and the lives of other characters in the film?
4. What do you think are the main character's unfulfilled needs, and what would be more appropriate ways to fulfill them?
5. Put yourself in the role of the main character. What would you do differently to find fulfillment?

Movies About Following One's Dreams

Billy Elliot (2000), directed by Stephen Daldry
Chariots of Fire (1981), directed by Hugh Hudson
Field of Dreams (1989), directed by Phil Alden Robinson
Flashdance (1983), directed by Adrian Lyne
Jonathan Livingston Seagull (1973), directed by Hall Bartlett
Legally Blonde (2001), directed by Robert Luketic
Miracle (2004), directed by Gavin O' Connor
October Sky (1999), directed by Joe Johnston
Real Women Have Curves (2002), directed by Patricia Cardoso
Rocky (1976), directed by John G. Avildsen
The Rookie (2002), directed by John Lee Hancock
Rudy (1993), directed by David Anspaugh
Whale Rider (2002), directed by Niki Caro
Working Girl (1988), directed by Mike Nichols

Questions to Answer

1. In the film, the main character is following a dream more powerful than life itself. What makes the main character know that he or she is on the right track? Is the evidence for this material, spiritual, or both? Name these signs.
2. How does the main character overcome each difficulty and obstacle on the way to fulfilling his or her dream?

3. Compare a movie from the first list with one from the second list. Those from the first list are about chasing fantasies, and those from the second are about fulfilling dreams. What differences do you see between the two movies in the main characters' lives and actions?

4. To pursue happiness, we must transform our dreams into reality, but this is not the same as chasing fantasies. In your life, how can you tell the difference between a dream and a fantasy?

5. What do you do to protect yourself from chasing fantasies and to encourage yourself to pursue your dreams?

6. What is the dream you are pursuing today?

Make Sense of Your Fantasies ▶ Exercises and Activities

The following exercises are designed to help you understand the meaning of your fantasies and their significance in your life. When you complete the exercises, you will have learned the following:

- Fantasies are symbolic pictures that trigger powerful emotions and can be used as tools to identify important unfulfilled needs.
- You can get the emotional meaning of fantasies by paying attention to the emotions they stir up in your body.
- These emotions reveal inner desires that you must fulfill through reality-appropriate actions.

▶ Your Biggest Fantasy Then

In this exercise, you will explore the significance of your favorite childhood fantasy. You will remember how your fantasy helped you to cope with your real problems.

1. Go back to your fantasy life as a child. Can you recall your favorite fantasy? Was it something you wanted to be when you grew up? Or did you live an imaginary life along with your real life? (*Hint*: perhaps you had an imaginary friend with whom you talked every night before falling asleep.)

2. Remember this fantasy. Make it vivid. Describe it in a short paragraph. Next, describe the feelings your fantasy evoked and how those feelings helped you cope with problems at home or school.

My favorite fantasy as a child was _____

_____ .

When I had this fantasy I felt _____

_____ .

I liked having this fantasy because it helped me _____

_____ .

▶ Your Biggest Fantasies Now

Now you will explore your current adult fantasy life. Think of three frequent or persistent fantasies. They can be yearnings or aspirations you have or simple fantasies that give you a really nice feeling.

1. Bring up your fantasies one at a time. Describe each vividly, just as you imagine it. Do not be embarrassed about the content of your fantasies, and do not try to pick "correct" or "reasonable" fantasies.

Fantasy 1: _____

_____ .

Fantasy 2: _____

_____ .

Fantasy 3: _____

_____ .

2. Now read each fantasy and feel yourself inside its imagery. What emotions does the fantasy stir in your body? Focus on your feelings one at a time. Don't try to make sense of them. Stay in the imagery of your fantasy for as long as it stirs up emotions, and write them down as you feel them. (*Note:* you may use the list of emotions in Appendix A as a reference.)

Feelings from Fantasy 1: _____

Feelings from Fantasy 2: _____

Feelings from Fantasy 3: _____

3. Read your emotion words a few times without thinking about them. Which ones grab your attention? Which ones evoke a physical, visceral response? Write down no more than three.

My predominant feelings from my three biggest fantasies are

   1. _____
   2. _____
   3. _____

4. Read again the feeling words you just wrote. What hidden, unfulfilled needs do they reveal to you? Name these needs. Do not write more than three. (*Note:* you may use the lists of needs in Appendixes B and C as a reference.)

The emotions that my strongest fantasies stir point to these unfulfilled needs (or desires):

   1. _____
   2. _____
   3. _____

5. Reread your three needs. They may all be pointing toward one main need that is the secret to your fulfillment, or they may be three distinct needs. In either case, you will have gained clarity about your inner needs, which will help you focus on ways to fulfill them one at a time. For now, choose one need and work only with this need for the rest of the exercises.

6. Now that you have identified your unfulfilled desire, ask yourself the following question:

What are some reality-appropriate scenarios through which I can fulfill my need?

    Write down three alternative scenarios that take realistic parameters into consideration. The following chapters will guide you as you follow through with your scenarios.

▶ **Your Favorite TV Commercials**

Commercial images almost always have the same effect on us as our inner fantasies: they are carefully designed to stir powerful emotions pointing to inner, unfulfilled needs. These are usually emotional needs, which the commercial message promises to fulfill through the advertised product. For example, notice how a commercial advertising an expensive, lavender-scented bubble bath promises to fulfill not the need for physical hygiene but the emotional need for inner purity and spiritual serenity.

In this exercise, you will learn how to get the emotional meaning of your favorite commercials and gain insight into your true needs. The process is very similar to the one you followed with your favorite fantasies.

1. Think of three commercials that you absolutely love because of how they make you feel when you watch them or think about them.

   Commercial 1: _____
   Commercial 2: _____
   Commercial 3: _____

2. Now imagine each commercial separately and feel yourself inside its imagery. What emotions does it stir in your body? Focus on your feelings one at a time. Do not try to make sense of them. Stay in the commercial's imagery for as long as it continues to stir up emotions. Write down your emotions as you feel them. (*Note:* you may use the list of emotions in Appendix A as a reference.)

   Feelings from Commercial 1: _____
   Feelings from Commercial 2: _____
   Feelings from Commercial 3: _____

3. Read your emotion words a few times without thinking about them. Which emotion words grab your attention? (Notice how you respond to them physically, viscerally.) Write down no more than three of these feeling words.

My predominant feelings from my three favorite commercials are

1. _____
2. _____
3. _____

4. Read the feeling words you just wrote. What hidden, unfulfilled needs do they reveal to you? Name these needs. Do not write more than three. (*Note:* you may use the needs lists in Appendixes B and C as a reference.)

The emotions that my favorite commercials evoke point to these unfulfilled needs:

1. _____
2. _____
3. _____

5. Read through the needs you identified. How possible is it to satisfy them through the purchase of products advertised in your favorite commercials? If it is not possible, can you think of other ways to satisfy these needs? What are these ways?

Things to Remember

- Fantasies and commercials are pictures aimed at stirring in the body emotions that point to unfulfilled needs.
- You can detect your unfulfilled needs if you identify the emotions stirred in the body through persistent fantasies or favorite commercials.
- The body never lies. The more in tune you are with your physical sensations, the closer you are to answers about yourself that you cannot find "out there."

Acknowledge Your True Needs

WE ARE PROPELLED through life by our needs. Our needs are the instincts, natural desires, genetic impulses, innate passions, and life cravings that spring endlessly from the very core of our existence. Not simple whims but forces of nature, these deep desires carry built-in patterns of emotional and intellectual behavior that drive us to attain their fulfillment. From the basic needs for air, water, and food to the most complex needs for personal meaning, a higher purpose, and self-awareness, our inner desires are the driving forces that propel us through life and motivate our growth. We are alive to fulfill needs and we fulfill needs to stay alive.

Nature has a way of letting us know that our needs seek fulfillment, thanks to physical sensations and spontaneous thoughts. For example, stomach cramps and visions of food make us realize we are hungry, which motivates us to look for something to eat. The same is also true for complex needs pertaining to our social, emotional, and spiritual wholeness. For example, we know that we have a need for love when we fantasize about being with a mate and sharing physical affection. Such spontaneous imaginings trigger both emotional feelings of tenderness and physical sensations that remind us of our need for love and motivate us to seek a mate.

Our happiness depends on how well aware we are of our inner needs and how committed we are to fulfilling them, while coping with our busy day-to-day lives. In our effort to reconcile conflicts between our inner needs and the demands of our external reality, many of us have lost the inner thread that connects us with our deep desires. Distracted and pre-occupied by the tasks and responsibilities of our daily lives, we forget how to first recognize and then fulfill our true, personal needs, our nature's inner commands for happiness.

As you seek inner clarity, certainty, and faith in yourself, it is essential to find this lost inner connection. This chapter is designed to help you reconnect with your inner nature by showing you how to recognize and honor your true needs. Naming your true needs empowers you to claim them. Being clear about them compels you to fulfill them.

Needs Are Not Always Wants

Many of us confuse the term *need* with *want*. A need is a physiological or psychological necessity that we must satisfy in order to ensure our well-being. For example, when you say, "I need a new, good car," this means that you have a necessity for transportation that is safe, comfortable, and reliable. Perhaps the car you have is old and unsafe. On the other hand, a want is a willful expression of a wish stating your intention to make it reality. Wants are not always related to our real needs. This is why your wants may often be harmful to your well-being. For example, you may say, "I want a new car," even though, in essence, your need is to feel secure by saving money for the future; or you may say, "I want to date new people," even though, in essence, your need is to improve your communication with your current mate; or you may say, "I want to marry a rich person," even though, in essence, your need is to reconnect with the love of your life, who is not so rich but adores you and brightens your days with smiles.

People who are perpetually unfulfilled pursue only wants, neglecting their needs. Wants are constantly prompted by social incentives and the media. This is why we give them more attention than our true needs: wants are closer to our awareness and easier to voice. Very often our wants seduce us into believing that if we pursue them, we will also satisfy our deep emotional needs. For example, we may think that if we marry for money, love will somehow come as a result. This is simply wrong. When you indulge in your wants, thinking that they may fulfill your true needs, you cannot have your cake and eat it, too. This is why being clear about your needs and distinguishing them from your wants is essential to building the goals that will bring you true fulfillment. The happiest, luckiest, and wisest people are not the ones who *need to fulfill their wants* but rather are those who clearly *want to fulfill their needs*, against the noise of the media and other social pressures. Such people concentrate their efforts to make their true desires a reality and are great examples of how inner clarity leads to success.

The Six Life Spheres of Human Needs

Our needs can be classified into six distinct categories, each representing a sphere of life. Ideally, we have to fulfill needs emerging from all six spheres of life in order to be truly happy.

- **Sphere of material and physical needs.** Clothing, financial prosperity, food, material and physical security, physical health, and shelter needs fall into this category.
- **Sphere of ego and identity needs.** Here the needs seeking fulfillment pertain to our ego and personal identity. Among them are the needs for achievement, challenge, competence, culture, distinction, freedom to express ourselves, independence, possession, privacy, property, and recognition.
- **Sphere of social needs.** Here we are moved to fulfill needs that satisfy our social being. Among these may be acknowledgment, affiliation, citizenship, community, competition, cooperation, hierarchy, history, justice, legacy, power, recognition, status, success, and work.
- **Sphere of knowledge and intellectual needs.** Here we strive to fulfill needs pertaining to our intellectual being. Such needs may include communication, ideas, information, intellectual explorations of all kinds, knowledge, language, science, strategy, organization, structure, and technology.

- **Sphere of emotional needs.** Here we strive to maintain emotional health as we fulfill needs pertaining to our emotional well-being. Such needs may include appreciation, belonging, community, entertainment, family, home, love, mating, play, pleasure, procreating, and respect.
- **Sphere of spiritual needs.** Here our emerging needs motivate us to fulfill our spiritual nature as our innate ability to express our inner connection with the Supreme Being through ideals, ritual, or creativity. Needs belonging to this sphere include art, beauty, creativity, dignity, faith, a sense of higher purpose, holiness, ideals, personal meaning, purity, religion, reverence, ritual, and self-awareness.

Inner Needs Are Often Revealed in Fantasies

While getting what you want requires primarily that you exercise your will to get it, fulfilling a need requires that you first exercise your ability to recognize it and then figure out what you have to do to fulfill it. This may be a problem when your unfulfilled needs are "hidden" from your awareness and the only indication that they exist is a persistent sense of dissatisfaction and a pervasive longing for joy.

Such was the case for Andreas, a client who asked for my professional help to learn what it was he needed, since he thought he had everything he wanted. Andreas, at fifty-two, had a successful business, a beautiful younger wife, and an illustrious social network. Yet for the past three years, he had felt a growing dissatisfaction with life and attempted to numb this with an increasingly frequent use of alcohol. Bordering on severe depression, Andreas went through his daily motions uninterested and joyless, until he decided to do something about it and contacted me for an appointment.

"How can I find out what I need to be happy if I can have everything I want?" he asked me during our first session.

"Let's take a look at your fantasies," I suggested.

"Oh, that's easy!" he answered. "I like fantasizing that I'm a spy, working for the intelligence service."

Andreas's fantasy occasionally embarrassed him but never failed to thrill him. It was especially active when he was at social functions with his wife, who gave great importance to public functions and society events. At least once a week, Andreas had to accompany her to such an event, even though he never enjoyed being there.

"The only fun thing about those receptions is fantasizing that I'm there undercover," he said. "As I mingle among the guests and overhear their conversations, I think of myself as gathering data for my mission."

"How does the fantasy of being a spy make you feel?" I asked.

"I *love* thinking that no one knows who I really am!" he said. "I feel free, unattached, independent, in control, *and* smarter than the other guests. I feel like I have a purpose for attending those functions. Otherwise, I get bored to death thinking that everyone knows me as Andreas and expects me to play a certain role. This suffocates me. But when I imagine I am a spy, I feel like I have options about who I am that others cannot control."

It was obvious that in his fantasy, Andreas fulfilled vital needs that he had neglected in his real life. He desired to be free from social conventions and from the persona he had to present in his wife's social circles. He needed to feel in control of his decisions and free to assert his own needs to his spouse. As I got to know him better, I realized that Andreas was an introverted intellectual, delighted by philosophy, poetry, and chess. His wife, on the other hand, was a socialite. Afraid that his intellectual needs might alienate her and create a marital crisis, Andreas had stifled his own desires by adapting his wife's social habits. As a result, he felt increasingly miserable.

"I need to stand up for myself and get back to doing the things I love," he said once he saw the meaning of his spy fantasy. "I had never thought that depriving myself of chess and Schopenhauer might have such an effect on me. Perhaps I had not taken my needs as an intellectual seriously," he concluded pensively.

Andreas is not the only one overlooking his needs and underestimating the importance of activities geared toward their fulfillment. Many of us commit similar injustices against our inner nature when we abandon fulfilling activities in order to please another person. Most of us ignore altogether that our life evolves in multiple spheres of existence and that each sphere represents a whole group of needs seeking fulfillment through appropriate actions. It is our responsibility to consider all aspects of our being as equally important and not repress any part of our inner nature only because it is not considered vital by others.

Honoring Our Needs Saves Our Spirit

Honoring our true needs is an exercise of courage and faith, often calling us to defy social conventions and external mandates. Blessed are the people who achieve this, for life returns their efforts not only with happiness but also with wisdom, self-knowledge, and an admirable sense of meaning and purpose. A great drama illustrating how honoring our deep, inner needs is a commitment to our spiritual nature is *Titanic*. In this epic, we are shown how two young people save their spirits by honoring their need for love. Heeding their inner call empowers them to challenge conformism, overcome social restrictions, and experience a deep spiritual bond outliving time, death, and oblivion.

The *Titanic*, of course, is the legendary ship that sank on its maiden voyage in 1912, after colliding with an iceberg in the North Atlantic. Some fifteen hundred people lost their lives as the boat plunged two and a half thousand miles beneath the cold waves. In the film *Titanic*, the ship is a metaphor for a society ridden by hypocrisy, injustice, and greed. Divided according to a rigid class system, the ship grants different privileges to its passengers based not on their moral merit but on their financial and social power. The wealthy passengers travel first-class, enjoying palatial suites with ocean views and superb entertainment that never seems to end. The poor travel third-class, packed in the bottom of the ship and forbidden to trespass on the upper decks or mingle with the rich.

The ship itself is portrayed as a product of blind ambition and greed. Built to satisfy outrageous expectations, the *Titanic* is the utopia of the rich and powerful, embodying an illusion of opulence and indestructibility. To fulfill this unrealistic vision, extreme emphasis has been given to the size and grandeur of the *Titanic*, conjuring a deceptive image of indestructibility. But in actuality, this facade has been created at the expense of the ship's structural integrity and prudent safety standards. As about two thousand innocent passengers board the seemingly impressive vessel amidst an uproar of festivities to launch their journey across the Atlantic, no one can fathom that the *Titanic* is a deadly vehicle, destined to become an underwater mass grave.

As this floating but doomed society of strangers begins its fatal journey, two young people, from backgrounds that are polar opposites, meet to live out a great love story. They are Rose DeWitt Bukater, a seventeen-year-old socialite traveling first-class with her mother and cold-blooded but wealthy fiancé, and Jack Dawson, a penniless but warmhearted artist bunking in the steerage, who jumped on the *Titanic* to seek his fortune abroad. Thanks to their courage to honor their love for each other, Rose and Jack transcend all divisions, restrictions, and conventions imposed by the society of the *Titanic* and let their spirits connect in the purest, most sincere union. Love forces them to push beyond the barriers of their respective social class and open up to each other's inner world. In a few hours, their new discoveries expand their individual horizons and give them new perspectives about life that will change them forever.

As we watch Rose and Jack fall in love, we sense that the world around them is about to collapse; seconds after they consummate their love, the ship hits an iceberg and suffers a giant gash in its hull. Just as a corrupt society begins to disintegrate once a scandal is exposed, the compromised *Titanic* begins to sink with amazing speed once it becomes public knowledge that no sufficient safety precautions exist to keep all passengers from drowning or freezing to death once they jump into the water. As the entire ship erupts in chaos and more than two thousand people scramble to save themselves, the love of Rose and Jack shines through and gives us hope that they can survive this catastrophe and spend many more years together. Indeed, what follows, though tragic, may separate them physically but will not have the power to kill the union of their spirit.

Eighty-four years later, when the 101-year-old Rose recalls the events of that night, she reveals that Jack has never left her. She likens the sinking of the *Titanic* to the doom of a society ridden by ignorance, greed, and ambition and declares that her love with Jack was the one true thing that remained unscathed. It saved her not only her life but also her spirit, by giving her the gift of an immortal union.

How to Honor Your Needs

If recognizing your neglected needs is not always easy, honoring them can be a challenge as well. The pressure to abide by the expectations of your surroundings—whether it be your family, your job, or your community—is usually so intense that the choice to follow your inner desires to fulfillment is often a lonely path. But if you do choose to honor your needs and walk the path to the end, the reward of having found the happiness you deserve will justify your entire journey and make you fully realize that the search for happiness is the noblest cause you were born to achieve.

To honor your true needs, you will have to face and conquer three challenges. First, you must heed your inner call. Second, you must defy the fear of rejection and be ready to walk the lonely path of fulfilling your desires, whether your familiar environment approves or not. Third, you must walk that path to the very end and not give up until you have fulfilled the needs that summoned you to take this life-changing journey. You will arrive at the end victorious and ready to celebrate your great success.

In the examples that follow, you will see how a number of mythical characters from popular films overcame these challenges and found the happiness they dreamed. Let their stories inspire you on your own journey.

Heed the Inner Call

In Chapter 1, you were introduced to Shirley Valentine and Frances, two film characters who responded to their need for happiness and heeded an inner call to create a new life away from their familiar surroundings in sun-filled Mediterranean countries. For Shirley, it was Greece; for Frances, Italy. Their stories illustrate how the journey of transformation begins with a single "yes" to an inner call.

Usually, the moment calling us to respond to the inner voice through an adventure of self-transformation is so private that no one else may take notice. Answering an inner call marks not only the beginning of a growth phase but also the moment that we accept our destiny. It is an extraordinary opportunity to become the person our inner nature desires us to be and find the wholeness we are created to enjoy.

Shirley Valentine experiences that moment at the airport in Greece, when she runs away from the boarding crowd and returns to her hotel. She heeds her desire, refusing to return to her dull life in England, and finds true bliss starting a new life in Greece. Frances, on the other hand, responds to the call while traveling on a tourist-filled bus through the Tuscan countryside. When the villa Bramasole beckons to her through the bus window, she jumps off the bus and embarks on a journey that will lead to her happiness.

As happiness calls Shirley to Greece and Frances to Italy, it summons stockbroker Jack Campbell, the main character of *The Family Man*, from a penthouse in Manhattan to suburban New Jersey. Young, single, and driven to success, Jack goes to bed alone on New Year's Eve and wakes up the next morning to a life that he might well have enjoyed, had he made different choices. This life is, in fact, a dream in which Jack finds himself married to Kate Reynolds, the love of his life, while in reality, he had abandoned her ten years earlier to pursue his business career. In his dream, he is not a broker but rather works in his father-in-law's business, selling tires and auto accessories to support his wife and two children. His dream presents a reality that is totally opposite his real life and shows him the possibility for happiness based on loving his family and honoring values other than financial success and social advancement.

As Jack gets more immersed in his dream, he becomes aware of two major truths about his real life: (a) he has never stopped loving Kate, and (b) in order for him to be complete, he must find her immediately and win her back. Jack does not waste time: he leaves a multimillion-dollar deal on the table, to the astonishment of his partners, and searches for Kate until he finds her. She has never married but instead has become a power attorney who is about to move to Europe, having accepted a job transfer. Jack knows that this is his only chance to be honest about his neglected needs. Following her to the airport, he begs her not to board the plane. And this is how the journey to his new life begins.

Defy the Fear of Rejection

In *My Big Fat Greek Wedding*, Toula Portokalos is thirty, single, and living with her family in a Greek neighborhood in Chicago. Every morning before dawn, she and her father open the family restaurant, where she works as a hostess. Toula's life revolves around that restaurant, an extension of her mother's kitchen. The Greek delicacies and the family feasts are the only tasty aspects of Toula's otherwise bland life. Though stifled by her family's traditions, she has stayed loyal to their Greek traditions, still living at home and working in the family business. With no friends or mate of her own, all she has to look forward to is the next order of moussaka she must serve.

Bored and dispirited, Toula plods through her daily routines until the day that Ian Miller walks into the restaurant. He is tall, handsome, and not Greek. One glance at him is enough for Toula to feel the arrow of Eros pierce her heart and awaken her to her own needs. All of a sudden, she realizes the degree to which she has abandoned herself all these years; she has neglected her physical appearance, her hunger for knowledge, and her desire to expand her horizons beyond her stifling Greek surroundings.

Toula does not waste time; she enrolls in accounting classes, changes her looks, and leaves her father's restaurant to work for her uncle's travel agency. She spends more time away from home and interacts with people who are not Greek. Then one day, much as it happened at the restaurant before, Ian Miller walks into her office. Minutes later, he asks her out. Days later, they are a couple. Toula is living a dream, the happiest one in her life. But it is not long before this dream becomes her family's nightmare.

When Toula's parents learn that she is seeing a non-Greek man, they cannot accept it. In their family, a non-Greek husband is an unfathomable idea. Her father almost falls ill. Her mother is angry. Her cousins make fun of her. Everyone feels betrayed and offended, as they cannot understand how Toula chose a man outside their culture. To them, this is not just disloyalty but desertion, and her love affair becomes an issue of conflict and strife. Her family feels rejected, so they in turn reject Toula.

Family rejection is one of the most painful experiences a person can endure, especially when precipitated by love for an "unacceptable" mate. Toula's need to please her parents collides head-on with her need to honor her choice of mate, and emotional pandemonium ensues, as feelings of guilt and fear of her parents' anger compete against her desire to be with Ian. Ultimately, she chooses to follow her heart and honor her need for emotional completion despite her family's criticism. She makes it clear that she loves Ian and is going to marry him. She proceeds to introduce him to the family and invites all her relatives to meet the first non-Greek who has ever set foot in their home.

Toula's choice to defy her family's criticism and do what is right for herself makes her a pioneer of a cross-cultural exchange that enriches and adds new meaning to her entire family's life. When Ian and his self-contained Anglo-Saxon parents visit Toula's loud Greek home, both families make an honest effort to transcend their cultural limits and accept each other in the name of love and their children's happiness. Once her father sees that love has no ethnicity, he transforms from an obstinate, ethnocentric Greek into a father who understands that the heart speaks a universal language and that happiness can transcend cultural differences. Wishing for his daughter the happiness that she deserves living with the man she loves, Mr. Portokalos consents to their marriage and welcomes his new son-in-law into the family. At the wedding reception, the moved father blesses his daughter's union to Ian, and in simple words, he imparts a profound message of universal acceptance and genuine warmth: "I was thinking last night, before my daughter's wedding to Ian Miller, that, you know, *Miller* comes from the Greek word *milo*, which means 'apple.' As many of you know, our name *Portokalos* comes from the Greek word *portokali*, which means 'orange.' So, OK? Here, tonight, we have 'apple' and 'orange'! We are all different, but in the end we are all fruit!"

Walk the Unbeaten Path

In another part of the world, an eleven-year-old boy fights for his creative need to become a ballet dancer, as he confronts his unsupportive family in the deprived environment of a small, blue-collar town. *Billy Elliot* is set in the 1980s and unravels in Durham Coal, a northern English village on the brink of economic disaster due to a prolonged strike by the local miners. Being raised by a miner, to become a miner, Billy is being forced to follow his grandfather's tradition and learn boxing, something the men in his family have done for generations. But he does not like boxing; Billy's creative nature pushes him instead to love music, play the piano, dance, and be sensitive to the needs of others. One day during his boxing class, he accidentally discovers that he loves to dance as he watches an all-girl ballet class being taught in his gym. Within minutes he joins the class and continues to attend the lessons every week in secret. Billy has found his calling: dance. Nothing can stop him from loving it, and no one can convince him that ballet is not a thing for boys.

It is not too long before his father finds out that the money he gives Billy for boxing classes goes to ballet lessons. An uneducated man, a financially stressed father, and a grieving widower, Jackie Elliot has no regard for ballet whatsoever. Enraged at Billy's love for it, he attacks his son and forbids him to attend ballet classes.

But Billy does not stop dancing. On a cold Christmas night, he sneaks into the gym with his friend Michael, a boy who has admitted his need for cross-dressing. Billy helps Michael to get dressed as a ballerina and starts teaching him ballet positions to the sound of music. Suddenly, Billy's father walks in on the scene and stares at his son, shocked. Billy does not flinch, but he does respond: he lets his dumbfounded father see who he truly is by expressing his feelings in a dance performance that is defiant, self-confident, proud, loving, powerful, honorable, and free. As his father watches him, Billy makes his statement clear: dance is all that he has; dance is all that he is.

And this is how Billy Elliot gains his father's respect. As Jack Elliot watches his son fight for what he loves, he realizes his responsibility to honor his son's creativity and support Billy until the Royal Ballet School accepts him. His son has become his hero and his source of strength, and as Billy goes off to London to study ballet, Jack returns to the depths of the coal mine. The strike at work is over. The strife in the family has ended, too. The right thing has been done. Billy has honored his need for creativity all the way. His dream to become a ballet dancer is now a reality.

Reel Fulfillment in Action

Movie Time! ▶ *Watch a Movie for Fun, Learn a Lesson of Life*

The movies in the following list describe the lives of characters who strive to fulfill inner needs as they overcome internal and external obstacles.

Choose a movie, and watch it alone or with your group. Afterward, think about the questions that follow the list of movies. Write down your thoughts, and share them with others.

Movies About Acknowledging Your True Needs

Ali (2002), directed by Michael Mann

Alice Doesn't Live Here Anymore (1974), directed by
    Martin Scorsese

All the President's Men (1976), directed by Alan J. Pakula

Bend It like Beckham (2002), directed by Gurinder Chadha

Billy Elliot (2000), directed by Stephen Daldry

Cold Mountain (2003), directed by Anthony Minghella

Educating Rita (1983), directed by Lewis Gilbert

Erin Brockovich (2000), directed by Steven Soderbergh

The Family Man (2000), directed by Brett Ratner

The Hurricane (1999), directed by Norman Jewison

Intolerable Cruelty (2003), directed by Joel Coen

Isn't She Great (2000), directed by Andrew Bergman

JFK (1991), directed by Oliver Stone

John Q (2002), directed by Nick Cassavetes

My Big Fat Greek Wedding (2002), directed by Joel Zwick

My Left Foot (1989), directed by Jim Sheridan

Norma Rae (1979), directed by Martin Ritt

Ray (2004), directed by Taylor Hackford

Real Women Have Curves (2002), directed by Patricia Cardoso

The Shawshank Redemption (1994), directed by
    Frank Darabont

Shine (1996), directed by Scott Hicks

Still Breathing (1997), directed by James F. Robinson

Sweet Home Alabama (2002), directed by Andy Tennant

Titanic (1997), directed by James Cameron

What Women Want (2000), directed by Nancy Meyers

Yentl (1983), directed by Barbra Streisand

Questions to Answer

1. In the movie you saw, what are the main character's inner needs, and what does he or she do to fulfill them?

2. How does the main character overcome external difficulties, adversities, and real obstacles in order to fulfill his or her needs?
3. What actions does the main character take to change what is within his or her control and find fulfillment?
4. How does the main character discover joy in the mundane, regardless of the difficulties and limitations he or she faces?
5. Which of the main character's qualities do you find most appealing? How can you apply this quality as you face your own issues?

Acknowledge Your True Needs ▶ *Exercises and Activities*

The following three exercises are designed to help you acknowledge your unfulfilled yearnings. As you work through them, you will be empowered to

- Take action and fulfill your neglected needs
- Change your attitude toward your everyday life and find joy amidst mundane activities
- Accept what you cannot change and take action to change what is within your control

▶ What Actions Do You Take to Fulfill Your Needs?

This week pay attention to what you do to satisfy the unfulfilled needs that you identified in the exercises of Chapter 2. For example, if you have an unfulfilled need for creativity, notice how much time you spend a week doing something creative. Do you have a creative habit, a hobby, or a creative outlet? Or do you spend your free time watching television or doing things for others? As you answer the following questions, be honest with yourself:

1. What needs did you identify in the previous chapter's exercises?
2. What actions have you taken toward fulfilling your needs?
3. What distractions have you chosen to forget, ignore, or postpone to satisfy your needs?

▶ How Much Joy Do You Get Out of Life?

1. This week observe yourself in your work, at your home, and in your social interactions. Notice how many of your activities on any normal day give you joy.

   On any given day, I receive joy from these simple activities, people, and environments:

   Activities that give me joy: _____
   People who give me joy: _____
   Environments that give me joy: _____

2. If you do not receive the joy you desire from everyday life and the simple things you do on any given day, please state how much of your time you spend fantasizing about experiences and situations that *would* bring you joy. Is this often, very often, almost always? How much does it interfere with your real life?

3. If your daily life does not give you the joy you desire, what do you do to find joy? Write down the activities, pursuits, or adopted habits that give you joy. How often do you practice them?

▶ How Much Do You Complain?

Our society encourages us to complain. This is why every good business has some kind of complaints and suggestions department, and there is a box for complaints in most reputable stores. As consumers, we are encouraged to complain because our comments help improve and refine the quality of service and products, which then results in our own satisfaction. But in our personal life, things are different. Complaining about things you *can* change without taking action to change them may become a destructive pattern, draining your energy and that of those around you. Similarly, complaining about things you *cannot* change without learning to cope with them slowly corrodes your natural ability to overcome adversities and pursue your goals.

Some examples of things that you *cannot* change but must learn to handle are the weather, the traffic, physical limitations, personal limitations of significant others, and past choices that influenced the course of your life and cannot be reversed.

Some examples of things that you *can* change by taking action are your physical condition, your living environment, your finances, the quality of your relationships, unrewarding habits, poor communication, and negative patterns causing you and others unhappiness.

The following exercise is designed to help you become complaint free by resolving to take action and change what is within your control—or to accept and handle with maturity what you cannot change.

▶ Become Complaint Free

This week notice how often you

1. Complain about things you cannot change. Make a list of those things.
2. Complain about things you do very little to change. Make a list of those things and your actions.
3. Use selected people as a sounding board (or target) for your complaints and what you achieve. Make a list of those people and the results your complaining produces.
4. Take actions to change the things about which you complain. Make a list of your actions and the results you achieve.
5. Use complaining as a way to do any of the following:
   - Attract attention to yourself
   - Join a group of "complainers" at work or school and feel included by peers
   - Avoid accepting what you cannot change or handling it with a mature attitude
   - Avoid taking action to change what is within your control

Copy, fill out, and sign the following "Freedom from Complaining" contract. By signing it, you resolve to stop complaining about things you cannot change and to take action to change what is within your control. Ask someone you trust to be your coach in changing your complaining pattern. Use the lists you made in this exercise to check your progress.

My "Freedom from Complaining" Contract

I, _____, resolve to stop complaining about the following things that I cannot change: _____

_____

_____.

Instead of complaining, I resolve to take the following actions to change the following things that are within my control: _____

_____.

This contract becomes effective today, _____.

Signature: _____

Things to Remember

- The secret to being happy is to fulfill your true needs.
- Acknowledging your true needs makes you accountable to them.
- It takes courage and concrete actions to find happiness.

Second Gain: Emotional Health

▶ **FULFILLMENT CANNOT EXIST** without emotional health. You are emotionally healthy when you are able to recognize the emotional patterns that destroy happiness and correct them through consistent, concrete, fulfillment-appropriate actions.

As an emotionally healthy person you will enjoy better physical health, a positive mental attitude, enhanced self-worth, and the ability to build and maintain fulfilling relationships.

The next three chapters are designed to help you achieve emotional health. Using examples from popular movies and special activities, you will learn how to:

- Identify the emotional pattern that sabotages your happiness
- Correct your negative emotional pattern
- Break free from Emotional Black Holes

4

Identify Your
Self-Sabotaging Pattern

HAPPINESS IS NOT handed to us. Rather, it is the trophy we earn once we prove to life that we have the ability to be happy, having overcome external and internal limitations along the way. You could say that we do not achieve true happiness unless we conquer internal limitations through a growth process in which we learn to control our self-destructive tendencies. In this process, we take specific actions to examine, admit, and transform our self-destructive patterns. Only when we master those harmful habits and replace them with successful behaviors can we be certain that our pursuit of happiness will be rewarding.

The big screen is filled with film heroes who strive for this very purpose: to follow an inner call and deliberately overcome external and internal limitations in order to fulfill their destinies. This is why we call them heroes. They leave a powerful imprint on our minds and hearts, inspiring us to follow their examples in our own lives. Two films exemplifying how a person's victory over inner limitations is a key element on the journey to fulfillment are *Erin Brockovich* and *The Color Purple*.

Erin Brockovich is based on the real life of an unemployed single mother of three who transformed her self-pity and anger into the courage to pursue a heroic fight against a giant California corporation involved in public fraud. Erin Brockovich is not a career woman; she dresses provocatively, uses foul language, has no formal training, and is very angry about her lot in life. But once she has realized her calling, she transforms herself into a warrior of truth by using all her socially unacceptable attributes to help her cause. Her anger becomes courage to confront the powerful, her abrasive manners become candor for tackling challenge, and her provocative looks become a tool to charm gatekeepers and gain access to classified information. In the end, Erin Brockovich wins; her victory not only brings fame, recognition, and wealth but also endorses her struggle to transform inner limitations into powerful assets that have proven indispensable to the fulfillment of her call.

The Color Purple is the account of the thirty-year journey of Celie, a black woman growing up in the Deep South at the beginning of the twentieth century, as she overcomes unfathomable difficulties with amazing courage and grace. For years, Celie tries to reconcile her earthly suffering with her faith in God, referring to him as her only friend when the males in her life crush her dignity, her self-esteem, and her identity as a woman. Raped and impregnated at fourteen by her father, Celie is destined to raise more children and suffer years of abuse and neglect by her husband, while developing an image of herself as an ugly, slow, unlovable person. When she meets Shug, another woman who has suffered injustice, Celie finds in her a friend, a lover, and a mentor. With Shug, Celie embarks on a journey to recover her ability to feel love for herself and another person, to embrace her womanhood, and, finally, to make peace with her extraordinarily difficult life.

These two heroines have something in common: they each fulfill a dream for happiness by overcoming self-limiting, self-sabotaging patterns originally developed as a way to cope with unfair and painful experiences. The movies show how they manage to transform those destructive propensities, becoming great examples to emulate in our own journeys to success.

On the other hand, the big screen offers examples of men and women whose self-sabotaging patterns cost them many losses in their personal and professional life. Usually, those heroes are portrayed as being social outcasts, members of the underworld, or plain criminals, plodding through misery that never seems to end. *Sideways* is a film portraying such a hero, living life as a series of self-sabotaging actions that lead nowhere. Miles, the main character, is a divorced forty-something author who lives alone and tries to get his novel published. But the problem is that he has no faith either in his work or his ability to get a publisher's attention. Every morning, Miles walks into life already feeling defeated. His favorite escape is wine-tasting trips to northern California from his home base in San Diego. This time Miles is about to embark on a seven-day trip to the vineyards of northern California with his ex-college roommate Jack, a frustrated forty-something actor who is about to get married. Jack sees this trip as his bachelor party and his last opportunity to indulge in endless sexual escapades. Miles, who loves wine tasting, sees this trip as his wedding gift to Jack and an opportunity to get away from his miserable life in San Diego. In order to finance this gift for his friend, Miles pays his mother a surprise visit on her seventy-third birthday, holding a cheap bouquet of flowers. While the old woman is on the patio with Jack, Miles enters her bedroom and steals a roll of bills from her dresser, looking at the photographs of him in earlier days that his mother lovingly keeps in her room.

What is gradually revealed in *Sideways* is that Miles is not only self-destructive but also too paralyzed to take action and fight for his dignity, values, or beliefs, which are repeatedly attacked by Jack's immature, self-indulgent actions during their trip. What will it take for Miles to put an end to this self-destructiveness? Will it be an internal decision or external circumstances leaving him with no choice?

Unlike *Sideways*, which portrays the relationship of two contemporary men with self-destructive propensities, *The Indian Runner* examines the relationship of two men (brothers) with polar opposite personal realities. Joe works as a police officer, is married, loves his family, and believes in the power of hope, faith, and honest work. Frank is a Vietnam veteran who returns from the war and tries to build his life with Joe's help. But Frank's self-destructive tendencies are so strong that they will create a downward spiral that no one can control and which seems to end only in death. Not a pleasant story, it is nonetheless an honest account of the psychological aftermath following the experience of war and its destructive spin in our lives, years after the war is over.

Affliction is another story in which the main hero, Wade Whitehouse, gradually sinks into an abyss of self-destruction that gets only deeper and darker as the movie progresses. Like Frank in *The Indian Runner*, Wade is also a war veteran, as well as being a small-town cop, who battles his demons with alcohol and actions that betray his deranged mind. Wade does not want help. The child of an abusive father, he has found police work as an excuse to perpetuate violence, inflicting it upon himself, others, and us as we watch him, wishing he could stop before it's too late. But Wade does not stop, through to the end. Even though he is a negative example, he still serves a purpose: he is showing us what can happen to us if we allow our inner demons to overpower our best judgment.

Like Wade in *Affliction*, Aileen Carol Wuornos in *Monster* is also gradually sinking into self-destruction. This film is based on the real story of a highway prostitute whose anger, self-hatred, and fear propel her to take actions causing her loss of dignity, sanity, and, eventually, the right to live. Again like Wade in *Affliction*, Aileen also suffered cruelty as a child, growing up in a self-destructive environment that abused her need for love and respect. But so did the heroine of *The Color Purple*, who, nonetheless, did not allow her negative tendencies to destroy her life. Her strength lies in her ability to master inner demons and transform self-hatred, shame, and anger through actions that bring success.

Anatomy of a Self-Sabotaging Pattern: THE SCAR Model

Recognizing that we engage in self-sabotaging patterns is an uncomfortable and self-confrontational experience. We usually prefer to blame life when things do not work out the way we dream them to. But admitting our share of responsibility in our seeming bad luck or miserable lot is, in fact, empowering because it gives us the choice of making changes.

A self-sabotaging pattern is an unconscious pattern of behavior that inevitably produces results contrary to our conscious intentions. To see how it operates, let us look at the example of Mary, a former client of mine. Mary's need was to find a soul mate and create a family. Her pattern was to end her relationships as soon as she and her boyfriend had a conflict. Mary saw each conflict as a challenge of "putting up with *him* or putting an end to *this*." The conflict reminded her of her parents' fights, which had led to divorce and caused Mary a very painful adolescence. Fighting with her boyfriend triggered in her the fear that should she continue the relationship, she would end up like her parents: miserable and divorced. Mary thought that she should never have to deal with conflict as a necessary growth challenge in every relationship. As a result, she ended a relationship as soon as conflict arose.

Mary's self-sabotaging pattern was set off once the external trigger of conflict activated negative emotions. Those emotions in turn activated negative thoughts about her ability to have a successful relationship and be happy. Being under the influence of negative thoughts, she took actions that sabotaged her initial desires.

Mary began working on her happiness by taking the first step of the model discussed in this chapter: she identified her self-sabotaging pattern. THE SCAR Model breaks down a self-sabotaging pattern into six elements, as follows:

1. **Triggering Hints.** These are external events, experiences, and interactions that activate powerful emotions.
2. **Emotions.** These are eight negative emotional states that are felt in the body and activate destructive thoughts. They are anger, apathy, envy, fear, greed, guilt, hatred, and shame. All other negative emotions activating self-sabotaging patterns are derivatives of these eight primary negative emotional states. (In Chapter 6, you will learn more about these eight negative emotional states and how to apply the tools provided there to break free from your "emotional black holes.")
3. **Sensations.** These are physical symptoms and changes in the body that we experience when we are in the grips of a negative emotion. Examples include a tight stomach, heart palpitations, pain in the chest, and clenched teeth.
4. **Cognitions.** These are painful memories, negative associations, and negative thoughts that are also triggered by negative emotions and prompt us to take relevant, destructive actions. They are usually unconscious and difficult to detect until after we have taken action. For example, anger triggers thoughts such as, "I must hurt him," "I'll show her," or "I must destroy it."
5. **Actions.** These are the actions that we take as a result of our negative thoughts. We take such actions hoping to alleviate the negative emotional state that initially activated our self-sabotaging

pattern. But instead, we achieve results that sabotage our original goal altogether, and we fail to free ourselves from the negative emotion.

6. **Results.** The results of a self-sabotaging pattern are always destructive, period.

Let us now examine the anatomy of Mary's self-sabotaging pattern by applying THE SCAR Model:

1. **Mary's fantasy.** "I am happily married; I have the perfect relationship with the perfect man."
2. **Mary's unfulfilled needs.** Love, family, marriage, home.
3. **Mary's pattern sabotaging her from fulfilling her needs.** She ends relationships within six months, as soon as she and her boyfriend have a conflict. She is constantly frustrated and heartbroken.

THE SCAR model of Mary's self-sabotaging pattern:

1. **Triggering Hints.** When conflict arises in the relationship, her partner's shortcomings are revealed to Mary, and her fantasy of the "perfect relationship" is crushed.
2. **Emotions.** Anger directed at boyfriend. Anger directed at self. Fear of the conflict. Guilt for not finding the perfect man and conflict-free relationship.
3. **Sensations.** Upset stomach, loss of sleep, physical tension, fatigue.
4. **Cognitions.** "This reminds me of my parents' marriage. I can't handle it. He's not what I wanted." "This is hopeless. I can't find the perfect mate." "I have to get out of this relationship and keep looking. I don't want to end up like my parents."
5. **Actions.** Uses conflict as an excuse to end relationship abruptly. Goes through a period of frivolous dating during which she appears to be detached, in control, and not interested in getting serious. Uses compulsive shopping as an escape from feeling lonely and disappointed, which increases her credit card debt.
6. **Results.** Mary cannot build a long-term relationship and is emotionally unfulfilled.

For Mary, recognizing her self-sabotaging pattern was a first step toward changing her behaviors. In time, she stopped fearing conflict and began dealing with it when it arose. She learned how to communicate her needs, embrace the other person's different viewpoints, and find ways to negotiate differences. Her efforts paid off: her last relationship has lasted three years and is only getting stronger.

Tim, another former client, sought my professional help when he approached the verge of bankruptcy. His dream was to buy his own home and create a home-based business. He craved financial security and professional success but sabotaged all this by using his credit cards to indulge in expensive restaurants, designer clothes, and pleasure trips. He had no savings, and he was chronically anxious about money. The first thing Tim needed to do was to clearly identify all aspects of his self-sabotaging pattern. Using THE SCAR Model, Tim created the grid in Figure 4.1 to give

FIGURE 4.1 ■ THE SCAR Grid of Tim's Self-Sabotaging Pattern

TRIGGERING HINTS	EMOTIONS	SENSATIONS	COGNITIONS	ACTIONS	RESULTS
Financial statements showing debt	Afraid	Tension, tight muscles	"I'll end up bankrupt."	Postpones self-discipline	Tim's debt increases.
	Hopeless	Loss of sleep	"My father never showed me how to budget."	Buys expensive clothes	Tim drifts farther away from financial security.
Collection notices	Apathetic	Frequent headaches		Eats out with "friends"	
	Angry at self				
Mounting credit card bills	Angry at father	Occasional chest and back pain	"I have to live for the moment."	Drinks in bars	Tim has an ongoing sense of failure.
	Desperate			Goes away on pleasure trips	
Social pressure to appear rich and successful	Inadequate		"I don't want anyone to know."		
	Ashamed			Develops unrealistic fantasies about miracles	
			"One day I'll be able to fix this, but not now."		
			"I have to wait for a miracle."		

himself a panorama of his triggers, emotions, sensations, cognitions, and actions and help him stay focused on their transformation.

Identifying Your Self-Sabotaging Pattern

In the first chapters of this book, you learned how to achieve inner clarity by identifying your unfulfilled, neglected needs. Now you have the opportunity to see how you sabotage yourself and keep yourself from satisfying those needs. In the exercises at the end of this chapter, you will learn how to create your own grid of THE SCAR Model and gain perspective on all the elements of your self-sabotaging patterns. As you acquire insight into your negative emotional habits, you must keep in mind the following four main points.

Know the Need You Desire to Fulfill

Being aware of the need you seek to satisfy keeps you motivated to watch for your self-sabotaging actions. What is your desire? Is it love that you sabotage with frivolous relationships? Is it creativity that you sabotage with endless hours of television watching? Is it a fit and healthy body that you sabotage with unhealthy eating and drinking habits? Is it financial security that you sabotage with compulsive spending? Is it professional success that you sabotage by associating with incompetent partners? Name your need. Stay aware of it. Claim it.

Identify Your Triggers

Knowing your triggers empowers you to gain control over your reactions. For this reason, it is crucial that you begin paying attention to all the triggers that set off your disturbing emotions. Are they certain people, places, events, or activities? Keep a log of your triggers and what they provoke. You will realize that though your triggers may be varied, they set off the same negative emotions. This is also your opportunity to assess the influence of your immediate environment on your emotions, especially if you cannot identify specific triggers or if it seems your negative emotion is identical with the trigger. In this case, it may be possible that your immediate environment is a constant trigger of disturbing emotions. An example would be feeling inexplicably depressed at work when nothing in the nature of your work or the cast of characters involved has actually changed. An examination of your environment could reveal that a recent move to a windowless office was the trigger for your emotional gloom.

Tune in to Your Body to Identify Emotional Reactions to Triggers

The body never lies. Every emotion that you feel has a physical manifestation first before it reaches your intellectual awareness and is able to be verbalized. If you are connected with your body and physical sensations, you are better able to identify your emotional reactions to external triggers. For example, anger manifests itself in the body as flushed cheeks, clenched teeth, tight fists, or heavy breathing. Panic manifests itself as shortness of breath, buckled knees, dry mouth, heart palpitations, or sweaty palms. Being alert to how negative emotions manifest themselves in the body by paying attention to your physical sensations will help you control those emotions before they trigger negative thoughts and self-sabotaging actions.

Begin by paying attention to your physical sensations in response to external triggers. Notice how different aspects of your environment affect you throughout the day. What physical reactions do you have to different experiences? Put a feeling word to your physical reactions.

Learn to Identify Your Pattern by Its Results

Because self-sabotaging patterns are mostly unconscious, very often you can detect a pattern only through your awareness of its results. To utilize this tool, examine areas of your life where you clearly do not enjoy results that fulfill your desires. Following is a simple example to help you understand this concept. Say you desire to buy a new car and provide yourself with safe transportation. To achieve this, you must save for a down payment, but by the second week of every month for the last six months, your bank account's balance has fallen to fifty cents. This upsets you; you cannot understand how it happens. Your initial reaction is to complain that it is not your fault, that you do not make enough money, that life is very expensive, and so on. But if you are certain that you want to fulfill your need for safe transportation, then you must acknowledge that your failure to save for a down payment is not due to life's unfairness and instead is the result of a self-sabotaging pattern, related to the way you handle your finances. Admit it. Then use THE SCAR Model to identify your pattern. The exercises at the end of this chapter will show you how to achieve this, and in the next chapter, you will learn how to transform your pattern into a fulfillment-appropriate plan of action.

Reel Fulfillment in Action

Movie Time! ▶ *Watch a Movie for Fun, Learn a Lesson of Life*

Self-sabotaging patterns have ripple effects that extend far beyond the self-sabotaging individual. They may stall, upturn, or even destroy the lives of others, such as family members, friends, colleagues, or neighbors who are innocent and undeserving of misfortune. The movies listed show how self-sabotaging patterns affect not only the story's main character but also the people whose paths he or she crosses.

Choose a movie, and watch it alone or with your group. The films on this list portray difficult life situations and may include adult subject matter. I recommend that you respect your sensibilities and make a selection after reading about each film (see imdb.com or mariagrace.com). As you watch the story evolve, observe the patterns that emerge in the main character's actions. Notice how they shape his or her own fate and affect that of the other characters. Answer the questions that follow the list of movies. Keep a log of your answers, and discuss them with others.

Movies About Self-Sabotaging Patterns

Affliction (1997), directed by Paul Schrader
Clean and Sober (1988), directed by Glenn Gordon Caron
Closer (2004), directed by Mike Nichols
Damage (1992), directed by Louis Malle
Eating (1990), directed by Henry Jaglom
Faithless (2000), directed by Liv Ullmann
Felicia's Journey (1999), directed by Atom Egoyan
The Ice Storm (1997), directed by Ang Lee
The Indian Runner (1991), directed by Sean Penn
Leaving Las Vegas (1995), directed by Mike Figgis
Less than Zero (1987), directed by Marek Kanievska
Money for Nothing (1993), directed by Ramón Menéndez
Monster (2003), directed by Patty Jenkins
Requiem for a Dream (2000), directed by Darren Aronofsky
The Shining (1980), directed by Stanley Kubrick
Sid and Nancy (1986), directed by Alex Cox
Sideways (2004), directed by Alexander Payne
The Sweet Hereafter (1997), directed by Atom Egoyan
28 Days (2000), directed by Betty Thomas
Unfaithful (2002), directed by Adrian Lyne
The War of the Roses (1989), directed by Danny DeVito
When a Man Loves a Woman (1994), directed by Luis Mandoki

Questions to Answer

1. Can you see clearly at least one self-sabotaging pattern in the actions of the main character? What is that pattern? What triggers it? What ensues once the pattern gets activated?

2. What are the character's unfulfilled needs?

3. How does the character avoid correcting the self-sabotaging pattern?

4. Does the self-sabotaging pattern get corrected in the story? How does this happen?

5. Does the character fulfill his or her true needs at the end? What happens?

6. What price does the character pay for not correcting the self-sabotaging pattern?

7. How do the main character's self-sabotaging actions affect the lives of the people around him or her? List the events that transpire and their consequences for everyone.

8. Put yourself in the role of the main character. What would you do differently to fulfill your needs? List the actions you would take.

9. List three insights you gained about a particular self-sabotaging pattern of your own from watching the movie.

10. List three things that are in your power to do to avoid repeating your own self-sabotaging pattern.

Learning to Use THE SCAR Grid ▸ *An Exercise for You*

The following exercise is designed in several steps in order to help you understand the anatomy of a self-sabotaging pattern. You will learn how to identify self-sabotaging patterns by working with THE SCAR grid, which is a practical tool for self-examination and measuring your progress. Learning how to use this grid is essential for assuming responsibility for your self-sabotaging behaviors. In the next chapter, you will learn how to transform those behaviors into fulfilling, success-oriented actions.

When you complete this exercise, you will know the following:

• The triggers of your self-sabotaging pattern
• The elements of your self-sabotaging pattern
• The negative results of your self-sabotaging pattern

Keep in mind that self-sabotaging patterns are unconscious and you realize them by becoming aware of negative results, not as they are happening. As you use the grid, you may fill it out in whatever order the elements of your pattern emerge, but once you finish, reread the completed grid several times in the order in which it is presented.

Note: in this exercise, you will work with the need you considered most important in the exercises of Chapters 2 and 3. Go back to your notes and recall that need. Identify the main pattern that sabotages your efforts to fulfill this particular need. In the future, you may use THE SCAR grid to identify other patterns sabotaging other needs.

Instructions: Take a few minutes and think of an incident that caused negative results in your efforts to satisfy your need. Recall what happened in as much detail as you can. This may also be a recurring pattern in your life that does not seem to stop, in spite of your efforts to understand why. Answer the following questions in the order they're presented:

1. What is your dream (or fantasy) of happiness?
2. What is your unfulfilled need?
3. How do you sabotage your own needs, and what is your resulting reality?
4. Fill out THE SCAR grid. Use any order that seems appropriate to you.

The following is an example of an author sabotaging his need to complete a book proposal for publishers, followed by THE SCAR grid (see Figure 4.2). Read the completed grid several times, and use it as your guide. You may copy the blank grid of THE SCAR grid from Appendix D for your work with your own self-sabotaging pattern.

Example: Roger, age thirty-one, wants to be a writer and has an idea for a book.

1. **Roger's fantasy.** "I am a famous writer."
2. **Roger's unfulfilled needs.** "I need to be creative, to feel successful, and to be recognized for my writing talent."
3. **What Roger does to sabotage his needs.** "I give up after page 10. Something always happens, and I never stick to my writing project.

FIGURE 4.2　■　THE SCAR Grid with Roger's Example

TRIGGERING HINTS	EMOTIONS	SENSATIONS	COGNITIONS	ACTIONS	RESULTS
What happened? (Describe an event or a series of events, coincidences, or incidents that activated the self-sabotaging pattern.) "A friend told me that it's impossible to find a publisher, unless you have important connections."	How did you feel? (Use the list of emotions in Appendix A for help.) "I felt discouraged, disappointed, and insignificant. I felt afraid that I will never make it in the publishing world."	What physical reactions did you experience? (Describe what you felt in your body.) "Tight stomach, clenched teeth, dry mouth."	What were your ■ automatic thoughts ■ painful memories ■ other associations "I'll never be published." "No one cares." "What good is it trying?" "My father used to tell me I would never amount to anything." "This world is a jungle—I can't handle it."	What did you do? "I gave up writing, again." "I decided to take a yoga class and learn to meditate." "I joined a book club, hoping to meet interesting people."	What results did your actions produce? (This is your resulting reality.) "I put off writing; instead, I spend my evenings in the yoga studio, reading for the book club, or chatting on the Internet."

My resulting reality is that I've never finished anything I've started, and I don't have a complete manuscript or proposal to present to publishers."

Congratulations on completing this exercise! You have taken a significant step by tracing your self-sabotaging patterns. In the next chapter, you will learn how to transform them by developing successful behaviors.

Things to Remember

- The trigger only activates the self-sabotaging pattern and is not the cause of it. By blaming or attacking the trigger, you do not change your pattern.
- The energy fueling a self-sabotaging pattern comes from disturbing emotions that activate negative associations, painful memories, or automatic negative thoughts that propel you to take destructive actions.
- As you become a conduit of negative emotional energy, you act accordingly and you invariably produce negative results.

5

Correct Your Self-Sabotaging Pattern

NOW THAT WE'VE identified self-sabotaging patterns, the time has come to stop and correct them. The most important part of correcting a destructive pattern is conscious practice. The more actively engaged you are with this process, the sooner you will transform negative behaviors into actions for success. It is important in this phase to use all the inspiration and support you can get from healthy sources, whether these are movies, people, or physical environments. As you transform your self-sabotaging patterns, try to limit self-analysis to a minimum and focus instead on your actions. In other words, focus less on *why* you engage in self-sabotage and more on *what* you can do to stop it. Remember that transforming a pattern is less about defining your pattern through exhaustive self-analysis than it is about taking actions to change it. Insight is good insofar as it gives us information about the causes of our behavior, but destructive behavior can only be changed through concrete, consistent, and fulfillment-appropriate actions.

In Chapter 4, the anatomy of a self-sabotaging pattern was explained via THE SCAR Model, and you learned to identify your self-sabotaging patterns with THE SCAR grid. In the first part of this chapter, you will learn how to transform a self-sabotaging pattern through a five-step model, outlined in the ABCDE Pattern-Correction Plan.

So that you can better understand the model, the steps are presented with examples from popular films in which a main character overcomes a self-sabotaging pattern and achieves set goals. The second objective of this chapter is to teach you how to break free from self-destructive behaviors using the LET GO Forgiveness Model, offering as an example a person from real life.

The ABCDE Pattern-Correction Plan

This model works. Its promise is freedom from self-destructiveness and the ensuing fulfillment of your desires, provided that you apply it consistently. Begin to implement the plan with one negative pattern that you are aware of and feel ready to transform. Over time, the positive results you achieve will motivate you to transform additional negative behaviors and discover happiness, one step at a time. The ABCDE steps are as follows:

> **A**dmit sole responsibility for your self-sabotaging patterns.
> **B**reathe before reacting to triggers.
> **C**leanse your life of negative emotional influences within your control.
> **D**evelop connections with sources of positive emotional energy.
> **E**xecute a plan of concrete and consistent fulfillment-appropriate actions.

Admit That You Have Sole Responsibility for Your Self-Sabotaging Patterns

It is easier to believe that you are a victim of your circumstances, past, heredity, or life in general than to admit that you are the only one responsible for your self-sabotaging behaviors. Admitting sole responsibility also means that only you are responsible for your actions. This insight takes away the right to say, "You made me do it!" to justify your destructive habits; so initially, it can be most uncomfortable to realize that you alone are accountable for creating your own unhappiness. But on the other hand, this insight empowers you to take charge of a transformation process whereby you have full control to become the happy person you desire to be. Nothing can stop you from attaining the happiness you deserve once you take this path.

An example of a person who conquers the "poor me" attitude and takes charge of transforming her life is Tess McGill, the central character in *Working Girl*. A hardworking Wall Street administrative assistant who craves success and hopes to get promoted for her brilliant business idea, Tess realizes that unless she changes her self-defeating patterns, her proposal will be appropriated by her boss, leaving her in the shadows and possibly unemployed. When she admits that everyone around her, including her fiancé, takes her for granted *because she allows it*, she changes her actions and masterminds a plan to take charge of her career and fulfill her need for success. Having no resources other than her wits, she decides to promote her own idea through actions that may be considered outrageous but under the circumstances seem justified. In the end, Tess teaches us the lesson that unless we take charge of our actions to find happiness, no one else will do it on our behalf.

Harry Sanborn in *Something's Gotta Give* is another character who realizes and admits that he must change his patterns—in his case, he must do so or he will never have love in his life. Harry is a confirmed bachelor in his midsixties whose life is changed, thanks to a heart attack that forces him to admit how he resists his need for love by avoiding the commitment required by a relationship. After having a brief affair with Erica, a successful playwright in her fifties who falls in love with him, Harry disappears and leaves her heartbroken. When he sees the Broadway play that Erica wrote to describe her painful experience following his desertion, Harry realizes that his noncommittal patterns have destructive effects not only on his own life but also on the women he seduces. He sees that if he wants to be happy, "something's gotta give" to reverse his self-sabotaging behavior. Harry takes immediate action: he looks for Erica everywhere and finds her in Paris. Humbled, vulnerable, and changed, he asks her for a second chance.

The beauty of this film is in its optimistic message: it is never too late to find fulfillment, as long as you want to achieve what you truly need.

Once Harry admitted his need for love and family and that he truly wanted to be happy, it was not too difficult for him to change his patterns to enjoy success. Contrary to the old saying, this movie clearly teaches that yes, an old dog *can* learn new tricks!

Breathe Before Reacting to Triggers

Chapter 4 explained how identifiable triggers set off our self-sabotaging patterns. Working with THE SCAR Model, you learned how to recognize the triggers of your own self-sabotaging patterns. Once you are aware that a trigger is prompting you to engage in a self-sabotaging pattern, it is essential to proceed with step B of the ABCDE Pattern-Correction Plan: breathe before you react to triggers. This also means slow down your reactions. Remember that if you repeat the destructive pattern once more, you will sabotage your own happiness all over again. You can never expect positive results from repeating a destructive method. So next time a trigger threatens to set off a *known* self-sabotaging pattern, breathe instead of giving in to it by reacting in your usual way. Focus your attention on your breathing consciously, intentionally, and deliberately. Make it a habit to count your breaths one at a time. Count up to twenty breaths. It may sound simplistic but it works!

In *The Karate Kid*, martial arts master Mr. Kesuke Miyagi mentors Daniel LaRusso on how to exercise patience to control his tendency toward reacting violently to people who trigger his anger. Numerous scenes in this film show how young Daniel transforms his reactions to triggers by deliberately slowing down and focusing on his body. Breathing is the key to achieving this; you can use it to begin a chain reaction of positive effects on your body, emotions, thoughts, and actions. We see Daniel use breathing to control his physical reactions to the bullies provoking him, by calming down his emotional energy. As a result, his thoughts slow down and he becomes clear about his next moves. This is how he triumphs over his opponents.

Just as Daniel learns how to win confrontations with a clear mind in *The Karate Kid*, the same holds true for real life: you cannot prevail in a confrontation or achieve a goal without having a clear mind. When confronted with a recognizable trigger of a self-sabotaging pattern, breathing is essential to clarify your thoughts so you can take appropriate actions and keep from sabotaging your purposes. To master this, you do not need to practice a special sort of breathing. Simply breathe in through your nose and exhale also through your nose slowly, staying focused on your breaths rather than the trigger.

The purpose of focusing on your breaths is to help you detach from the trigger and its negative emotional influence as quickly as possible. As you pay attention to your breathing rather than the trigger, you will notice a shift in your physical sensations. Your heart palpitations will slow down, the flush on your cheeks will dissipate, your clenched jaws will loosen, and your body temperature will return to normal. As your physical sensations change, so will your attitude; a sense of inner clarity will replace the need to engage a negative reaction, and you will be able to act in ways that you will never have to regret.

As you practice this approach in dealing with emotionally upsetting triggers, keep a log of the instances in which you choose to breathe before reacting. In time, breathing will become a healthy habit replacing your old, self-sabotaging reactions.

Cleanse Your Life of Negative Emotional Influences Within Your Control

This step requires boldness and determination. But it is an essential step to take if you really want to succeed in your plan to find fulfillment: make deliberate efforts to cleanse your life of external influences conducive to negative emotions, to the degree that it is in your power to do so. To cleanse your life of negative emotional influences, you must examine the following three areas: people, places, and activities.

People

You may often be subjected to interactions with toxic people who do nothing to support your efforts to transform your life. Be aware of their negative energy and how it affects your emotions, thoughts, and actions. Limit your interactions with them to the minimum amount of contact necessary. Do not share your correction plan with such people, do not seek their support or understanding, and do not discuss ideas for personal change with them, especially if they are not asking for help. All such efforts would be futile, and in all instances, you would be wasting time and energy, period. When you interact with toxic people, always stay focused on your reason for the interaction and do not expand into other areas.

Unfortunately, toxic people very often have a crucial role in your life: they may be your boss, your child's spouse, a close relative, your parents or parents-in-law, or even your own spouse. In such cases, the patterns in your relationship may be so firmly ingrained that it may seem impossible to get rid of their toxic influence on your emotions. A film showing how closely related people can become lethally enmeshed in a harmful pattern is *The War of the Roses*; Oliver and Barbara Rose are married and in the grips of an irresolvable crisis that becomes progressively destructive. While both want a divorce, neither one is willing to leave or sell their matrimonial home. Their pattern of trying to retain control of the house as "power territory" while trying to drive the other away becomes a compulsive addiction. Oliver and Barbara end up locking themselves inside the house, where they continue their fight to the bitter end, when it becomes clear how dangerous destructive relationships can be.

An example of how to resolve the toxic relationship quandary in real life can be found in the case of my client Lynn, who for forty years suffered a relentless sibling rivalry with her twin, Bonnie. The two sisters were so immersed in a love-hate relationship that when Lynn began executing the ABCDE Pattern-Correction Plan, she consistently "failed" at step C. On one hand, she could not extricate her sister from her life, but on the other hand, she could not resist engaging in the familiar and destructive interactions that perpetuated emotional defeat and misery.

As Lynn worked her way through step C, she had to learn to see Bonnie as her teacher rather than her rival twin. She devised a little game in which she mentally assigned Bonnie the role of a difficult examiner whose role was to test Lynn's ability to learn healthy behaviors. Every time she had an interaction with Bonnie, Lynn resolved to ask herself two simple questions:

- "What is my purpose in this interaction with Bonnie; that is, what need am I seeking to fulfill in my interaction with her?"
- "What are the limitations of this relationship in fulfilling my need?"

As Lynn repeatedly explored these two questions, she realized that her relationship with Bonnie was limited in fulfilling her need for unconditional love and acceptance. Lynn also admitted that this was not entirely Bonnie's fault, because Lynn herself was unwilling to give unconditional acceptance to Bonnie. This realization freed her from unrealistic expectations that perpetuated the love-hate patterns. Lynn gained an adult outlook toward her rapport with Bonnie, in which she respected their mutual limitations and focused on the positive aspects of their sisterhood.

Places

To the degree that it is within your control, avoid frequenting places with negative energy, and instead make an effort to situate yourself in places that rejuvenate and inspire. This, of course, includes making necessary changes in your own home to maximize its energizing effect on your emotions and spirit. Your home is the temple of your personal and emotional existence, the sanctuary of your dreams, and the refuge in which you and your loved ones share a life and, together, create memories. Respect and cherish it. Keep it clean and orderly. Look for its positive aspects rather than dwelling on its negatives. Complete those long-overdue repairs and discard unnecessary clutter. Give it warmth and care and make it your haven, a place where you can feel safe and fulfilled.

A home is more than just a building. It is the shelter of our spirit, which often remains in it long after our physical presence is gone. This gives a house a life of its own that closely resembles the spirit of its occupants. Innumerable and always-popular movies about haunted houses illustrate the truth that homes can contain the energy of former residents and have the ability to heal or damage the energy of new ones. *The Shining* recounts the ability of a gorgeous dwelling that was once the scene of murder to drive Jack Torrance (an author who moves in with his family, hoping to heal his writer's block) into madness. On the other hand, in *The Ghost and Mrs. Muir*, the energy inhabiting the house where the young widow Lucy Muir moves guides her to write a bestselling novel that not only brings her wealth but also changes her life forever.

What is the type of energy you want your home to have? What can you do to make your home a healing, inspiring place? The time to begin is now, and the rewards you will enjoy are worth all the time and effort. Start with these three things to give your home a head start toward becoming your haven: (a) get rid of clutter, (b) make sure your kitchen and bathroom are always clean, and (c) make your bed every morning.

Whether you live alone or with roommates or family, if everyone in your household follows these three "rules of conduct" over several weeks until they become a habit, you will notice a change in your home energy that will lift your spirit and the spirits of those who visit you.

Activities

Eliminate activities that drain your emotional energy, activate negative patterns, or fail to produce positive results. We all engage in such activities and overlook their cumulative negative effect on our energy. Notice which of your activities fall into these categories. Make a list and begin with the easiest ones. A former client named Flora decided to limit her news intake once she acknowledged her increasing distress and rage over the carnage in the Middle East and noticed how it affected the rest of her day. Unable to do anything about the violence overseas, Flora found a better use for the time she would otherwise have spent watching news: she chose something within her control and joined a program of volunteers teaching English as a second language in the public library system. Helping people in need gave Flora a sense of self-empowerment, and this constructive activity lifted her spirits, banishing any trace of despair.

Develop Connections with Sources of Positive Emotion

To become emotionally healthy, you need to be nurtured by sources of positive emotional energy in your environment and to cultivate these within yourself. As you develop connections with such sources, the power of negative influences that trigger self-sabotaging patterns will gradually weaken.

Seek out people who give you healthy emotional energy and inspire fulfilling qualities, and form mutually helpful relationships with them. A film that illustrates how such a relationship can change both parties' lives is *Finding Forrester*. It is the story of a friendship between the young Jamal

Wallace, an inner-city African-American writing prodigy, and his writing mentor, reclusive Pulitzer Prize winner William Forrester. As we watch Jamal reach out to Forrester for help, he also invites his mentor on a journey of healing and growth, in which they both benefit from each other.

Once you are clear about your need, it becomes your obligation to seek the support of people who can help you fulfill it. Reach out and seek a mentor. Do not be embarrassed to ask for guidance from those who can offer it. Offering help feels as good as receiving it. There are many people who would love to be a source of inspiration in your path to fulfillment, even though some may initially seem hesitant.

Develop spiritual fitness and use your mind to avoid the trap of emotional black holes. Learn to generate healthy emotional energy through meditation and prayer. Chapters 7, 8, and 9 are designed to help you achieve this, offering guidance, helpful exercises, and activities through which to gain inner strength.

Inner strength is needed during life's most unexpected moments, when we are left to our own devices to overcome crucial challenges. Two film heroes showing us their own admirable inner strength in surviving an extremely difficult call are Rubin Carter in *The Hurricane* and Kevin McCallister in *Home Alone*. *The Hurricane* is a social drama based on the real story of Rubin Carter, a grown man and boxing champion who spent his adult life in prison for an alleged triple murder, having fallen victim of a racist conspiracy. *Home Alone* is the entertaining adventure of eight-year-old Kevin McCallister, who spent Christmas defending his home and his life from two dangerous burglars, having no one else home to help him.

The purpose of juxtaposing these two polar opposite movies is to stress their key message: inner strength is a quality that life always demands of us, regardless of our age or social circumstances. Rubin Carter relied on himself alone to draw amazing courage and faith in his innocence, even though the entire world had abandoned, betrayed, and rejected him. Little Kevin relied on himself alone to show amazing bravery and strategic genius against the two criminals, when everyone in his neighborhood was away on Christmas vacation. Both characters came out winners. They did not win thanks to a magical intervention every time their battle seemed lost (as it happens in most adventure stories) but thanks to their unflappable inner strength, which was their only source of courage.

Execute a Plan of Concrete, Consistent, Fulfillment-Appropriate Actions

You can satisfy your needs only through concrete actions that remain consistent, in spite of the transformation process's tests of your stamina and willingness to persevere. Furthermore, to satisfy your needs, your actions must be fulfillment appropriate. This means that they must produce results without causing physical, spiritual, or emotional harm to yourself or others. Otherwise, your actions are destructive, period. For example, taking diet pills and starving oneself in order to lose weight are not fulfillment-appropriate actions because they cause physical harm. In this case, fulfillment-appropriate actions include following a sensible eating plan and exercising regularly.

A film character who overcomes enormous difficulties and fulfills his dream by implementing a plan of concrete, consistent, and fulfillment-appropriate actions is Andy Dufresne in *The Shawshank Redemption*. A young, successful banker living in the 1940s, Andy suddenly suffers a tragic twist of fate when he is sentenced to life imprisonment for the murders of his wife and her lover, neither of which he committed. Entering the prison system, Andy holds no expectations for parole; instead, he holds on to his own plan for freedom and never loses hope. Over time, we watch how he stays focused on his plan until he succeeds.

Andy masters his reactions to provocations and attacks from the inmates. He does not become violent or allow them to intimidate him. He never attacks, but he does defend himself when he is attacked. He develops a friendship with Red, an old-timer serving a life sentence who becomes his mentor and ally. Andy also avoids the trap of negativity and despair by doing what is in his control to improve his circumstances. Instead of spending energy complaining about his unfair incarceration, he makes himself useful to the prison system by offering his banking skills. This empowers him to rely on his own abilities to earn his freedom, rather than daydreaming about the unrealistic "miracle" of being granted parole. He keeps his plan secret, being fully aware of the prison reality and the risk of sabotaging his goals by confiding in a fellow inmate, no matter how trusted. Without harming anyone and by showing extraordinary patience, he perseveres for twenty years, always keeping alive the hope that one day his dream of freedom will be fulfilled. Only minutes before the movie ends do we finally see what happens to Andy, as he astounds us with the surprising outcome of his genius, patience, and self-determination.

Given that self-sabotaging patterns are mostly unconscious, you are likely to notice them only after they have been activated, because of their negative results. When this happens, do not get disappointed. Go back, correct your behaviors, and follow the ABCDE steps. Stay connected with sources of positive emotional energy, and take fulfillment-appropriate actions. This is how you will be able to transform your negative patterns one at a time, fulfill your desires one at a time, and find the happiness you deserve.

Correcting a Self-Sabotaging Pattern Through Forgiveness

Forgiveness is not simply a religious value or a trait of personal kindness. It is the art and discipline of transforming destructive patterns triggered by pain and anger into actions of love for yourself, for your life, and for others. Practicing forgiveness is also your duty to your physical, emotional, and spiritual health. When you transform the destructive patterns propelled by anger, hatred, pain, and resentment into fulfillment-appropriate behaviors, you are free to experience happiness. No longer trapped inside an emotional black hole, you will be free to pursue your desires and accomplish the human destiny that will fulfill your spirit.

You can master the art of forgiveness over time and through practice by implementing the LET GO Forgiveness Model. You will learn how to move through its five stages, from feeling victimized and disempowered to being fully connected with your inner purpose and free to create happiness and experience joy.

There is not a definite time frame in accomplishing the steps of LET GO. It depends on how profound your loss is, how willing you are to forgive, how motivated you are to move on, and how ready you are to give up destructive behaviors. Completing this process may take weeks, months, or even years. But once you choose to follow the steps of LET GO and achieve forgiveness, you will enjoy the rewards of a fresh beginning with a lighter heart and strengthened hope.

The five steps of the LET GO Forgiveness Model are illustrated by the example of Kate, a former client whose progression through each step allowed her to forgive the betrayal of her fiancé and best friend. Like Kate, you, too, can accomplish these steps and become empowered to reclaim your dignity, your direction in life, and your ability to follow your dreams.

The five steps of the LET GO Forgiveness Model are as follows:

Lament the harmful events.
Emote safely.
Tell your real losses.
Get clear about your needs.
Open yourself to fulfillment-appropriate actions.

Lament the Harmful Events

Focus more on *what* was done to you than *who* did it. Speak about the harmful events that took place, and name the physical, material, emotional, and spiritual harms they caused for you. Read here how Kate laments the real harm she suffered:

> *Kate: "My fiancé cheated on me with my best friend. Then he told me he wanted to break up with me in order to be with her. This was a betrayal of my trust, love, and innocence. I broke up with him, and I ended my friendship with her. I lost my best friend and the man I thought would be my husband."*

Emote Safely

This phase may be challenging because you must allow yourself to experience all the pain-related emotions caused by the harmful experience as they arise. Make sure you do this with safety. In other words, give yourself space and time to emote, and surround yourself with people you trust. Avoid further harm by not making yourself vulnerable to people who do not care. Be gentle with painful emotions. When they are intense, rest and sleep well. Do not strain yourself when you are in emotional pain. Respect your need to emote, and make this phase of LET GO as safe as possible.

> Kate: "At the beginning I was shocked; I couldn't believe it. Then I felt betrayed, angry, and fooled. Then I felt hurt and depressed. I slept for hours, did not want to eat, and did not care about how I looked. Then I felt like I had to hurt both of them, and take revenge. But every time I felt this vengeful wrath, I asked for my therapist's help and went running to burn off my anger. Now I don't feel vengeful, but lonely and very sad. I can't trust anyone."

Tell Your Real Losses

Once you have allowed yourself to emote safely, it is time to tell your real losses. These are the current financial and physical damages—those that are within your control to recover—that were caused by pain-driven actions. In this step, you must answer these two questions:

- How is your pain affecting your current relationship with your finances?
- How is your pain affecting your attitude toward your physical health?

Now name your current pain-driven behaviors and how they damage your financial and physical health.

> Kate: "I lost my trust in people. I am suspicious and paranoid, and this makes me doubt my own judgment. My self-confidence has hit rock bottom. To make myself feel better, I go on shopping sprees. I charge clothes and jewelry on my credit cards, and then I feel worse. I am anxious about getting into debt, but I can't help it. I also eat junk food and drink quite often. The junk food is not so bad, but the drinking is really dangerous, and I know it."

Get Clear About Your Needs

In this step, you are called to identify what needs you must fulfill in order to recover your emotional and spiritual losses caused by the harmful experience. Such losses may be your innocence, trust, enthusiasm, love, hope, power, sense of control, faith in justice, sense of security, and so on.

Answer the following question as concisely as you can by identifying the emotional and spiritual losses you suffered and expressing them as needs that you must fulfill: What spiritual or emotional loss did this harmful experience cause in you that you need to give back to yourself?

> Kate: "This experience took away my self-confidence, sense of control over my life, and trust in my judgment about others. I need to feel self-confident, recover my sense of control, and trust my judgment about people again."

Open Yourself to Fulfillment-Appropriate Actions

In the final step of LET GO, you are called to open yourself to actions that fulfill the needs you identified in the previous step. Here you must recover your emotional and spiritual losses and create abundance, avoiding acts of revenge or self-destruction. Few things are more destructive in life than the emotional and material energy spent on actions of revenge. But if you empower yourself to recover your losses instead of being vengeful, you will give a powerful thrust to your growth, creating emotional, spiritual, and material abundance.

> Kate: "In order to fulfill my need for self-confidence, I will do something that makes me feel happy with myself without hurting anyone else. Something that would make me happy—and healthy—right now is dancing. I will take dance classes.
>
> "In order to fulfill my need for control over my life, I will get a handle on my finances. I will stop using my credit cards until I have paid off the balances.

"In order to fulfill my need for trusting my judgment, I will stop compromising myself. I will not ignore my gut feelings, and I will honor my hunches about others. I was not very good at honoring my intuition, but now I know that I must not betray it."

Notice that this approach to forgiveness does *not* focus on forgiving the persons who have harmed you. Rather, it empowers you to forgive the damages you suffered by learning how to recover your emotional and spiritual losses and preserve your physical and financial health. In fact, this approach makes clear that you should not spend energy and money on vengeful acts but focus deliberately instead on creating happiness. This does not mean that you should not also forgive those who harmed you but means that you should consider the recovery of your happiness as the best form of revenge and decline to waste your energy and your life on avenging those who have harmed you.

Reel Fulfillment in Action

Movie Time! ▸ *Watch a Movie for Fun, Learn a Lesson of Life*

The following films are stories of transformation and healing. Choose a movie, and watch it alone or with your group. Observe how the main character takes action to transform sabotaging patterns and how this also changes the lives of other characters. Pay attention to the critical events that start the transformation process and the ones that influence its course. As you watch the film, keep in mind the questions that follow the list. Afterward, write down your thoughts and share them with others. You may repeat this with all the movies on the list.

Movies About Correcting Self-Sabotaging Patterns
Catch Me if You Can (2002), directed by Steven Spielberg
The Color Purple (1985), directed by Steven Spielberg

Erin Brockovich (2000), directed by Steven Soderbergh
The Family Man (2000), directed by Brett Ratner
Finding Forrester (2000), directed by Gus Van Sant
The Fisher King (1991), directed by Terry Gilliam
Garden State (2004), directed by Zach Braff
The Ghost and Mrs. Muir (1947), directed by Joseph L.
   Mankiewicz
Home Alone (1990), directed by Chris Columbus
The Hurricane (1999), directed by Norman Jewison
Intolerable Cruelty (2003), directed by Joel Coen
The Karate Kid (1984), directed by John G. Avildsen
Million Dollar Baby (2004), directed by Clint Eastwood
Norma Rae (1979), directed by Martin Ritt
The Prince of Tides (1991), directed by Barbra Streisand
The Shawshank Redemption (1994), directed by Frank Darabont
Something's Gotta Give (2003), directed by Nancy Meyers
28 Days (2000), directed by Betty Thomas
25th Hour (2002), directed by Spike Lee
The Verdict (1982), directed by Sidney Lumet
What's Love Got to Do with It? (1993), directed by Brian Gibson
What Women Want (2000), directed by Nancy Meyers
Working Girl (1988), directed by Mike Nichols

Questions to Answer
1. What is the main character's unfulfilled need, and is there a self-sabotaging pattern?
2. What events trigger the character's transformation process?
3. What phases of transformation does the character go through?
4. What actions does the character take to fulfill his or her need?
5. What adversities does the character encounter during his or her transformation?
6. What lessons does the character learn from his or her transformation?
7. What prices did the character pay for his or her transformation?
8. How does the character's transformation change the lives of the people around him or her?

9. Which scene in the film do you find most touching and for what reason?

10. How does the film inspire you to correct your own self-sabotaging patterns?

Correcting Your Self-Sabotaging Pattern ▶
Exercises and Activities

▶ **Implementing the ABCDE Pattern-Correction Plan**

Following is a contract for you to sign as you take step A of your ABCDE Pattern-Correction Plan: admit sole responsibility for your self-sabotaging patterns.

Copy, complete, and sign the contract, and then keep it in a private but easily accessible place so you can read it often.

The ABCDE Pattern-Correction Plan Contract

I, _____,

Admit that I am the only one responsible for the following self-sabotaging pattern: _____.

By repeating this pattern, I sabotage my need for _____.

I am accountable for my need and I promise to fulfill it. Effective today, _____, I resolve to:

Breathe before I react to triggers.

Cleanse my life of external negative emotional influences within my control.

Develop connections with sources of positive emotional energy from within myself as well as my environment.

Execute a plan of concrete, consistent, and fulfillment-appropriate actions to satisfy my inner desires.

FIGURE 5.1 ■ ABCDE Pattern-Correction Steps with Roger's Example

ADMIT SOLE RESPONSIBILITY	BREATHE BEFORE REACTING TO TRIGGERS	CLEANSE YOUR LIFE OF NEGATIVE EMOTIONAL INFLUENCES	DEVELOP CONNECTIONS WITH SOURCES OF POSITIVE EMOTION	EXECUTE A PLAN OF CONCRETE, CONSISTENT, FULFILLMENT-APPROPRIATE ACTIONS
Self-Sabotaging Pattern: *"I look for social distractions when I feel discouraged or uncertain about my writing."* **Unfulfilled Need:** *"I need to feel successful and recognized as an author."*	**List of Triggers:** *"Critical remarks about my writing."* *"Discouraging comments about publishing."* *"Other authors' successes that overwhelm me."*	**People:** *"George: he reminds me of my father—always negative."* **Places:** *"Happy Hour every Friday: I'm hung over all Saturday."* **Activities:** *"Book club, chat rooms: they are a waste of time."*	**In Your Environment:** *"Classical music instead of chat rooms."* **In Yourself:** *"Daily breathing, meditation. A massage per week."*	**List of Actions:** 1. *"Write two hours a day, every day."* 2. *"Complete a book outline in three weeks."* 3. *"Take a course on writing book proposals."*

▶ **ABCDE Pattern-Correction Grid with Example**

The grid in Figure 5.1 offers an example of an author wishing to correct the self-sabotaging pattern of procrastinating on a proposal for publishers (see also Chapter 4). Read the grid several times, and use it as a guide for your own ABCDE Pattern-Correction Plan. You may make copies of the blank grid in Appendix E and use them as needed.

Congratulations on completing this exercise! Continue to practice the ABCDE Plan, and keep a log of the results that you achieve. Notice how your life will begin to change as you transform your pattern. Celebrate every improvement you make, and share your victories with people you trust and who can support your progress.

Things to Remember

- Breathe: breathing regulates your energy and keeps you calm.
- We never get it right the first time, or the second, or the third. In implementing your ABCDE Pattern-Correction Plan, do not give up when you make a mistake. Go back and correct it.
- Living a fulfilled life is the best form of revenge.

6

Break Free from Emotional Black Holes™

You will significantly speed up your progress in transforming self-sabotaging patterns if you learn how to break free from Emotional Black Holes (EBHs). These are eight destructive emotional states responsible for a number of self-sabotaging patterns and self-debilitating behaviors. This chapter is meant to be an indispensable complement to Chapters 4 and 5. Here we will identify Emotional Black Holes and learn a practical and efficient method of breaking free from their destructive influence with specific antidotes for each EBH.

Each EBH, along with its destructive effects, is illustrated with examples from popular films. Both reading about these films and watching them will sensitize you to other people's EBHs and make them easy to spot in your own life.

Mapping Emotional Black Holes

In the universe, black holes are negative stars. Formed by the core of collapsed stars that have exhausted their fuel, they are regions of space where gravity is so strong that not even light can escape. Having tremendous gravitational pull, black holes are capable of absorbing anything that approaches their orbit and crushing it into nonexistence. Similarly, in our psychological universe, Emotional Black Holes are states of negative emotional energy with a tremendous gravitational pull on our thoughts, attitudes, and actions. Descent into such negative emotional states activates only negative thoughts, which in turn provoke harmful actions against ourselves, others, and nature. The results are consistently destructive.

You cannot avoid falling into an EBH. It happens again and again, as part of your human journey of self-discovery. The only positive aspect of falling into an EBH is that you can remember its destructive influence on your life, so you can choose to avoid it the next time you feel attracted to its pull. You can do that if you learn to neutralize negative emotional energy and take responsibility for your Emotional Black Holes, which are anger, apathy, envy, fear, greed, guilt, hatred, and shame.

- **Anger** fuels the propensity to destroy ourselves, others, and nature. It activates negative thoughts that always provoke destructive actions. In order to thwart anger, you must learn how to transform it into a constructive force.

  Two films that demonstrate the blind destructiveness of anger are *Falling Down* and *Do the Right Thing*. In *Falling Down*, defense worker William Foster gives in to anger and lashes out at the evils of society through acts of terrible destruction. In *Do the Right Thing*, the violence incited by anger ruins an entire community in Brooklyn. Both films show clearly that raw anger, expressed through destructive acts, can never have constructive outcomes.

- **Apathy** is generally the indifference and lack of responsibility toward our own well-being, with the consequence that important inner needs are neglected. As a result, we feel disconnected from others and exempt from our responsibilities toward their well-being. Apathy absorbs all the vital energy and potential to fulfill our dreams, corrodes our ability to care, and petrifies our spirit. Apathetic people do not hunger for happiness; their zest for life has been transformed into cynicism, into words and actions of indifference toward both their own well-being and that of others.

A film that illustrates the destructive results of apathy is *House of Sand and Fog*, in which Kathy, a main character, wakes up one morning to discover that her home is up for auction and she is being evicted because she has not paid property taxes for years. She is a recovering drug addict with a broken marriage who has clearly been apathetic toward herself and her life. Abruptly confronted with homelessness when she learns that an Iranian immigrant family has purchased her house, Kathy enlists the help of her lover, a police officer, to reclaim her home. Presenting her apathy as helplessness, she convinces him to instigate an illicit plot against the new owner that results in a tragedy of epic proportions. It is shocking to see how Kathy's EBH of apathy causes her life to implode and eventually destroys everyone who crosses her path.

- **Envy** is the pain and resentment from knowing that another person enjoys a privilege that is absent in our own life. It is also coupled with the desire to possess the same advantage. Envy propels destructive actions against those we envy: we want to destroy or take away what they have because we want it for ourselves.

  In order to break free from envy, you must learn to decipher its message and transform it into inspiration to fulfill neglected needs.

  In *My Best Friend's Wedding*, envy launches the main character, Julianne, on a mission to destroy her best friend's plans to marry the woman he loves. Her envy shows that Julianne has a neglected need for romantic love that she strives to fulfill by seducing Michael hours before his wedding. She breaks free from envy only when she admits that her actions are fulfillment inappropriate and she is forced to repair the damage she has caused, which is a humbling but self-empowering experience.

- **Fear** is the state of inner paralysis rendering us incapable of taking fulfillment-appropriate actions. It can cause irrational worrying, compulsive doubting, and generalized negativity about the future.

Actions propelled by the EBH of fear are typically reactive rather than proactive, are never fulfillment appropriate, and almost always have damaging results. In order to break free from fear, you must start by taking baby steps and learn to be proactive in fulfilling the desires that you have been unable to satisfy due to being paralyzed by fear.

Arlington Road illustrates how fear corrodes our ability to think or act rationally and how it instead makes us give in to destructive actions. The main character, Professor Michael Faraday, teaches classes on terrorism and is the widower of an FBI agent who was killed while on an antiterrorist mission. When he meets his new neighbor, Oliver Lang, Michael begins to suspect that he is a terrorist and then allows himself to fall into a black hole of fear, which causes him to resolve his suspicions alone. Handling his fear inappropriately, Michael takes actions that progressively make matters worse and worse. An essentially well-intentioned man, Michael falls into the EBH of his own fear and destroys himself.

- **Greed** is the blind, insatiable hunger for acquisition and possession of money, objects, power, love, attention, fame, and so on. When we are greedy, a voice in our heart yells, "I want, I want, I want!" This EBH corrupts our ability to feel satisfied and leaves us with a perpetual sense of emptiness and lack. It can propel us to immoral and inhumane actions in order to increase our acquisitions, and its ripple effects spread unhappiness through relationships, communities, organizations, and societies. To break free from greed, you must replace the voice yelling, "I want, I want, I want!" with the quiet mantra, "I am thankful for . . . , I am grateful for . . . , I am happy for. . . ."

  The silent film *Greed* is a powerful epic about the dangers of being trapped in this EBH. Set in California at the beginning of the twentieth century, the story describes how greed destroys a woman's mind once she wins the lottery, and then it drives her husband to madness and murder for the sake of the money. Originally eight hours long, this film is four hours long in its current version and worth watching as a visual saga about the irrational suffering and excruciating pain greed can cause us.

- **Guilt** can be described as the unjustified state of culpability and self-reproach for imagined offenses, coupled with a pervasive sense of inadequacy and unworthiness. The most insidiously destructive EBH, guilt absorbs all life's pleasure and annihilates any possibility for experiencing contentment and joy. It corrodes our sense of self-value, damages our natural ability to feel pleasure, and replaces joy with a debilitating sense of failure. Guilt exacerbates our grief for significant losses and taints our excitement for successes, perpetually inciting self-sabotaging actions with destructive results. Survivor's guilt frequently causes withdrawal from life and retreat to addictive behaviors involving drugs, alcohol, or work, and guilt for being fortunate or successful often propels senseless acts of self-contempt that ruin success or fortune.

  In *Fearless*, the irrational and destructive effects of guilt are manifested in Max Klein and Carla Rodrigo, two survivors of a plane crash, in which Carla lost her little son but Max managed to save several people's lives, including that of a baby. Once they rejoin their families, survivor's guilt becomes unmistakable in their behavior: for Max, guilt causes the denial of his human limitations, propelling him to dangerous, grandiose acts of daring, and for Carla, guilt debilitates her ability to relate to her husband and communicate with the world. Ignoring their families, the two seek each other out and embark on a healing journey that saves them from guilt and allows them to enjoy life.

- **Hatred** is the hostility and animosity that keeps us estranged and divided from ourselves and each other. Hatred kills our natural capacity for empathy and compassion. It can be instilled as a learned behavior from one generation to another, and it is the reason for senseless acts of destruction against ourselves, others, and nature. To break free from this EBH, you must question your rationale for hatred and practice conscious acts of kindness toward the ones you claim to hate, as well as their families.

  American History X shows how a father teaches racism to a son, encouraging him to commit acts of hatred that cause devastating results. A true portrait of hatred's potential for destruction, this film forces us to reevaluate our ability to commit acts of hatred and use thought and reason as countermeasures against this EBH.

- **Shame** is the pain caused by an inner sense of humiliation, disgrace, and regret. This EBH causes expressions of self-reproach through remorseful actions and self-humiliating attitudes. Persons suffering from shame deny their human right to visibility, recognition, and success, and deeply seated shame may be the cause for creating a false persona in order to avoid authentic relationships. Shame imprisons us in loneliness and isolation, cripples our potential for intimacy, and steals our freedom for self-expression.

  Real Women Have Curves is a film about gaining freedom from shame. The main character, Ana, is a first-generation Mexican-American teenager growing up in a Latino community in East Los Angeles who is awarded a full scholarship to Columbia University upon graduation from high school. While any other family might beam with pride over such a success, Ana's family reacts with reproach and resentment, causing her to give up her plan and join them in a sewing factory. There, realizing that the women of her family are immersed in shame, Ana rebels: she takes off her clothes, flaunts her full-bodied figure to the other women, prompts them to remove their own clothes, and empowers them to be proud of their bodies. Through her symbolic act of rebellion, Ana proclaims that "real women have curves," curves for which they must be proud. This statement frees her from shame and awakens her to her need to do more with her life.

Breaking Free from Emotional Black Holes

You will break free from your EBH as you continue to work on transforming your self-sabotaging patterns, following the steps given in Chapters 4 and 5. To achieve this, you must continue using the grids, both for reference and to monitor your progress.

Additionally, it is advisable to choose one or more of the following five approaches to transform the energy of destructive emotions and avoid their damaging results. Make a routine of whichever method of transforming negative energy suits you best.

- **Physical activity.** There is no limit to the different kinds of physical activities available today through courses, classes, clubs, and associations, and their benefits to our emotional health are widely known. From dancing lessons to martial arts, to skydiving, to rock climbing, to power walking, there is a physical activity for every body type, age, and constitution. Join in and enjoy the rewards!

- **Video games.** This is a useful way to act out destructive emotions without causing real harm to yourself, others, or nature when you are in the grips of an EBH. For example, when you are in the grips of anger, playing a video game allows you to feel as though you are destroying your enemies in the "as if" reality of the game. This activity allows negative emotions to run their course while you are under their influence. As long as you do not use video games as substitutes for real life, it is preferable to use them as outlets for negative emotions rather than to allow these emotions to run amok with destructive results in your real life.

- **Creativity.** Developing a creative habit will help you to channel destructive emotions into activities that keep you occupied and challenged as they give you the reward of creation. Choose a creative habit that appeals to you, and begin practicing immediately; for example, you can learn how to draw, paint, dance, sculpt, bake, dig, garden, build, tutor, become a sports coach, and so on. In Chapter 11, you can read more about the benefits of practicing creativity.

- **Play.** Through play, negative emotions lose their destructive power as we enter an "as if" reality. Choose a playful activity that appeals to you, and engage in it regularly. Play with a kitten or puppy, take an acting class, write your negative thoughts in the form of a funny poem, turn an unpleasant experience into a funny skit and act it out with friends or family, play with kids, have a game night with friends, or devise your own way to play.

- **Prayer and meditative practices.** Developing spiritual fitness is the fast track to freedom from negative emotional energy. Over time, the consistent practice of prayer and meditation brings amazing results. The longer you practice prayer and meditation, the stronger your mind becomes in its capacity to resist the power of negative emotional energy. In Chapter 9, you will learn more about practicing effective prayer and meditation.

The Antidotes to Emotional Black Holes

When you fall into an EBH, you can pull yourself out by applying an antidote. The sooner you do this, the faster you can break free from destructive emotions and their effects on your thoughts and actions. Following are step-by-step instructions on how to apply antidotes for each EBH.

Anger

When you are caught in anger, breathe and count your breaths one at a time. Do not react until you count twenty breaths. As you breathe, use your imagination to picture yourself in the future, away from the current, anger-provoking situation. If it helps, walk away from the situation until you can address it without anger. I have worked with a couple who learned to use this rule every time they have a conflict that is about to turn into a fight: the husband, who can easily lose his temper and use foul language, says to his wife, "Before I lose my cool, I'll take a break. Back in five." This is how he stops himself from saying things that he will later regret.

When you feel angry, blood rushes to your brain and you cannot think clearly. It is better to wait and speak or act until anger is no longer active in your body and you are lucid. In the meantime, try to express your anger in a physical or creative activity, such as exercising, writing, painting, sculpting, and so on.

In case you have acted in anger and caused damage, as soon as you realize it, let the person you have treated with anger know that you are really sorry, ask for forgiveness, correct the physical damages, and do not repeat the same behavior again. Treat others kindly whether they are superior or inferior to you in status or power.

Apathy

The antidote for apathy is taking action to fulfill your neglected needs. Admit that being cynical and indifferent has destructive effects on your relationships and your environment, and transform your apathy with acts that show care for yourself and others. Do get interested in your well-being and involved with your life in the here and now. Name your neglected needs, and set goals to fulfill them. Each day, do one thing toward achieving your goals. Reward yourself as you go.

For example, if you simply don't care and you are tired of it, ask yourself what kind of a life you would have if you cared. Write down a full description of that life: describe your home, your job, your relationships, your financial situation, and your physical appearance. Then pick an area in your current life that you can transform according to your description, starting now. Take your home, for example: if you cared, your home would be uncluttered, serene, and welcoming. Begin working immediately to make this happen: get rid of clutter, paint a wall, change those dingy blinds, refinish an old piece of furniture, clean the windows, cook for friends. As you involve yourself physically in your life, your apathy will subside and you will feel alive.

Envy

The pain of envy is a clue that you are neglecting certain of your needs. The first antidote for envy is to discover which needs it hints you are neglecting, after which you should then pursue their fulfillment through actions appropriate to your own life. For example, when you envy a friend for having won a trip to an exotic country, ask yourself which of your unfulfilled needs this envy reveals: it may be a need for diversion, rest, vacation, adventure, or all of the above. Rather than wallow in pain over your friend's good luck, take action to provide the diversion you lack in your own life. Perhaps you lack the resources for exotic travel, but you can take a weekend off to go camping and in doing so learn, exercise, and enjoy your ability to provide for yourself the entertainment you lack, within your own means.

A second antidote for envy is to turn it into inspiration for success by asking the people you envy how they maintain their blessings. For example, if you envy a friend for her wonderful marriage, rather than covet her husband or indulge in self-pity about your less successful relationships, ask her what she does to maintain a good marriage. Then ask yourself to what extent her approach to her marriage resembles your own approach to a relationship, and determine if you can learn something new to create and maintain a happy relationship. Also ask yourself to what extent you are willing to change your ways in order to find the happiness you perceive in others. Once you have clear answers to these questions, proceed with actions. Staying busy in the pursuit of your happiness will keep you free from envy.

Fear

The antidote for fear is to take baby steps toward fulfilling your desires. When you are paralyzed and unable to take action, you can extricate yourself from paralysis with baby steps. Use baby steps also to slow yourself down as you resist the temptation to react to fear with gigantic, panicked leaps. If you stay focused on the need you are seeking to fulfill, envision it in spite of your fear, and take baby steps toward its fulfillment, you will considerably offset the destructive effects of fear. Remember that feeling fear is natural. It is all right to feel fear as you take baby steps—but keep walking, one baby step at a time.

For example, most of us are afraid of the future. The unknown petrifies us, period. This fear paralyzes many of us from managing our finances now, with a plan to secure our future. We soothe our fear, hoping that something magical will happen and our finances will take care of themselves. If this sounds familiar, then you must face your fear with baby steps, keeping in mind that only you are responsible for satisfying your need for financial security. Face your fear and empower yourself. Begin with four baby steps: (a) take a money management course, (b) set up a savings account, (c) save $100 a month for the next six months, and (d) take a course on retirement planning. Notice how much less afraid you feel after you take these steps and how motivated you will be to take more.

Greed

The antidote for greed is to make a conscious effort to count your blessings and express gratitude for what you have through the act of sharing with those in need. Learn to say, "I have enough of . . ." and "I am grateful for. . . ." Use giving to those in need as an act of gratitude that will liberate you from the fear of being deprived. Focus also on fulfilling neglected emotional and spiritual needs by creating genuine relationships with people and developing a spiritual practice.

For example, spend a day counting how many times you say, "Yes, but . . .," and how many times you say, "I want more. . . ." These are signs of greed: material, emotional, or spiritual. Then decide to say, "Yes" and omit "but," and try to say, "I have enough for now," when you feel like saying, "I want more." Try this exercise for a day or two. See what it does to your attitude. During these two days, fulfill a promise you gave to someone a long time ago. We have all given promises that we never fulfilled. What is yours? Notice the changes you bring to your life by fulfilling your promise. Enjoy!

Guilt

The antidote for guilt is to allow yourself to enjoy that which gives you true pleasure and makes you happy. This is harder than it sounds. It takes honesty and boldness, as the voice of guilt will persist at filling you with pain, remorse, and self-deprecation for crimes you didn't commit, hissing in your heart that you should not be happy. If you want to break free from guilt, you must firmly say no to your own tendency to create misery and deliberately indulge in being happy. You must also allow others to enjoy pleasure and support them in their efforts to find their bliss.

For example, if you love dancing but feel too guilty to indulge in it without your significant other, who hates dancing, *do it*, in spite of your guilt. Take a dance course now. Buy a pair of dance shoes and a comfortable outfit, put them on, and go to the class. Enjoy it! Remember that it is good to make yourself happy doing things you love and which hurt no one. Then encourage your significant other to indulge in something that makes him or her happy, of which you had disapproved in the past using guilt as a weapon.

Hatred

The antidote for the toxic burden of hatred is to put yourself in the position of the person you hate and try to see the world through his or her eyes. Once you realize that he or she is a human being like you, with his or her own desires, fears, and shortcomings, you can transform your hatred into understanding. This way of relating will transform your hatred into empathy and compassion. The same approach works with self-hatred. You, too, are a being made by the Creator to be loved and happy. Love yourself and forgive yourself for not being perfect. Instead of punishing yourself for your shortcomings, focus on all the positive aspects nature has gifted you and use them to create happiness.

For example, pick a person you say you hate. Put yourself in his or her shoes, and write down ten things that you know this person has suffered in his or her life. (*Note:* if you truly hate this person, you should know his or her history; otherwise, you don't hate the person, but you hate your impression of that person or the ideas and values that person represents in your eyes.) Then write down ten things you have suffered in your own life. Compare the two lists. How similar are the listed items, and how deep is the pain they have caused in both of you? Write down three things you are discovering about that person that are freeing you from hating him or her. Now write down five positive qualities you recognize in that person that you would like to have in yourself.

Shame

The antidote for shame is pride. To break free from shame, you must accept that which you have no power to change and focus on changing what is within your control. Doing this will give you the opportunity to see yourself as effective, worthy, and proud of all the good associated with you, your actions, and your life. Name your points of pride. Show your self-appreciation by making yourself visible and heard. Show self-respect as you educate others to recognize your self-worth regardless of your individual differences.

For example, if you suffer from irrational shame, make a list of three things you are secretly proud of. They must be things directly related to you (that is, not your children's achievements or other things you do not control). Now plan a special occasion to celebrate them. Make a list of your guests, and send them an invitation in which you describe the purpose of your party. Ask them to come prepared to speak about three things that make them secretly proud. At the party, present your secret points of pride as a group. Then ask each guest to share in what ways you have been an inspiration to them. Bask and rejoice! You may also implement this exercise with your own family. The rewards will be tremendous!

Reel Fulfillment in Action

Movie Time! ▶ *Watch a Movie for Fun, Learn a Lesson of Life*

Destructive emotions cause human tragedy, and tragedy is the essence of drama. This explains the multitude of films that dramatize the effects of Emotional Black Holes. The biggest blockbusters of all time are usually the stories of characters trying to break free from an EBH that consumes their lives.

Following are eight lists of movies, each list corresponding to an EBH. Many of the films portray difficult life situations, and they may include adult subject matter. Choose a movie from each list, and watch them alone or with your group. Afterward, think about the questions that follow the lists. Write down your thoughts, and share them with others.

Movies About Anger

Anger Management (2003), directed by Peter Segal
Dolores Claiborne (1995), directed by Taylor Hackford
Do the Right Thing (1989), directed by Spike Lee
Falling Down (1993), directed by Joel Schumacher
Gladiator (2000), directed by Ridley Scott
Monster (2003), directed by Patty Jenkins
Mystic River (2003), directed by Clint Eastwood
The Patriot (2000), directed by Roland Emmerich

Movies About Apathy

The Accidental Tourist (1988), directed by Lawrence Kasdan
Garden State (2004), directed by Zach Braff
House of Sand and Fog (2003), directed by Vadim Perelman
The Kid (2000), directed by Jon Turteltaub
Lost in Translation (2003), directed by Sofia Coppola
Sideways (2004), directed by Alexander Payne
Slacker (1991), directed by Richard Linklater
Unbreakable (2000), directed by M. Night Shyamalan
The Virgin Suicides (1999), directed by Sofia Coppola

Movies About Envy

All About Eve (1950), directed by Joseph L. Mankiewicz
Cruel Intentions (1999), directed by Roger Kumble
Envy (2004), directed by Barry Levinson
Gossip (2000), directed by Davis Guggenheim
My Best Friend's Wedding (1997), directed by P. J. Hogan
What Ever Happened to Baby Jane? (1962), directed by Robert
   Aldrich

Movies About Fear

Alien (1979), directed by Ridley Scott
Arlington Road (1999), directed by Mark Pellington

Gaslight (1944), directed by George Cukor
Mad Max (1979), directed by George Miller
Mystic River (2003), directed by Clint Eastwood
Rebecca (1940), directed by Alfred Hitchcock
Sleeping with the Enemy (1991), directed by Joseph Ruben

Movies About Greed

Boiler Room (2000), directed by Ben Younger
Confidence (2003), directed by James Foley
The Croupier (1998), directed by Mike Hodges
Double Indemnity (1944), directed by Billy Wilder
Greed (1924), directed by Erich von Stroheim
Intolerable Cruelty (2003), directed by Joel Coen
Jean de Florette (1986), directed by Claude Berri
Manon of the Spring (*Jean de Florette II*; 1986), directed by Claude
  Berri
The Man Who Would Be King (1975), directed by John Huston
Payback (1999), directed by Brian Helgeland
The Postman Always Rings Twice (1981), directed by Bob Rafelson
Wall Street (1987), directed by Oliver Stone

Movies About Guilt

The Accidental Tourist (1988), directed by Lawrence Kasdan
The Door in the Floor (2004), directed by Tod Williams
Fearless (1993), directed by Peter Weir
In the Bedroom (2001), directed by Todd Field
Million Dollar Baby (2004), directed by Clint Eastwood
Ordinary People (1980), directed by Robert Redford
The Sweet Hereafter (1997), directed by Atom Egoyan
Unbreakable (2000), directed by M. Night Shyamalan
Unforgiven (1992), directed by Clint Eastwood

Movies About Hatred

American History X (1998), directed by Tony Kaye
Boys Don't Cry (1999), directed by Kimberly Peirce
Cape Fear (1962), directed by J. Lee Thompson

Carlito's Way (1993), directed by Brian De Palma
The Devil's Advocate (1997), directed by Taylor Hackford
Gangs of New York (2002), directed by Martin Scorsese
The Godfather trilogy (1972, 1974, and 1990), directed by
    Francis Ford Coppola
Heathers (1989), directed by Michael Lehmann
The Indian Runner (1991), directed by Sean Penn
In the Bedroom (2001), directed by Todd Field
Kill Bill Vol. 1 (2003) and *Kill Bill Vol. 2* (2004), directed by
    Quentin Tarantino
Mad Max (1979), directed by George Miller
Monster (2003), directed by Patty Jenkins
Mystic River (2003), directed by Clint Eastwood
Open Range (2003), directed by Kevin Costner
RoboCop (1987), directed by Paul Verhoeven
With a Friend like Harry (2000), directed by Dominik Moll

Movies About Shame

Affliction (1997), directed by Paul Schrader
Bastard Out of Carolina (1996), directed by Anjelica Huston
Maria Full of Grace (2004), directed by Joshua Marston
The Prince of Tides (1991), directed by Barbra Streisand
Raising Victor Vargas (2002), directed by Peter Sollett
Real Women Have Curves (2002), directed by Patricia Cardoso
Sideways (2004), directed by Alexander Payne
Sleepers (1996), directed by Barry Levinson
Sleeping with the Enemy (1991), directed by Joseph Ruben

Questions to Answer

1. Which Emotional Black Holes compromise the characters' lives?
2. What triggers the negative emotional energy to begin operating in the story?
3. How does it cause tragedy and destruction? How do the characters respond?
4. Which characters become its conduits, and which ones oppose it? Who wins?

5. As the story develops, how does negative emotional energy spread? Which words, actions, thoughts, random events, or conscious decisions propel it? Who is affected by it and how?

6. Are there any moments in the story when the characters break free from EBHs? How do they achieve that? List the events that precipitate their change and their actions in response to those events.

7. Very often, the actions the characters take in order to break free from EBHs are unconventional, even amoral. In the context of the story, to what extent are these actions acceptable? How acceptable are they in a real-life context?

8. What were your major emotional reactions to the movie? Which scenes impacted you the most, and how?

9. Choose a main character of the movie, and put yourself in his or her role. Describe what you would do differently to break free from the EBH in a real-life context.

10. What major lesson about EBHs from this movie can you apply to your own life?

Breaking Free from Emotional Black Holes ▶
Exercises and Activities

Gaining freedom from EBHs is very rewarding and worth any effort. The exercises in this section will help you to recognize how an EBH affects your thoughts, attitudes, and actions. You will learn how to emerge faster from your EBHs and thus avoid their destructive effects. With practice, you will learn how to transform destructive emotions into positive energy that propels you to take constructive and meaningful actions toward fulfilling your dreams.

▶ **Are You Stuck in an Emotional Black Hole? A Survey**

Read the following ten statements, and note if they apply to you or not. Give each True answer 1 point, and give each False answer 0 points.

1. I often avoid mentioning or telling the truth about certain parts of my life.
2. I procrastinate a lot and it's hard for me to finish a project.
3. Every so often, my way of handling anger sabotages my efforts to reach my goals.
4. I have noticed that every time I am very close to success, something happens and things fall apart.
5. I often feel that if one of these things about me were different, I would be a much happier person (check one or more):
   □ my family
   □ my race
   □ my gender
   □ my physical appearance
   □ my nationality
6. I often feel used and unappreciated; people should feel very guilty for the way they treat me.
7. I am not optimistic about the future. In fact, I worry a lot about what will happen to me.
8. I am very critical of myself.
9. I have a hard time feeling content with my life; I always want more and it's never enough.
10. I don't want what I have in my life; I envy other people's lives and I want what they have.

Check your score: the higher it is, the more important it is that you begin taking steps to get free from the Emotional Black Holes that keep you stuck and drain your energy.

7–10: You create a lot of suffering for yourself and others that only you can alleviate by taking freedom steps, starting now.

4–6: Go through the exercises in this chapter and name your EBHs. At the end of this chapter there is an EBH Self-Rescuing Action Kit; copy it and apply the antidotes through concrete actions.

1–3: Free yourself completely from the habits that sabotage your happiness. You deserve the best life you can have, and it is in your power to achieve it! Follow the exercises and enjoy the results of your good work.

► **Taking Freedom Steps**

You may complete this exercise over time. Read the eight EBH grids (Figures 6.1 through 6.8), which outline all the different aspects and antidotes of the eight Emotional Black Holes. Choose to work with the one that resonates most with you. Refer to the EBH grid of Appendix D for your personal work. When you fall into an EBH, refer to these grids immediately and take the antidotal steps. Your happiness is in your hands, and so is your freedom from destructive emotions!

FIGURE 6.1 ■ Anger

THOUGHTS	ATTITUDES/ACTIONS	RESULTS	ANTIDOTES
■ *"I can't stand X in me/ you/them, and I want to do something to hurt me/you/them for that."* ■ *"I can't rest if I don't hurt X/myself."* ■ *"Get away from me, or I'll show/hurt you."* ■ *"Your feelings don't matter to me."* ■ *"I must hurt you."* ■ *"You deserve to be hurt."* ■ *"I must hurt myself."*	■ Abusive parenting ■ Spouse battering ■ Crimes ■ Destructive acts against self, others, and/or nature ■ Dogmatic, dictatorial leadership ■ Fanaticism ■ Impatience ■ Lack of ability to listen to other points of view ■ Lack of cooperation ■ Passive or deliberate neglect of personal or other people's needs ■ Poor results in assigned projects	■ Alienating instead of attracting people ■ Judging, belittling, and rejecting others ■ Judging, belittling, and rejecting self ■ Poor communication and rapport building ■ Poor relationships ■ Communication breakdowns ■ Health problems (heart, ulcer, high blood pressure, chronic pain, etc.) ■ Drug and alcohol abuse	1. Recognize the trigger and count 20 breaths. 2. Visualize yourself in the future, away from the anger-provoking situation. 3. Walk away from anger and revisit the situation when you can communicate with clarity. 4. Get clear about your needs.

FIGURE 6.2 ■ **Apathy**

THOUGHTS	ATTITUDES/ACTIONS	RESULTS	ANTIDOTES
■ *"Why bother? Life stinks anyway."* ■ *"Who cares?"* ■ *"Yeah, right."* ■ *"I get a kick out of watching others run to fix their lives—especially when they stumble and fall."* ■ *"I'm not the one to change the world."* ■ *"Get me a better job, a better family, a better body, and then I'll do the rest to be happy."* ■ *"I don't get how people can say, 'I love my work!'"* ■ *"I don't care what the team needs—to each his own."* ■ *"I'd rather watch TV than deal with this world."*	■ Cynicism expressed in remarks, attitudes, and acts of indifference ■ Lack of motivation to begin or carry through with a project ■ Chronic procrastination and avoidance of responsibilities ■ Expectation of miraculous changes without participation ■ Grandiosity about being special and blaming external reality without taking action to change one's circumstances ■ Sabotaging collective efforts for change and progress with no concern about the outcome ■ Using television and/or drugs to escape reality	**Apathy** ■ can kill all zest for life and the desire to achieve ■ kills enthusiasm, joy, love, and compassion ■ forms the habits of cynicism and chronic procrastination ■ can kill the vital energy needed for projects, relationships, and all life-forwarding actions **Apathetic People** ■ have little or no concern about how they affect others ■ drain others' energy with their indifference ■ are incompetent managers, poor parents, inept partners, and destructive friends	1. Identify your neglected needs. 2. Claim responsibility and shun the victim role. 3. Make a fulfillment plan. 4. Do one thing a day to fulfill your plan.

▶   **What Works for You?**

In this chapter, you learned about five categories of helpful activities that you can choose from to break free from Emotional Black Holes: physical activity, video games, creativity, play, and prayer. From these five categories, make a list of three things you can do to diffuse the negative energy of your EBH. Write them in your personal EBH grid. Begin practicing immediately. With persistence, you will see amazing results.

FIGURE 6.3 ▪ Envy

THOUGHTS	ATTITUDES/ACTIONS	RESULTS	ANTIDOTES
▪ *"If I had a life like X...."* ▪ *"If I were born with the advantages of X...."* ▪ *"Why is X better, richer, luckier, happier, and more successful than I am?"* ▪ *"I must have what X has."* ▪ *"X doesn't deserve such a great life."*	▪ Desiring to have another person's life instead of living one's own ▪ Coveting other people's possessions and not appreciating one's own ▪ Using other people's achievements to measure one's self-worth ▪ Negating one's self-worth ▪ Backstabbing colleagues, family, and friends ▪ Being bitter ▪ Defaming others ▪ Bickering ▪ Gossiping ▪ Committing intentional acts of malice	▪ Misery ▪ Poor self-image ▪ Poisonous interactions ▪ Mistrust ▪ Pain ▪ Destroyed relationships ▪ Damaged friendships, marriages, partnerships, finances	1. Name what you envy in person X. 2. Name how you would feel if you had what you envy. 3. Detect the unfulfilled needs revealed by your emotions. 4. List your actions that sabotage or neglect those needs. 5. List actions you must take to fulfill your neglected needs. 6. Become inspired by the people you envy: learn from them how they maintain their happiness, and emulate their qualities in your life.

▶ **Your Emotional Black Hole Self-Rescuing Action Kit**

Create a bookmark or a personalized card from the table in Figure 6.9. Carry it with you, or put it on your desk at work. Use it to rescue yourself from negative emotions.

FIGURE 6.4 ■ **Fear**

THOUGHTS	ATTITUDES/ACTIONS	RESULTS	ANTIDOTES
■ *"I can't do this."*	■ Anticipating failure and disaster	■ Sense of inadequacy to pursue dreams	1. Check your fear against reality by gathering data.
■ *"I dread this person/experience/ thought."*	■ Avoiding responsibilities	■ Staying stuck in unfulfilling jobs and relationships	2. Surround yourself with sources of hope.
■ *"I must protect myself against the unknown."*	■ Discouraging, sabotaging, or forbidding progress that involves risk taking	■ Lack of hope	3. Take baby steps toward fulfilling your needs with manageable projects.
■ *"I won't be able to handle this."*		■ Pessimism, worry, and anticipation of the worst	
■ *"If I try to do anything about X, I'll be destroyed."*	■ Obsessive preoccupation with own health, money, or possessions		4. Celebrate your successes.
■ *"This is stronger than I am."*	■ Obsessive worrying	■ Fear-based relationships that are uneven, manipulative, controlling, and often abusive	
■ *"This paralyzes me."*	■ Pervasive anxiety or panic attacks	■ Fear-based decisions that thwart fulfillment	
■ *"I'm afraid of what will happen if…."*	■ Being overly controlling		
■ *"I must attack before getting attacked."*	■ Abusing and exploiting the weak		
■ *"I must protect myself against everyone trying to get close."*	■ Controlling others		
■ *"I am afraid of people/life."*	■ Refusing intimacy and commitments		

Things to Remember

- Getting free from Emotional Black Holes is a process that unfolds successfully as you correct your self-sabotaging patterns.
- There are five ways to transform destructive emotional energy: physical activity, video games, creativity, play, and prayer.

FIGURE 6.5 ■ **Greed**

THOUGHTS	ATTITUDES/ACTIONS	RESULTS	ANTIDOTES
■ *"I can't have enough of X."* ■ *"I constantly need more of X."* ■ *"Consequences are not important: when I need more of something, I just need it and I must have it."* ■ *"I don't pay attention to what I already have. I am only interested in how much more I can get."* ■ *"I feel complete only when I chase what I want; as soon as I get it, I feel empty."* ■ *"I must get the most for the least."* ■ *"I'm never satisfied; I'm never content; I always demand more."*	■ Compulsive accumulation of material objects or money ■ Grandiose fantasies of being indestructible and above all human morals ■ Illegal or immoral business dealings aimed only at profit ■ Inability to connect with others or reciprocate a kindness ■ Moral confusion and loss of human values that result in illicit affairs with destructive consequences ■ Inability to manage possessions or money ■ Tax evasion	**Greed** ■ instills a pervasive sense of lack that imitates poverty ■ kills feelings of satisfaction, contentment, and gratitude ■ distorts our innate morality and our ability to see the consequences of our actions on the common welfare ■ destroys families, communities, organizations, and societies ■ impairs leadership skills ■ muddles our thinking and critical judgment ■ isolates us and kills our humanity	1. Acknowledge and cherish your acquired possessions. 2. Express gratitude through acts of giving. 3. Tell the truth.

FIGURE 6.6 ■ **Guilt**

THOUGHTS	ATTITUDES/ACTIONS	RESULTS	ANTIDOTES
■ *"I deserve to suffer for all the mistakes I've made in the past."* ■ *"I must suffer for my successes."* ■ *"I should not honor my needs—they are less/not important."* ■ *"I must not indulge in what makes me happy—that is too selfish."* ■ *"I should always give others the best of me, even against my own wishes."* ■ *"I should not feel fulfilled as long as there is so much suffering in the world."* ■ *"It's not important to be clear about my needs right now."* ■ *"Money is not for me; I don't deserve to be rich or happy."*	■ Causing incidents to induce guilt for own and others' success ■ Choosing financially needy, failure-prone partners and friends ■ Compulsive work habits ■ Negative stereotyping of wealthy or successful people ■ Sexual oppression of self and/or others ■ Grandiose fantasies of saving the world through self-punishing behaviors ■ Using guilt to control and manipulate others ■ Saying yes when meaning no	Guilt ■ can kill all life's pleasures, from the smallest to the most significant **Guilt-Ridden People** ■ impose their suffering on others by building guilt-based relationships ■ resent others' happiness and avoid their own ■ are not authentic with their emotions (i.e., their actions do not represent how they truly feel) **Guilt-Based Relationships** ■ are not healthy and eventually explode in destructive conflicts with long-term effects	1. Accept pleasure as an essential, normal, and healthy experience. 2. Claim your neglected needs and fulfill them. 3. Learn to do what feels good and makes you happy.

FIGURE 6.7 ■ Hatred

THOUGHTS	ATTITUDES/ACTIONS	RESULTS	ANTIDOTES
■ *"Even if I could help him/her/them, I refuse to—their misery pleases me."*	■ Premeditated or spontaneous acts that invalidate others or harm their welfare	■ Hate crimes	1. Visualize being your enemy.
■ *"He/she is my enemy—I must hurt him/her."*	■ Compulsive behaviors of self-inflicted pain	■ Ongoing strife	2. Feel the pain of your enemy.
■ *"I am my own enemy—I must hurt myself."*	■ Premeditated or spontaneous acts of violence, crime, destruction, neglect, torture, or abuse against self, others, and/or nature	■ Pain	3. Practice conscious acts of kindness.
■ *"I refuse to accept X."*		■ Misery	4. Connect with your enemy through your mutual humanity.
■ *"I must destroy X."*		■ Bitterness	
■ *"I cannot accept myself or part X of myself."*	■ Receiving pleasure or being entertained by others' pain, suffering, and/or demise	■ Psychosomatic illnesses	
■ *"I cannot accept part X of my life."*	■ Violence, abuse, or systematic crime	■ Hate-induced madness	
■ *"I enjoy seeing X suffer."*			
■ *"I wish the worst to happen to X."*			
■ *"I'll never rest as long as X exists."*			
■ *"I will make X suffer at all costs."*			

FIGURE 6.8   ■   Shame

THOUGHTS	ATTITUDES/ACTIONS	RESULTS	ANTIDOTES
■ *"I must hide X about me."* ■ *"I should not be visible; success would make me visible; therefore, I should not succeed."* ■ *"I do not deserve to be proud of who I am/what I have."* ■ *"I am embarrassed about myself."* ■ *"There are parts of me I avoid talking about; people would hate me if they knew these things."*	■ Denying or hiding own sexual orientation, origins, or past ■ Avoiding social contact ■ Avoiding success and visibility ■ Resorting to grandiose fantasies with no reflection on reality ■ Illicit business dealings ■ Presenting a false persona to others ■ Choosing partners who sabotage personal success ■ Choosing jobs below one's potential ■ Sabotaging efforts for social and career advancement	**Shame** ■ undermines our natural need to feel proud of ourselves, our identity, and our accomplishments ■ sabotages our efforts to become visible and accepted within a community ■ alienates and isolates us from others ■ is the emotional black hole that drains our efforts to succeed socially and professionally **Shaming People** ■ use shame to control others **Shame-Based Relationships** ■ are perverse and have destructive long-term effects	1. Change what you can and accept what you cannot change about yourself. 2. Name and claim your points of pride. 3. Terminate shaming relationships. 4. Refuse to be shamed—educate others to respect and recognize you.

FIGURE 6.9 ■ EBH Self-Rescuing Action Kit

EMOTIONAL BLACK HOLE	ANTIDOTE
Anger	Breathe and express your anger constructively.
Apathy	Connect with your neglected need.
Envy	Fulfill your neglected need within the context of your life.
Fear	Take baby steps toward fulfilling your need.
Greed	Stop saying "I want more!" and say "I am thankful for. . . ."
Guilt	Do what makes you truly happy, and let yourself and others feel pleasure.
Hatred	Question your rationale for hating, and treat your enemy as you would like to be treated.
Shame	Be proud to be yourself, and do what makes you happy.

Third Gain: Spiritual Fitness

▶ JUST AS YOU achieve physical fitness thanks to regular exercise, you can achieve spiritual fitness thanks to regular mental routines that enhance your spiritual health.

The mind is the tool for mastering emotions. This is why you need spiritual fitness to enhance your emotional health and maintain a sense of inner safety and calm. As a spiritually fit person you will have self-confidence, inner strength, and consistent focus on accomplishing your goals with success.

The next three chapters will teach you how to develop spiritual fitness amidst your busy, noisy life. Using examples from movies and special activities, you will learn how to:

- Stay grounded in the present
- Use creative imagination to solve problems
- Practice effective prayer and meditation

[7]

Get Grounded in the Now

ABOUT SCHMIDT'S HERO, Warren Schmidt, is a widower and recent retiree who at age sixty-six makes a very painful discovery. He realizes that he has spent his life repeating routines and following a script that has made him a husband, father, and vice president of his company but has given him no real personal fulfillment. Warren always went through the motions but was never present in his experience: he spent his years watching life happen to him as he adhered to a daily schedule and did the right things, much like a well-functioning robot, with no emotions, no desires, and no dreams of his own. Now at this age, he has to face the consequences of his chronic self-alienation. Seeing that he has let his life go by without really living it, he recognizes his unfulfilled need for a meaningful existence and decides to take his first steps to fulfill it.

Will he succeed? What miracle will be required for Warren to take back his lost time, his lost opportunities to be present in his life, and his right to experience his own humanity that he has never exercised before?

Warren Schmidt is an example of a person who discovered late in life the joy of being connected with the present moment. The movie does not show how he will use what he learned along the way in the rest of his life, but you can use his example for your own sake and apply his lesson for your own benefit. Getting grounded in the now, *now*, will save you years of meaninglessness and self-alienation, and it will empower you to fully participate in your life as you live it in the present. A life fully lived is a life lived in the present, not one lived in our memories of the past or our anticipations of the future.

There is a great deal of talk about living in the present, trusting the moment, and being open to the unknown without worrying about it. But rarely do we discuss why it is so difficult to live in the now or how to get grounded in the now through specific actions, rather than just attitudes. This chapter is designed to help you understand why you get—and stay—disconnected from the present and learn what you can do to get grounded in the now and live life to the fullest as you pursue your dreams, goals, and desires.

The three main reasons for not being engaged in the present are explained later in the chapter. Before reading them, you must know that being grounded in the now requires a specific mental attitude, emotional involvement, and specific actions that demonstrate your full participation in life as it happens in the present. All three components must be active in order for you to be present in the now. Keep this in mind as you work with the exercises at the end of the chapter. Remember that you are working on turning the abstract notion of living in the now into concrete experiences leading to fulfillment. You must learn to engage your mind, emotions, and actions in order for this process to be successful.

Living *in* the Now Is Different from Living *for* the Now

The first distinction you must make as you learn to ground your life in the now is that living in the present is not the same as living for the present. The following 2,600-year-old short story by the Greek fabulist Aesop distinguishes between the two different attitudes using the metaphor of the Ant and the Grasshopper:

In a field one summer's day, a grasshopper was hopping about, chirping and singing to its heart's content. An ant passed by, bearing along with great toil an ear of corn he was taking to the nest.

"Why not come and chat with me," said the Grasshopper, "instead of toiling and moiling in that way?"

"I am helping to lay up food for the winter," said the Ant, "and recommend you to do the same."

"Why bother about winter?" said the Grasshopper. "We have got plenty of food at present." But the Ant went on its way and continued its toil. When the winter came, the Grasshopper had no food and found itself dying of hunger, while every day it saw the ants distributing corn and grain from the stores they had collected in the summer. Then the Grasshopper knew: it is best to prepare for the days of necessity.

In Aesop's story, the Ant is living *in* the now. He is aware of his need for nourishment and his responsibility to keep his needs satisfied in the winter when food will be scarce. So he actively engages in storing it away during the summer, when food abounds. He shows his involvement in the present through his mental attitude, emotional involvement, and specific actions. Using action, he works in the now to find and store abundant food for the time he knows it will be scarce. Emotionally, he feels proud of his industrious activities to the point of urging the Grasshopper to do the same, and mentally, he believes in what he is doing, knowing it is the right thing. Apparently, he has done the same in the past and has benefited from it; therefore, he is happy doing the right thing for himself again, being fully engaged in the present moment.

The Grasshopper, on the other hand, is living *for* the now. Not only does he lack vision, but he also seems to ignore his responsibility toward his future need for food. Seduced by the ease of feeding himself right now, he forgets that when winter comes, he won't be able to find food as easily and he will be hungry. So while the Ant is fully engaged in the present moment as he stores food for the future, the Grasshopper lives for the now, gratifying only his present hunger with the food he finds available. His mental attitude is shortsighted and arrogant, his emotional involvement with the present is limited to instant gratification with no concern for the future, and his actions show that he ignores the true value of the present. While the Ant sees the value of summer as an abundance of food that he can store for the days of scarcity, the Grasshopper sees summer's value only in the pleasure of consuming his food right now, with no thoughts of the future.

Catch Me if You Can tells the tale of a Grasshopper living in a perpetual summer at other people's expense—that is, until he is forced to see that living *for* the present is destructive not only for him but also for everyone coming into contact with him and society at large. The film's story profiles a real person, Frank Abagnale Jr., who was one of the most successful con men in the history of the United States and who managed to forge checks for millions of dollars and successfully impersonate a doctor, a lawyer, and an airline pilot. He cashed checks in more than twenty countries and in all fifty states and accomplished all this before the age of nineteen.

Being gifted with extreme intelligence, wit, and charm, Frank decides to leave home as a teenager and live life to the fullest. He puts his genius to work by committing one fraud after another while indulging in pleasures only money can buy. As we watch Frank live for the now at the expense of others, we see him create a trail of destruction that involves more and more innocent people. Frank is reaping the fruits of seeds he never sowed and manipulating others' emotions as he steals their love, trust, and money. He has an insatiable need for approval, recognition, and acceptance but does nothing the right way to fulfill his needs. He does not work for his fulfillment, show his true self to others, risk his own emotions, or build honest relationships. Instead, he steals his fulfillment by appropriating foreign identities, and he feels no remorse or concern about others. This will eventually catch up with him.

Grasshoppers exist everywhere: they are the ones with the maxed-out credit cards, the ones who have difficulty balancing their own checkbooks, and the ones who complain about life's unfairness because they cannot pay their bills. They are the ones who always cite their circumstances as the reason they are unable to achieve their dreams and as an excuse for hurting other people. They are the ones asking for a loan that will never be returned, the ones who spend the company's budget for personal expenses, and the ones who will leave a relationship when it stops gratifying their impulses.

Grasshoppers do not commit to anything because commitment requires a full presence in the now and this is too difficult for them. The truth is that Grasshoppers are a lot of fun to be with because they are the life of the party, as long as the party lasts. But when it is over, you had better be prepared because the Grasshopper will then want you to keep him or her entertained, happy, and fed. This is why keeping a Grasshopper close to you—or following his or her ways—is draining and eventually destructive for you, your family, your work environment, and your community. If you care about yourself or your loved ones, stay away from the ways of a Grasshopper.

Reasons for Not Being Grounded in the Now

Ignoring Your True Needs or Trying to Fulfill Them Through Inappropriate Actions

Knowing your true needs gives you an impetus to fulfill them, and this automatically grounds you in the here and now. On the other hand, ignoring or not paying attention to them is a reason for perpetual daydreaming, frequent escapes into the past or the future, or avoidance of reality through various addictions. In addition, when you are not consciously aware of your true needs, you are more vulnerable to succumbing to social pressures and pursuing needs that are not truly yours. For example, people who ignore their need for love try to fulfill this need through their work: instead of getting mentally, emotionally, and actively involved in creating a nurturing family or intimate relationships, they get completely immersed in work. As they are seeking recognition, fame, or money to fulfill their ignored need for love, they allow deadlines and PalmPilots to keep them focused on the future. These people are not in touch with the present but live in a time and space that do not exist.

Lester Burnham, the hero of *American Beauty*, is a character who spent years being disconnected from the now. As the story begins, we hear Lester describe his life as being in a perpetual coma, going through each day's motions completely severed from any real experience. Even though he lives in an expensive suburb, has the right furniture, drives the right car, and wears the right clothes, Lester is an unfulfilled husband, estranged father, and unsuccessful employee. His needs for intimacy, authenticity, and meaning are stifled, and this hurts him. Nothing around him seems to hold his attention to the here and now, and he sees no reason to be involved in his life until, unexpectedly, he falls in love with his teenage daughter's classmate.

This is Lester's awakening in all sorts of ways; it forever changes his attitudes, emotions, and actions and pushes him into reliving his lost adolescence. Acting like a teenager, he comes into constant conflict with his environment, provoking everyone's confusion, exasperation, anger, and hatred.

As the rift between Lester and his environment deepens, we sense that he has gone too far and that an ominous event is about to befall him. When this happens, Lester has no choice but to recognize the beauty of his life unconditionally and be thankful for it. This revelation gives him the completion he craved and frees him from his inner prison. As we watch his controversial journey to the end, we have mixed feelings of sadness and relief. We are relieved that he has finally fulfilled his need for authenticity by discovering the beauty of his life, but we are also sad that he had to pay so dearly for his discovery.

Can our quest for authentic living be successful without our having to pay a price as high as Lester's? Absolutely! What, then, is the law of success governing our journey to fulfillment? The answer is simple: knowing our true needs and pursuing them through fulfillment-appropriate actions. Lester did acknowledge his needs, but he took inappropriate actions to transform his life, showing immaturity and lack of vision. If you want success in creating a life you love, you must choose appropriate ways to fulfill your desires and evaluate the effectiveness of your actions based on the results you are getting; otherwise, life will teach you a lesson to show you that you cannot violate its laws.

Unlike Lester, who pays a price for disobeying the laws of fulfillment in *American Beauty*, Andrew Largeman, the young hero of *Garden State*, does the right thing to fulfill his need for a real life. Having spent almost twenty years disconnected from himself and his true emotions, Andrew reclaims his life when he finally forgives his father and accepts himself and his life with no conditions.

"We may not be as happy as you always dreamed we would be, but, for the first time, let's just allow ourselves to be whatever it is that we are," he tells his father, relieving both of them from the pressure of being their "best selves" to make up for past regrets.

But Andrew does not stop there. When his heart calls him to take the path to happiness and leave behind him a lonely and emotionally starved past, he hesitates for only a moment, and then he goes right ahead. Even though he cannot control how things will turn out, he is positive that this is the path he has to take. Andrew has come into his life by choosing to do the right thing, which is to listen to the call of his heart. His example clearly shows that in order to live an emotionally full life, we must follow our heart when it calls us—and we must be ready for this opportunity because it may never happen again.

Not Being Free from Emotional Black Holes

As we've seen, Emotional Black Holes not only drain your energy, but they also pull you out of the present, making you a prisoner of the past or a fugitive into the future. Grounding your life in the present requires freedom from their destructive pull. There is an abundance of films about characters who broke free from Emotional Black Holes and reconnected with the present or learned life lessons that grounded them in the now.

Phone Booth is one such film. The hero, Stuart Shepard, learns a lesson that forces him to start living an authentic life. Stu, as his friends call him, is a New York publicist in his thirties whose Emotional Black Holes dictate his life, causing him to be absent from the here and now. Greed for social recognition causes him to live in the fast lane, exploiting his young, innocent protégé and lying at others' expense. Shame for his personal flaws causes him to present a false persona to the world. Fear of being emotionally open to his wife causes him to have an affair, and guilt for his transgressions pushes him to conceal them using deception and lies. Trying to prevent his wife, who reads their phone bills, from finding out about his calls to his girlfriend, Stuart doesn't use his cell phone to call her but goes to a phone booth in the Upper West Side. This is his routine until one day the phone rings as he enters the booth. At the other end of the line is a sniper, calling from nearby and watching Stu's every move while he talks. The sniper embodies Stuart's conscience and knows him very well. He commands Stuart to expose his true self to the world; otherwise, he will shoot Stuart.

Phone Booth is a story in which a person's nemesis becomes his messiah. In other words, the extreme situation facing the hero of this film threatens to end his physical existence but, in essence, gives him a chance to begin a new emotional and spiritual life. Some of us may be so fortunate as to have such an encounter with fate. Others may have a completely different experience: while being fully engaged in the present, we may suddenly receive from life a blow so cruel that our world is torn apart and we are thrown into a vacuum that seems abysmal, unable to move on. In such instances, we may have to make choices that seem extreme in order to get back what has been taken away from us, come to terms with life, and reconnect with the now.

The big screen is filled with stories about heroes struggling to reclaim their life after an unfair and tragic loss. Most often those are films about revenge. They usually show how the main hero avenges the murder of a loved one by taking justice into his or her own hands through extreme, violent actions that culminate with killing the murderer(s) and destroying their accomplices. Such movies present the idea of an eye for an eye as a viable way to break free from the Emotional Black Holes of anger, hatred, and guilt through destructive actions that know no limits.

Widely known, much loved award-winning films *Gladiator, The Patriot, Braveheart, Mad Max, The Salton Sea, Kill Bill, RoboCop, Rambo, Unforgiven*, and *In the Bedroom* are all stories about revenge. Because of their enormous appeal to billions of viewers around the world, it is useful to put these movies in perspective. Here are some helpful points about the role of these movies in your own process of breaking free from Emotional Black Holes:

- Movies are visual myths. As such, they give you the opportunity to live vicariously in extreme situations, identify with extreme emotions, and watch extreme ways of handling them in a mythical context, without causing harm to yourself or others. If you try to replicate those actions in reality, you will suffer serious consequences. *Always keep in mind the distinction between myth and reality.*

- The societies portrayed in those movies are always corrupt and devoid of justice. Their rules are basic and survival oriented. The hero is left to his or her own means to enforce what seems fair to him or her. *A real society is much more complex, multilayered, and subtle than any mythical society. It is influenced by psychological and spiritual variables that can never be revealed in a two-hour action movie.*

- In real life, premeditated murder as an act of personal revenge is generally forbidden and always prosecuted by the law. *As members of a real society, we must follow rules and use proper channels to get justice restored when we have suffered injustice.*

- The psychological value of revenge movies is in the cathartic experiences they catalyze on the viewer's intense, destructive emotions, such as anger, hatred, shame, and guilt. This experience is supposed to last as long as the film itself so you can reenter reality feeling relieved. *Under no circumstances should you replicate in real life the violent and murderous acts of personal revenge you watch in a film.*

It is true and perhaps inevitable that as you try to heal your Emotional Black Holes, reclaim your life, and live it in the present, you may have to make unconventional choices or take radical actions. What these actions will be depends on your discernment, moral judgment, and common sense. If you want to see how a Native American culture handles betrayal, adultery, and murder without having to retort with acts of vengeance, watch *The Fast Runner*. It is the visual tale of the heroic struggle of Atanarjuat, leader of a primitive Inuit tribe, to save his spirit and his people from the attacks of evil without having to commit vengeful acts of murder.

Not Having Faith in Life's Inherent Wisdom

The more tuned in you are with your true needs, the more encouraged you feel to do the right things to fulfill them. As you ground your life in the here and now and focus on making your inner desires your reality, you will see the future and the unknown not as threats to your happiness but as carriers of possibilities. Confident that you are doing your part to create the happiness you deserve, you trust that life, thanks to its inherent wisdom, will respond accordingly. The more faith you show in life's inherent wisdom, the more you trust *your own* wisdom, and vice versa. Trusting that life knows and delivers when you also know what you need from life and how to pursue it relieves you of the irrational need to control the future.

When you do not try to control the unknown, you live life as the Ant of the Greek fable: you stay grounded in the now. You prepare for the future using knowledge from past experience and common sense, which is how you practice faith in life's inherent wisdom. Knowledge from past experience includes the legacy inherited from our ancestors' generations throughout the millennia until the present day, as well as our own knowledge gained from personal experiences. Common sense is the knowledge that nature instills in each of us, irrespective of schooling or training. It is instinctive and reflects our inherent ability to discern and make choices that ensure our own well-being and that of our community. When you exercise knowledge and common sense in pursuing your yearnings, life's challenges are opportunities that enrich your self-knowledge, strengthen your character, and allow you to fully experience your humanity.

A film that illustrates how a person can practice faith in life's inherent wisdom by staying focused on pursuing his own happiness and doing good to others is *The Simple Life of Noah Dearborn*. Noah, the main character, is a ninety-one-year-old man who has always been loyal to his values, practicing them throughout his life. As a result, at his venerable age, he enjoys perfect health, the love of his community, and the joy of living a natural life according to his beliefs on his thirty-five-acre estate. His peace is interrupted when a team of real estate developers threatens to seize his property and build a shopping mall. Noah is faced with the biggest challenge of his life and handles it by remaining authentic to his truth, strong in his beliefs, and fearless of the invaders despite their efforts to harm him. As the intruders get to know Noah, they discover that the secret of his power and well-being is his ability to live a life he truly loves. This humbles them and prompts them to reconsider their own lives and definitions of happiness. Noah triumphs over the intruders by challenging them to discover their true needs, and he inspires them to find happiness by living simpler lives, yet lives that are full of meaning and authenticity.

Noah Dearborn's mythical character impersonates the ability to live in the now by being authentic to one's needs, staying true to one's values, and focusing on one's goals. He shows us that by being grounded in the now, we can overcome difficulties, resolve problems, deal with unexpected challenges, and celebrate our victories, as we trust life's inherent wisdom and are thankful for its blessings.

Reel Fulfillment in Action

Movie Time! ▶ *Watch a Movie for Fun, Learn a Lesson of Life*

A number of movies show how different characters from all walks of life discover that life is best lived in the present. Choose a movie from the following list, and watch it alone or with your group. Afterward, write down your answers to the questions that follow the list of movies, and discuss them with your group. Repeat the same with other films on the list, as your time permits.

Movies About Living in the Present
About Schmidt (2002), directed by Alexander Payne
American Beauty (1999), directed by Sam Mendes
As Good as It Gets (1997), directed by James L. Brooks
Catch Me if You Can (2002), directed by Steven Spielberg
The English Patient (1996), directed by Anthony Minghella
The Fast Runner (2001), directed by Zacharias Kunuk
Fearless (1993), directed by Peter Weir
Garden State (2004), directed by Zach Braff
Gladiator (2000), directed by Ridley Scott

In the Bedroom (2001), directed by Todd Field
It's a Wonderful Life (1946), directed by Frank Capra
Liar Liar (1997), directed by Tom Shadyac
Matchstick Men (2003), directed by Ridley Scott
Phenomenon (1996), directed by Jon Turteltaub
Phone Booth (2002), directed by Joel Schumacher
Regarding Henry (1991), directed by Mike Nichols
The Salton Sea (2002), directed by D. J. Caruso
The Simple Life of Noah Dearborn (1999), directed by Gregg
    Champion
Terms of Endearment (1983), directed by James L. Brooks
21 Grams (2003), directed by Alejandro González Iñárritu
Wrestling Ernest Hemingway (1993), directed by Randa Haines

Questions to Answer

1. How does the main character in the story learn the lesson that life must be grounded and lived in the now?
2. What discoveries does the character make as he or she is forced to learn his or her lesson?
3. How does the character influence other people around him or her? How do others respond to his or her changes?
4. Did the story give you any insights about your way of fleeing the present? What are they?
5. List three things that you do to avoid living life in the now. Share them with your group.
6. List three things that you can do to ground yourself in the now. Share them with your group.

Getting Grounded in the Now ▸ *Exercises and Activities*

When you complete the following exercises, you will have learned how to practice a concrete, step-by-step approach of grounding yourself in the now and living your life in the present.

▶ **Take Care of Your Physical and Financial Health Now**

Taking care of your physical and financial health will help you stay grounded and focused in the present and will alleviate your tendency to worry about the future.

- Examine your health and begin a fitness routine. Get a physical examination and take stock of your current health habits. How healthy are they? Are there any needs for improvement? Take responsibility for your health and begin making those improvements now.
- Take stock of your current finances. Get the real data of your financial situation and your financial habits. How healthy are they? Take stock of your assets and liabilities. Create a budget and learn how to balance your checkbook. Actively participate in how your money is invested or managed. Create financial goals and begin working on them now. As you do so, stay focused on the present and check off your accomplishments. As you improve your financial habits and you become financially healthier, your worries about the future will diminish and you will feel more able to enjoy the present.

▶ **Determine Which Triggers Propel You to Escape from the Present**

Very often, urges to flee from the present are reactions to external triggers that we react to unconsciously. Identifying those triggers empowers us to take charge of our reactions to them and, when it is within our control, to change them. For example, a dark wall color in your office may be a trigger for daydreams about a sunny beach, which in turn habitually interfere with your work. Changing the wall color or hanging a poster of a sunny beach may satisfy your need for a pleasant environment and help you focus on your work.

FIGURE 7.1   ■   Fleeing from the Present

TRIGGER	OVERWHELMING EMOTIONS	FLEEING THOUGHTS	REACTIONS
1. A rich cousin bragging about her money	1. Overwhelmed, Inferior	1. *"My life stinks—hers is much better."*	1. Watch soap operas and neglect the household
2. Credit card debt	2. Overwhelmed, inadequate	2. *"I'll deal with it later."*	2. Go shopping and incur more debt
3. Recent divorce—having to pay alimony	3. Overwhelmed, angry, sad	3. *"I need a break from this."*	3. Drink a lot and occasionally do drugs

Based on the example outlined in Figure 7.1, make your own list of three triggers, the overwhelming emotions, and the fleeing thoughts they elicit. In the last column, write three behavioral reactions you use to flee from the present.

▶ **Practice a Grounding Routine**

Disturbing thoughts and overwhelming emotions accompany our escapes from the present. In such instances, we feel helpless as we dwell on moments long gone or become consumed with worry about the future and fear of the unknown.

Every time you feel overwhelmed and ready to flee the present, practice the following grounding routine:

- **Get grounded in your body.** Turn your attention from your disturbing thoughts to your body. Concentrate on your breathing for two minutes, until the overwhelming emotion subsides.
- **Get grounded in your mind.** Use your mind for self-empowerment by asking yourself this question: *What is my source of strength right now?*
  Identify three sources of strength in your life now. Focus your attention on these sources, one at a time, to draw strength. These

sources can be *internal* or *spiritual* (for example, an inner guide, your religious faith, or your love for someone), *external* or *material* (for example, a mentor, a person supporting you, or your material accomplishments), or *both*.

- **Get grounded in your life.** Complete the routine by asking yourself this question: *Who are the people and what is my purpose right now for the sake of which I must not escape the present but stay actively involved in it?*

  Answering this question brings your attention to a person, a project, an interest, or a commitment *outside yourself* (for example, your children, your spouse, someone whose welfare depends on you, your employees, a work project, or people you mentor). When you think of a commitment that requires you to be present, strong, and available, you reconnect with life and bring your attention to the now. When you remember what you are here to do and for whom else you are here besides yourself, you will free yourself from being excessively self-absorbed and entangled in your own worries.

▶ Breathe

- Create a habit of breathing deeply every time you notice your heartbeats rising due to stress, anxiety, worry, fear, or excitement.
- Use breathing to ground your mind in the now. Become aware of your breathing pattern.
- Take a breathing course and learn how to breathe.

▶ Count Your Present Blessings

In a page or two, write down what you have learned about yourself and your life since you began this course. Answer these questions:

1. What major strengths have you discovered within yourself?
2. What are your present external sources of strength?

3. Which sources presently give you inner peace and clarity?
4. What everyday joys do you presently appreciate?

Things to Remember

- You can notice your progress and count your blessings only when you are present in the now.
- The best way to be prepared for the future is to be actively involved in the present.
- Being grounded in the now is not only a mental attitude but also a practice that requires emotional involvement and specific, consistent actions.

8

Practice Creative Imagination

When I was a little girl, I loved to draw. Every evening, I would open my sketch diary, take my crayons out of their box, arrange them neatly according to color (from lightest to darkest), grab the shade of my choice, and begin drawing. I liked drawing scenes from my day, especially events from my school or home life that had affected me emotionally. I drew when I was anxious, upset, or scared; I drew when I was lonely, afraid, or confused; I drew when I was impressed, excited, or happy.

Each time I finished a drawing, I felt much better than I had before. If I had been cheerful before I started to draw, afterward I was elated; if I had been upset, afterward I was calmer; if I had been afraid or lonely, drawing made me feel reassured and accepted. This was because the figures I drew had human thoughts and spoke with a human voice. To illustrate this, I would write in what my drawings were either thinking or saying, putting words into little bubbles I drew over the figures' heads.

Those word-filled bubbles were what I loved most about drawing, because inside them, I could put the words I wanted my figures to speak or the thoughts I wanted them to have. My drawings described my daily experiences but allowed me to see them from a completely opposite point of view. During the day, I participated in the world of adults, trying to adjust to new things and cope with the reality around me. I was a tiny actor on a huge stage, learning to perform in a world I did not always like. But in the evening, my sketchpad was *my* stage, the adults were now *my* tiny actors, and *I* was telling them how to act. Without knowing it, I was using my creative imagination to create scenarios in which I would give the world of adults a second chance to behave in ways that always made me feel better. The rescripting of my real life into a mythology of speaking drawings was not only a fun activity but my biggest source of strength and inspiration.

By the time I finished second grade, my hobby of making "talking" sketches had ended and was replaced by reading. My new friends were now the characters in novels and short stories. When I felt alone, I called on them to keep me company, cheer me up, or even give me advice. My best fictional friend was Francie Nolan from Betty Smith's novel *A Tree Grows in Brooklyn*. We were so much alike, we could have been twins! We both loved to read, and we each stowed away the petty cash we had earned or received from relatives on holidays. We both had a spoiled younger brother and a family that didn't always treat us fairly. We both loved observing the world of adults, and we sought out truth and beauty in our daily experiences. When life got hard, we both used imagination to soothe ourselves, dreaming of a bright, happy future. Francie stayed with me and helped me through the difficulties of my childhood and early adolescence. She showed me how to be courageous, stay honest, and become resourceful. Every time I needed help, I would call on her, and she would be there for me, always with helpful and encouraging ideas.

Can you remember what you did to overcome difficulties as a child? Was creative imagination one of the tools you used to cope with the world of adults? Did you have an imaginary friend or an activity in which you used imagination to gain strength and inspiration? Today, when external support is inadequate to help you handle stress, what do you do? Do you ask for help from inner guides, or do you resort to antidepressants, tranquilizers, alcohol, tobacco, or daydreaming?

This chapter will help you rediscover and use your creative imagination. It will show you how movie heroes as well as real people have used imagination to draw on their inner resources and overcome life's crises. Following their examples, you will add creative imagination to your tool kit of inner resources available to help you achieve your goals.

Creative Imagination Is the Source of Divine Inspiration

Everything that has ever been created was first imagined. Thanks to our ability to imagine, we have created paintings, sculpture, poetry, and architecture. Imagination has also been the source of every intellectual achievement, including philosophy, mathematics, science, and, most important, language. From the realm of imagination sprang every technological miracle, enabling us to master nature, develop communication systems, explore the planet, and conquer space. From the Egyptian papyrus to today's Internet and from the Sumerian wheel to the American space shuttle, every human accomplishment has been inspired by imagination.

Creative imagination is the means of communing with the Creator and receiving inspiration. The verb *inspire* comes from the Latin *inspirare*, which means "to breathe into something." From the same verb comes the word *spirit*, which, in essence, means "breath." Inspiration then is the experience of being filled with spirit or being filled with the Creator's "breath" that moves us to bring forth divine ideas into reality.

For the ancient Greeks, engaging in creative imagination was a religious ritual, performed with great reverence. It started with a prayer to the Muses, the nine deity-protectors of the arts, letters, and sciences, daughters of Zeus and Mnemosyne ("Memory"). Their leader was Apollo, the patron of reason, music, and harmony, whose help was also traditionally invoked. Authors and historians, musicians and poets, playwrights and actors, astronomers and philosophers, dancers and sacred lyricists always began their work by praying for inspiration. The ideas that followed the prayer were the divine answers and the second part of the ritual. The third part was following and developing the ideas through creative work.

A modern story about our need for divine inspiration is told in the movie *The Muse*. It is the story of Steven Phillips, a Hollywood screenwriter whose creative output has lost its edge and who desperately needs help. Heeding a friend's advice, he seeks the help of "the Muse," an unusual woman with bizarre manners who presents herself as the daughter of Zeus. As soon as she agrees to help Steven, she demands his total devotion, time, and a considerable amount of money in exchange for her inspiration. As the story unfolds, her demands increase, but so does her influencing power. She not only inspires Steven to write his script but also inspires his wife, who starts a bakery enterprise. While the Muse changes the lives of everyone who surrenders to her advice, no one knows who she really is. Everyone is shocked and surprised when her true identity is ultimately revealed.

Beneath the surface of this lighthearted movie lie two perennial truths about our intention toward creative imagination:

- **Creative imagination requires total surrender and patience in order to produce ideas.** The Muse's impossible demands illustrate how creative imagination requires surrender, devotion, and patience. As soon as Steven Phillips and his wife surrender to the Muse and trust her ideas, they start to realize the benefits. In the process, Steven has to learn to be patient, let go of his expectations, and allow a timetable he may not have anticipated to play out and bring the desired results.
- **Sometimes creative imagination produces ideas that may seem crazy; instead of judging them, we must apply them using common sense.** Some of the Muse's ideas initially seem crazy to Steven and his wife. But they don't judge her suggestions; they simply try to implement them using common sense. As a result, Steven writes a brilliant script and his wife launches a successful business.

The Muse's modern story demonstrates the ancient practice of surrendering to the guidance of creative imagination to achieve a fulfilled life. It also illustrates the perennial truth that the path to happiness requires hard work and faith in the inherent wisdom of life, which in turn, in its own time frame, always rewards our efforts.

Using Creative Imagination for Fulfillment

Creative imagination not only offers inspiration for creative output, but it can also guide your personal growth. Learning how to use it for inner mentoring can help you develop inner strength, resolve daily problems, overcome personal crises, and face the unknown as you tackle life's new phases.

Using Creative Imagination for Inner Strength

No innocent man should meet a fate as unfair as that of Giuseppe Conlon. A good Irishman who lived in Belfast, loved his family, and practiced his religion, he was never prepared for the tragedy that befell him late in life. In 1974 he was wrongly accused of being involved in an IRA bombing of two pubs in Guilford, England, that killed several people. Also implicated were his son, Gerry Conlon, two other family members, and three of his son's friends. Coerced by the British police to confess to crimes they had never committed, the "Guilford Four"—Giuseppe, his son, and two of his son's friends—were sentenced to life imprisonment. During their sentencing, the judge declared that it was unfortunate that Britain no longer had the death penalty.

Giuseppe spent his last fifteen years in a prison cell, where he finally died of a heart attack. His story is told in Gerry Conlon's autobiography, on which the film *In the Name of the Father* is based. The film adds dramatic effect to the documented facts by showing Giuseppe sharing the same cell with his son. As they live in the confined space, we watch them develop an intense and touching relationship in which Giuseppe's character shines radiantly. Modeling faith and inner strength for his son, he challenges Gerry to keep alive his inner freedom using the power of his mind. As his son laments his life inside the stifling cell, Giuseppe says, "All they've done is block out the light." Then pointing to his head, he adds, "They can't block out the light in here."

Giuseppe's secret lies in his ability to use creative imagination. Seeing his end approach, he confesses to his son how he has stayed strong after all those years in prison. "Listen," he tells Gerry, "every night I take your mother's hand in mine. We go out the front door, into Cyprus Street, down the Falls Road, up the Antrim Road to Cave Hill. We look back down on poor, troubled Belfast." And looking straight into his son's eyes, he says, "I've been doin' that every night, for five years now. As if I never left your mother."

This is how Giuseppe's character never broke under his ruthless fate. Thanks to his creative imagination, he kept his inner horizons endless, and in spite of being confined to a small, dark cell, his spirit continued to soar. His daily mental routine of connecting with his wife protected his inner freedom and saved his dignity as an innocent man. Seeing her in his mind's eye and feeling her love every day nourished his soul and kept intact his capacity to love himself, his son, and his life.

Giuseppe's mythical character is based on the life of a real person whose myth survived long after his death. The real Giuseppe did not leave the legacy of a great inventor, an artist, or a visionary politician who enjoyed fame or profit thanks to his creative imagination. His own creative imagination served as the source of a free inner life when his external freedom was taken away. Thanks to his ability to draw on the power of his inner intelligence, this simple man coped admirably with a dreadful reality that he could not change. His life was not one of privilege and material success but an example of how a person can successfully keep the inner light shining amidst external darkness, never knowing when the darkness will end.

There are people like Giuseppe everywhere in the world. They are men, women, and children who survive ruthless conditions by keeping their spirit free, thanks to their ability to imagine freedom. One of them is Jennie, a former client of mine, with whom I worked for two years, helping her overcome a fear of intimacy and forgive her mother for a difficult childhood.

Jennie's father died when she was four, leaving her mother alone to raise Jennie and her two brothers. Her mother held sporadic jobs and depended on the support of relatives and occasional boyfriends who never stayed longer than six months. Jennie remembers her mother going through regular bouts of depression followed by periods of hyperactivity. When she was depressed, she would stay in bed, sleeping or watching television. When she was hyperactive, she would get short-tempered and violent toward her children, especially Jennie. To cope with the pain of growing up in such an environment, Jennie began imagining that her real mother was another woman, from whom she had been separated at birth due to a doctor's mistake. When she first imagined this story, she was six years old. She continued to believe it as true until she was thirteen. Over the years, as the relationship with her real mother grew more difficult, the bond with her imaginary mother became unbreakable.

The mother of Jennie's fantasy had all the qualities a child needs from a guardian in order to feel accepted, protected, and loved: she was kind, available, affectionate, and always present. For years Jennie kept a drawing of her underneath her pillow, and she talked to it before falling asleep. Later, she started clipping photographs of women who, according to her, looked like her imaginary mother, and from these she made an album that she named "My Mom's Faces." One Christmas Eve, her real mother had one of her violent tantrums and tore that album to pieces. Beginning that night and for the following four years, Jennie wrote hundreds of letters to her imaginary mother, asking for love, help, and support. As she finished each letter, Jennie read it to herself, and then she wrote the response to her own pleas on behalf of her imaginary mother. She never kept the letters, fearing her mother's violent reaction if they were discovered. Instead, she memorized and then destroyed them, saving in her memory the echo of her "other" mother's words. By keeping this extraordinary correspondence active, Jennie survived years of emotional neglect and abuse, until her mother was finally hospitalized and Jennie moved in with a relative.

Jennie knew that her emotional scars would take time to heal. Embracing the past and forgiving her mother were bold tasks, and she often felt intimidated by the healing process. Her turning point was when she stopped judging the imaginary game of her childhood and saw its crucial value for her emotional development. Jennie realized that engaging in creative imagination as a child was her only means of staying resilient in a severely dysfunctional environment. Her next step in therapy was to learn how to exercise the qualities of her imaginary mother in nurturing herself. She gradually learned how to practice self-love, to pay attention to her emotional needs, and to develop relationships that honored her.

Using Creative Imagination to Overcome Crises and Tackle Life

In his midthirties, Allan Felix is a married, mild-mannered film critic living in New York City. His personality is not what you would call exciting nor are his looks considered dashing. He is a small man with big glasses and red hair that never stays combed. When he does not think, talk, or write about movies, he ruminates about his unattractiveness and inability to be an exciting lover.

One day two years into his marriage, Allan's wife announces, "I need to laugh really hard and go skiing. I want a divorce." Unable to free her from boredom, Allan lets her go. The next morning, he wakes up with the painful realization that he is, once again, a bachelor. Even though he feels unbearably lost and too inadequate to attract women, he knows that he must learn how to date all over again. So he seeks the best advice he can get from a man who has all the charisma, rugged virility, and power that he feels he lacks. That man is Humphrey Bogart, starring as the tough, cynical loner Rick Blaine in *Casablanca*. Faced with the challenge of tackling bachelorhood anew, Allan summons Bogart as his inner mentor and embarks on a real journey of personal growth that leads to self-love.

Allan, the hero of the comedy *Play It Again, Sam*, is a self-inhibited, feeling-phobic man who is helped by his imagination to take risks and blossom in the real world. As Bogart mentors him on the strategies of a great lover, Allan dreads and resists the process as he struggles to reconcile the two realms. "Tell her she's beautiful! Go on, kiss her. Go on!" Bogart prods him in his fantasy, while a panicky, hysterical Allan struggles to combat his fear and take action with the woman in front of him. His clumsiness as he tries to emulate the qualities of the mythical Bogart is so funny that it can make us laugh until we cry.

Allan's journey takes him through several failed attempts to convince various women of his animal magnetism, until he realizes that he is in love with Linda, his best friend's wife. As he faces the dilemma of whether or not to consummate his love for her, he tackles the most important challenge of his journey: to expose his feelings to Linda, not knowing if she will leave her marriage to be with him. Allan responds to the challenge and does not regret his choice. The experience helps him conquer his fears and affirm his masculinity, as he expresses his emotions and fully accepts himself.

In *Play It Again, Sam*, we see how a movie star can be a very powerful inner figure who can inspire us to grow as people. In my practice, I have often helped clients address personal issues using their favorite movie characters as inner mentors. Of them, Elena is a client who turned her fascination with a movie star into a mentoring experience that gave her guidance, confidence, and clarity about her patterns with men.

Elena asked for my help following her breakup with Greg, who was her boyfriend for six years and the man she had hoped to marry. At thirty-eight, Elena had already been married once, for four years in her twenties. After her divorce, she had a series of short unsatisfying relationships, the last of which was with Greg. Elena described him as a forty-year-old, very handsome, incredibly witty, irresistibly charming man whose playfulness always made her laugh. They both liked the outdoors, shopping, going on cruises, and listening to jazz. But there was a problem that Elena kept over-looking: in the five years of their relationship, Greg had changed jobs eight times and could not commit to marriage. His constant refrain was that he needed more time to find his purpose in life and explore life in other countries.

Their last trip, to Prague, was the best vacation they had ever taken. For ten days, Greg enchanted everyone and gave Elena endless delight. But the spell broke two hours before they were to leave for the airport to return home. Elena was packing their luggage when Greg held her by the shoulders, looked into her eyes, and gravely announced that he would not be returning home with her. He said he was instead staying in Prague indefinitely to "check out the European way of living." At first, she thought she was dreaming, but her nightmare was real: Greg was breaking up with her and sending her to the airport alone.

When she returned, Elena discovered that Greg's decision to stay in Europe was not spontaneous. Not only had he been planning it for months, but his scheme included Elena's close friend Marisa, with whom he had begun an affair while still involved with Elena. Everything became clear when Marisa announced a job transfer to Czechoslovakia a few weeks after Elena broke up with Greg, followed by a confession that she and Greg were going to live together. This news devastated Elena but also served as her wake-up call. For the first time, she saw that instead of blaming Greg for "what he did to her," she should examine her own patterns and see how she had contributed to her own unhappiness.

As I got to know Elena better, I realized that she had a fascination for actors with the same attributes she had described in Greg. During one session, she confessed that she had a huge crush on the actor George Clooney.

"How huge?" I asked.

"I dream of him very often, I think of him at work, I read everything that mentions his name, I own all his movies, and I fantasize that someday I'll run into him and he'll be my boyfriend. In the meantime, I am jealous of all the women he's kissed on-screen, and I hate his current girlfriend. I hope he'll *never* marry her!" she said in one breath.

"Indeed, this sounds like a crush," I agreed, unable to hide my chuckle. But at the same time, I saw how I could help Elena use her fascination with George Clooney to transform her patterns with men. "So, until you meet George in real life, you get involved with men who are like him?" I asked.

"How did you know?" she answered. "Yes, the guys I fall for are a lot like him, but not *exactly* like him. They're cute and funny and very adorable at the beginning, but they ultimately break my heart."

"And how is George Clooney different?" I asked.

"Deep down he's sensitive," she answered. "He may tell the press that he likes his freedom and that he's commitment phobic, but with *me* he would be different. He would never hurt me like this."

"Then, if he is so present in you, why don't you ask him to help you see what *you do* to get hurt by men in reality?" I asked her.

"What do you mean? Start having counseling sessions with George Clooney in my mind?" she reacted, her eyes wide open.

"Well, you *do* talk to him in your fantasies, don't you?"

"To tell you the truth, I do."

"Then why don't you let George talk back and answer the questions you cannot solve on your own? He may have some interesting points," I encouraged her.

Elena followed my suggestion and began to practice creative imagination. Because the persona of George Clooney was very active in her, it did not take her long to receive the answers she needed. Over time, his image in Elena's fantasy was transformed from an object of obsession to an inner mentor who helped her see how her choices led to repeated heartbreaks.

One day during session, Elena said, "He's telling me I need to grow up."

"What do you mean?" I asked.

"George says that I have to take responsibility for my weak spots regarding men and protect myself," she responded calmly.

"And what are your weak spots?" I prompted.

"I like being seduced by charm, but I forget that I have much more important needs from a relationship with a man, like a sense of security. I have never felt secure in a relationship. All the men in my life were charmers; they kept me enchanted, stimulated, fascinated, but no one made me feel secure. This is my weakness and I won't let it happen again," she explained.

"So, is George advising you to beware of guys like him?"

"Yes, that is exactly what he's telling me. He says I should never give a man high points just for being charming, but should always determine whether he makes me feel secure with real actions. I know, from now on, charm is not the first thing I'll be looking for in a man."

With these words, Elena described the great breakthrough her creative imagination had catalyzed in her healing process. Using as a conduit the mythical figure of George Clooney, she had tapped into her inner intelligence and accessed valuable self-knowledge. Today Elena is aware of her patterns and her own responsibility toward her happiness. She no longer sees herself as the victim of unreliable, immature men but as a self-aware woman who can make intelligent choices to avoid old mistakes.

How to Practice Creative Imagination

Engaging in creative imagination is a practice that follows a specific process. To do it successfully, keep in mind that for centuries in ancient times, it was performed as a sacred ritual, with great reverence and according to explicit rules. Today imagination is no longer considered the gift of Muses but is seen as a mental function studied by scientific research. However different our approach to it may be, the process of tapping into our creative imagination today follows exactly the same steps as in the Greek religion almost three millennia ago. The following steps will help you complete the exercises at the end of the chapter:

1. **Define the problem you need help with.** This may be a project that is not progressing, a dilemma you are having a hard time resolving, a difficulty you are facing regarding the future, and so on. Be specific in naming the problem. Do not make a list of issues that bother you, but write in

one sentence what seems to be *the* problem. This may be more difficult than you think, because you may have to examine several issues troubling you until you pinpoint the one that captures the essence of your difficulty. The exercises in the previous chapters should help you pinpoint this core issue.

2. **Engage in the realm of imagination, invoke the helping figures, and open a dialogue.** Set a specific time aside, sit in a quiet, private space, close your eyes, and stay silent for a few moments. Gently ask yourself who can help you with your problem (describing the problem as you have defined it in the first step). Wait in silence for a few moments, as images will appear in your mind's eye. Continue waiting until a figure appears and calls your attention. This figure can be anything: a person, an animal, an object, a natural element, a color, or even a hybrid of different people or animals. Do not try to understand the way it looks—just trust your reaction when it appears. When the right figure appears, you will feel energized. That's your hint. Allow the figure to speak. Stay quiet and keep a written record of your dialogue. Write down your questions one at a time. Wait for a few moments, until an answer comes up. Continue with the next question, followed by its answer. Do not rush it. Write your entire conversation as it happens. Throughout the process, you are free to ask questions, seek clarifications, and express opinions. Write the dialogue as it happens within your allotted time. Do not judge its content.

Note: if you have a specific figure that you wish to use as your inner guide (as Allan had with Humphrey Bogart and Elena with George Clooney), you may just call upon that figure.

3. **Read the dialogue, and apply common sense to distill its value.** Read the dialogue carefully, and see how you feel as you assess it. When the advice you receive from your inner mentor is helpful, you will feel energized and animated. Trust the body; it never lies. Also, exercise common sense to evaluate the ethical value and applicability of the advice you received. To do this, answer these questions: If you follow this advice, will you forward your life in the direction you desire without harming yourself or others? How can you make this happen considering the limitations of reality? Examine your answers to these questions. If your body energy and common sense indicate that you should follow the advice, proceed

with the next step. Otherwise, ask your inner guide for more practical advice, or invoke another figure from the endless repository of your imagination, and repeat the process.

4. **Take action and evaluate the outcomes.** Engaging in active imagination only for the pleasure of talking to inner figures becomes equivalent to daydreaming. In order to benefit from this activity, you must complete it by taking action. Once you become clear about what you must do to improve your real situation, you must act on it. Follow the examples of the movie characters and cases studies in this chapter and proceed. Only by taking action can you change your real situation. Keep evaluating your progress. Is your life improving? Are you falling into old patterns? Are you staying focused on your goals? Are you using your own advice? Are you walking the talk?

Never abdicate your personal responsibility to the power of creative imagination in solving your problems. Always keep your feet firmly grounded in reality, and always check the real data when applying advice from your imaginary guides. They may offer very wise advice, but in the end, your actions in the real domain carry *your* name and *you* are accountable for them.

Reel Fulfillment in Action

Movie Time! ▶ *Watch a Movie for Fun, Learn a Lesson of Life*

Choose a movie from each of the following lists, and watch them alone or with your group. Keep notes of your answers to the questions that follow each list, and discuss them with your group.

Movies About Imagination
Being There (1979), directed by Hal Ashby
Flawless (1999), directed by Joel Schumacher

Goya (1999), directed by Carlos Saura

In the Name of the Father (1993), directed by Jim Sheridan

Julia and Julia (1987), directed by Peter Del Monte

Passion of Mind (2000), directed by Alain Berliner

Play It Again, Sam (1975), directed by Herbert Ross

The Purple Rose of Cairo (1985), directed by Woody Allen

Rosie (1998), directed by Patrice Toye

The Secret Lives of Dentists (2002), directed by Alan Rudolph

Questions to Answer

1. What are the main character's problems, and how does he or she use creative imagination to overcome them?
2. Is there a point in the story where imagination and reality must be separated? What happens when they are not?
3. Can you think of moments in your life when you used creative imagination to resolve or cope with serious problems? What happened? Share your answers with your group.

Movies About Mentors or Inner Guides

Dead Poets Society (1989), directed by Peter Weir

Finding Forrester (2000), directed by Gus Van Sant

The Ghost and Mrs. Muir (1947), directed by Joseph L. Mankiewicz

Good Will Hunting (1997), directed by Gus Van Sant

Harry Potter and the Sorcerer's Stone (2001), directed by Chris Columbus

Lean on Me (1989), directed by John G. Avildsen

The Legend of Bagger Vance (2000), directed by Robert Redford

The Lord of the Rings trilogy (2001, 2002, and 2003), directed by Peter Jackson

The Matrix (1999), directed by Larry and Andy Wachowski

Mona Lisa Smile (2003), directed by Mike Newell

Mr. Holland's Opus (1995), directed by Stephen Herek

The Muse (1999), directed by Albert Brooks

To Sir, with Love (1967), directed by James Clavell

The Wizard of Oz (1939), directed by Victor Fleming

Questions to Answer

1. How does the mentor influence the life of the main character?
2. What are the most important qualities of their relationship?
3. Did the mentor of the film have a gift for you? What is that?
4. Who have been your mentors so far and in what areas of your life?
5. Who was your most important mentor, and what was his or her gift for you? Share it with your group.

Practice Creative Imagination ▸ *Exercises and Activities*

When you complete the following exercises, you will know how to creatively use your imagination to gain inner strength and resolve problems.

> ▶ **Create Your Inner Mentor: An Exercise on Creative Imagination**

What qualities do you need to develop or strengthen in yourself to fulfill your goals?

1. _____
2. _____
3. _____

Imagine a Figure That Inspires You

In your journal, create a grid similar to the one in Figure 8.1. In the first column, write the qualities you need to develop. For example, you may need to develop discipline, focus, lightheartedness, and so on. In the second column, identify one person (he or she can be a celebrity, a character from a film or a novel, or a mythical figure that your imagination conjures) you feel embodies these qualities. (*Prerequisite:* imagining this figure must give you energy and courage; it must inspire in you the quality that you imagine this figure to have.)

FIGURE 8.1 ■ Create Your Inner Mentor

QUALITIES YOU NEED	PERSON WHO EMBODIES THOSE QUALITIES

Bring Your Inner Mentor Alive

Use one of the following three approaches to give your mentor a real presence:

- Find a photograph or another piece of memorabilia that evokes the image of your inner mentor.
- Draw your inner mentor, if it is a composite of several other figures.
- Make a collage using pictures that represent the characteristics of your inner mentor.

Keep the visual image of your inner mentor close to you, in a visible and private space so you can look at it when you need to do so. It is important to keep an accessible visual connection with your inner mentor.

Talk to Your Inner Mentor

Write a letter to your inner mentor and ask for help:

"I need you to show me how to be _____ [name quality], when I am faced with _____ [trigger of inner blockage]. Tell me what to do."

1. Now, keeping your connection active with your inner mentor, use his or her voice *as you are imagining it* to write a letter to yourself, with your mentor's answers, instructions, and advice.
2. You may mail this letter to yourself. When you receive it, read it daily for a few days. Concentrate on the advice of your inner mentor and how you can apply it to your life. After a few days have lapsed, does it still ring true? What have you done during this time to implement the advice, and what are the results it gave you?
3. Refer to your inner mentor's image every time you need to gather inner strength and inspiration.
4. Remember that your inner mentor is a *symbol* of the qualities you want to develop and that this symbol inspires you to practice those qualities in your life.

Look for Your Inner Mentor's Qualities in Real People

Use your mentor's advice to notice and attract people with the qualities you need to develop in yourself. Begin practicing these qualities one at a time.

Example: you need to develop responsibility and discipline in handling your money. Your mentor has advised you to stop using your credit cards. To act, put this advice into practice and destroy your credit cards. Then begin to consciously seek out people who are financially responsible and can support you in your efforts to develop this quality in yourself. This is yet another way your inner mentor's qualities can become your own qualities.

▶ **Your Problem-Free Self: An Exercise on Imagination and Problem Solving**

You may do this exercise when you feel stuck and need to tap into your inner wisdom for advice and helpful hints to move on. When you are faced with a problem that seems irresolvable or difficult to tackle and it drains your energy, follow these steps:

1. **Define the problem.** Write down your current problem and what difficulties it creates for you in fulfilling your inner desire.

2. **Activate your imagination and connect with your problem-free self.**

    1. Close your eyes and imagine yourself having fulfilled your dream.
    2. See yourself past your current problem and having fulfilled your dream.
    3. Imagine yourself living your dream and feel the bliss of your fulfillment.
    4. Let the energy of happiness run through your body as you imagine yourself having successfully accomplished the process, until you feel completely freed from the worries of your current problem.
    5. Write down this scene, or you may draw it or create a collage of it.

       This process will help you reconnect with your own helpful energy. Give this scene a date. It must be a date from the future.

3. **Speak to your problem-free self.** Begin a dialogue with your future, problem-free self. Date your dialogue with today's date, and ask the following questions. As you ask them, imagine your future self answering them one at a time.

    Dear Self,
    1. What were the biggest challenges you faced to achieve this goal?
    2. What were the major strengths you developed during the process?
    3. How did you overcome the problem X that I am facing right now? (Describe the problem you are currently having, and then list the ways that your problem-free self used to overcome it.)
    4. What kind of help did you receive to resolve this problem? (List as many forms of help as possible that are coming through your dialogue.)
    5. How do you think I should stop sabotaging my efforts to resolve my current problem? (List as many ideas as possible that your problem-free self is suggesting.)

4. **Evaluate the answers of your problem-free self and use them in real life.** Read carefully the answers you wrote, and evaluate how they can be applied in your life. Follow your own advice accordingly to successfully face your current challenges and reach your goals.

Things to Remember

- Imagination is not the world into which we escape to avoid reality but the world of infinite ideas that helps us improve reality.
- If we cannot imagine being good, we cannot do what is good.

9

Practice Effective Prayer

FOR MOST OF US, prayer is communication. We pray to talk to an entity within and beyond us and send messages in hopes that they will be received. The entity that receives our prayers is invisible but omnipresent and, depending on our beliefs, omnipotent. When we pray, we authorize this entity to influence important life matters that we have limited ability to affect. For example, we might pray to get easy questions on an important exam for which we are not very well prepared. In our prayers, we also communicate our deepest desires, some of which we may never utter to another human being. For example, we might pray to meet our soul mate at our cousin's party so we can end the boring relationship we are currently in, to win the lottery so we can get out of debt, or for our boss's personality to change and become pleasant.

We also use prayer to make requests for things we consider important for our happiness. The less control we have over our happiness, the more likely we are to summon the entity's help. We ask for a promotion so we can put the salary increase toward a new car, that someone to whom we are romantically attracted will reciprocate and fall in love with us, or that a policeman will fail to notice we have run a red light so we can avoid a ticket.

Finally, our prayers express positive or negative acknowledgment of the entity with whom we communicate. When our requests are granted and we feel rewarded, we pray to acknowledge the entity's presence and its kindness in our lives. But when the opposite happens and undeserved misfortune befalls us, we pray to express our indignation at the entity's lack of compassion or total indifference. "Why did you do this to me? Do you care about me or not? Why can't you listen to my prayers for a change? Are you up there or not?" We call out, questioning the entity's benevolence, accusing it of causing the pain we feel, or doubting its existence altogether.

This is how most of us use prayer in our everyday lives, as we struggle to attract the Almighty's attention and summon higher help with our problems. But regardless of how often we pray, very few of us know how to practice *effective prayer*. In this respect, we are a little like Bruce Nolan, the main character of *Bruce Almighty*. This profound film was advertised as a comedy and received mixed reviews. However, it is a modern parable about God's faith in our free will and our innate ability to have most of our prayers answered if we learn how to pray effectively and act accordingly.

Bruce Nolan, a mediocre news reporter from Buffalo, New York, with a short temper and a self-involved manner, is at the end of his rope. Life, for him, is pointless; it seems that God consistently ignores him in all spheres of his life. Instead of being promoted at work, he gets fired. When he tries to help a homeless man on the street, a gang attacks him. At home, where he lives with his girlfriend, Grace, he cannot sit on his couch without having to worry about his dog's toilet habits, which ignore all housebreaking rules. Incensed at God for allowing all this to happen to him, Bruce lets his anger explode and challenges the Almighty to a duel. "Smite *me*, oh mighty Smiter!" he yells up at the skies, desperate and anxious for a response. And a response he gets, from the Almighty himself. Bruce is given the opportunity to meet God, who appears in the form of a contemporary African-American man. Bruce confronts him and questions God's ability to grant people's prayers and run a happy universe. "And since when does one know what people want?" is God's response; in other words, God seemed to be saying, "If people are not clear about their own needs, how can I be responsible for their happiness?"

God sees that Bruce still does not understand that God is not responsible for people's unhappiness. So he allows Bruce to become God for a while, to see firsthand how people act to stay unhappy and to see why God, despite being omnipotent, does not interfere with human acts or try to effectuate universal happiness.

"You can do whatever you like, except for one thing," he advises Bruce, as he lets him take over his office. "Never interfere with free will."

Bruce-turned-God fails to comprehend God's only request and uses the power to perform miracles for his own agendas, interfering with the laws of nature and cosmic order. He alters his girlfriend's appearance to his taste, brings the moon close to their balcony to accent a romantic dinner, and turns his dog into a humanoid to finally get him house-trained. He avenges the gang who attacked him by causing indescribable suffering to their leader and ruins his professional rival by making him completely lose control of his speech and utter senseless gibberish during a live television news broadcast. However, Bruce-turned-God soon discovers not only that his personal miracles have global repercussions but also that he cannot answer the billions of requests made through people's prayers, varying from grave to ludicrous and flooding his mind every second of the day. Overwhelmed, exhausted, and fed up with people's infantile dependency on God to solve their problems, he dismisses all prayers by answering a flat, all-inclusive "*Yes!*" as a way of saying, "Leave me alone!"

Revolted by Bruce's abuse of power, Grace breaks up with him. Then, devastated and humiliated, Bruce looks for God, admits his failure to keep Grace, and surrenders his godly powers, becoming human again. "Welcome to my kingdom, my son," God responds kindly. His answer alludes to the paradox of a spiritual awakening, in which our failure to control the universe as though we were God forces us to surrender our expectations and embrace free will as God's will.

Acceptance that he cannot manipulate free will is Bruce's biggest lesson from his failure to be God. He realizes that God's power does not lie in controlling the universe but in allowing it to evolve based on free will. As Bruce surrenders, he recognizes his awful behavior, acknowledges Grace's reasons for leaving him, and sees that he cannot make her come back against her will. For the first time, Bruce accepts what he cannot change and recognizes the only thing he can change: himself. Keeping his eyes fixed on God, he opens his heart and prays selflessly for Grace to meet someone who, unlike him, will honor her kindness and give her the happiness and love she deserves.

"Now, *this* is a real prayer," answers God, looking back at him with a smile.

Bruce's prayer transforms him. No longer acting *like* God but being *with* God, he opens his eyes and his heart and begins to value what is truly important. In his prayer, loving Grace is the most important thing for him, so his prayer is granted. As soon as he is able to recognize how precious Grace is, he transforms his behavior and becomes the loving man Grace deserves to have in her life. His release of agendas and display of love through actions bring Grace back into Bruce's life. In fact, the aptly named Grace had never left him; her love for Bruce was always present, even when he was too blinded by his own self-serving intentions to see it. This is how it happens with grace, the virtue, in real life as well. It never leaves us but only appears when we are ready to acknowledge life as is, surrender our expectations of how things should be, and realize what is truly important for our happiness. Grace, then, empowers our actions in a universe blessed with free will.

Practicing Effective Prayer for Fulfillment

Communication is the key to any relationship. When you communicate effectively, you send clear messages designed for your listener to easily hear and understand. Another crucial element of effective communication is your deliberate effort to hear what is being said to you, by paying attention and listening. Effective communication also requires that you know your audience and address them in a manner appropriate to their age, status, and ability to understand your language. Finally, it requires your ability to answer questions from—and clarify misunderstandings for—your audience and the knowledge that you will not have all the answers or understand all the questions.

With prayer, you also build a relationship based on communication, in which you try to send clear messages and hear the responses you receive. You address an audience that you cannot see, but you believe does exist. The stronger your faith is that the audience is present, the more comfortable you feel and the less inhibited you are to express yourself openly and without fear.

It may seem radical to suggest that prayer is a form of communication between you and a higher entity, in which that entity is the audience of your intimate thoughts, claims, and various requests. Yet prayer is an authentic form of communication of high significance. When you pray, you address the Great One as your audience, using a special, revered name, such as God, Jesus, Yahweh, Buddha, Muhammad, Allah, Tao, Atman, Krishna, Holy Mother, Father, Lord, Great Spirit, Mother Nature, Universe, and so on. When you pray, you invite a response, and knowing how to listen to the Great One's responses to your prayers is as essential as knowing how to handle your audience's responses to a very important speech. The following two key requirements of effective prayer can help you strengthen your communication with the Great One and give you tools to hear answers to your prayers when you think that they have not been heard.

Effective Prayer Requires Clear Intentions and Responsible Actions

"I've been talking to God every day for a month and a half now. He doesn't listen!" exclaimed my client Linda one day as we began our session. A deeply religious woman, she had an unfulfilling marriage that ended in divorce and was followed by a long period of celibacy. For the past four months, she had been working with me on developing dating skills.

Linda's strong religious sentiment had been cultivated by her mother, a Sunday school teacher who had taught Linda that God would always answer her prayers as long as she was God's servant. A volunteer in several organizations and an active member in her religious community, Linda had been praying to God for an honest and kind man to cross her path. Two months ago, Linda thought God had answered. During coffee hour at church, she met Rolando, a new parishioner who had just moved to town. He seemed to fulfill Linda's requirements to perfection: he was kind and polite and seemed honest. Two weeks later, when he asked her out for coffee, Linda was thrilled. She had a great time with him, but that was also the only time she had with him. Subsequently, Rolando seemed to avoid her at church, preferring to talk to other people. Linda felt confused, then hurt, then angry. Fearing rejection, instead of approaching Rolando, she prayed to God to make Rolando ask her out again.

"God brought him to me the first time, why can't he make him ask me out again?" she said, almost in tears.

"Linda," I asked, "when you pray to God to make Rolando ask you out again, what is your intention behind your prayer?"

"My intention?" She paused, startled. "My intention is to attract Rolando's attention. I like him a lot, and I want him to like me, too. I want to see him again."

"So, besides speaking to God, have you made your intention clear to Rolando?" I asked again.

"No, I haven't. I'm too scared that he will say no, and then I will feel very bad," she said.

"If your intention is to get Rolando's attention, you cannot make it happen by avoiding him," I said. "It seems that God's silence *is* answering your prayers. Now that you are clear about your intention, *you* must take responsible actions to get the results you have been asking God to deliver," I explained.

"And risk rejection?" she asked.

"Linda, the point here is that you must take responsible actions to help God answer your prayers in reality, instead of doing nothing while imagining the worst," I answered.

Linda listened. She realized that taking risks, approaching others instead of avoiding them, and communicating her intentions were necessary and responsible actions in finding a romantic partner. She trusted that God wanted her happiness and supported her efforts to find it, so she considered talking to Rolando as an exercise in communication. The following Sunday, she approached him at church and invited him to a concert. Linda's prayers were answered: Rolando accepted and Linda learned that defining a clear intention and following through with responsible actions were both essential for her prayers to bring results.

Linda's initial approach is rather common. Many of us often pray for miracles while we avoid claiming our true intentions or taking responsibility for our actions. We then hold God responsible for how our life turns out. This is a very childish attitude to have toward the Almighty. This attitude also comes into play when we ask God to cause others harm on our behalf. In doing so, we act like delinquent teenagers who ignore the dangerous consequences of our intentions. The paradox is that even though we may not trust our own or others' good intentions, God's faith in our innate ability to do good is unconditional.

An example of how someone can use prayer to ask God to harm a fellow human is Antonio Salieri in *Amadeus*, an account of the life and rivalry between Salieri and Wolfgang Amadeus Mozart. Based on real facts, the film adds a fictional element to portray Salieri's relationship to God as that of a resentful child's attitude toward a punishing father. Salieri feels punished by God for not having Mozart's musical genius. He envies Mozart with passion and secretly wishes for his demise. But even more so, he envies Mozart's confidence in his musical genius that he so unabashedly makes public. In Salieri's eyes, this self-assurance constitutes blasphemy against God, who gave Mozart his genius. Like a scornful child who feels neglected, Salieri asks God to punish Mozart, to take away his genius and give it to him, thus making Salieri the greatest composer of his era. Salieri goes so far as to make an arrangement with God: in exchange for acquiring Mozart's genius, he pledges God his lifelong loyalty, devotion, and chastity by promising to never touch a woman.

In the film, Salieri's true intention is to destroy Mozart. This is why his prayer is devious. Salieri's prayer is not a heartfelt plea for the courage to forgive his opponent's superiority and accept his own imperfections. Instead, he connives to convince God to penalize his competitor, under the false pretense that Mozart deserves punishment for his arrogance. Furthermore, Salieri justifies his rival's anticipated demise as God's punishment for Mozart's transgressions, rather than the consequence of his own hateful acts. But in spite of Salieri's contract with God to destroy Mozart, God's universal justice did not concede to his intentions; Salieri never enjoyed recognition as a first-class composer, while Mozart's music became immortal.

Like Salieri, there are people who believe that God answers their prayers for assistance in committing illicit or evil deeds by helping them conceal their crimes and not get caught. Such people abuse the gift of free will and exploit the Creator's faith in our inherent goodness. Even though criminals sometimes escape punishment, universal justice always prevails in due time, enforcing laws that are beyond human control. An example of how universal justice eradicates a family that, for three generations, evaded punishment for its crimes is the film trilogy *The Godfather*.

Effective Prayer Requires the Willingness to Embrace Reality

One of life's paradoxes is that we live in an imperfect world but constantly strive for perfection. Being perfect is not only a desire that consumes most of us, but it is also an expectation that alters our view of reality. The more we desire to be perfect, the more we expect reality to conform to our expectations. As a result, we chase perfection everywhere, expecting to find it in ourselves, our relationships, and the universe. In fact, we do not simply expect it, but we demand it, as though perfection had been promised to us at birth. We demand perfection of ourselves, and we ask the same of our significant others. At work, since we cannot directly ask our superiors to be perfect, we expect perfection at least from our subordinates. On the road, we expect others to drive perfectly and allow the slightest mistake to enrage us and ruin our day. When we travel abroad, we expect the weather to be perfect and the hotel service to be perfect, and we even expect natives of foreign countries to speak our language with perfection. To many of us, reality is acceptable only when it is perfect.

In my work as a therapist and coach, I meet a number of people whose need for perfection has become a self-imposed tyranny and the principal cause of misery for themselves and others. One of them is John, a tall, handsome, and successful architect in his fifties who asked for my help in dealing with a number of issues, among which were relationships. A divorced father of three boys, John had been a bachelor for ten years and spent most of his time working and traveling around the world for business.

"I am a very busy man, and I love my work," he told me in our first session. "I live out of a suitcase, and when I'm in town, I sleep in my office. Going home to an empty apartment takes away my motivation to work."

"What does your empty apartment trigger that discourages you to work?" I asked.

"Well, you know," he said with a sad smile, "it's an empty apartment. No housemate, no soul mate, no kids, no dog, no noise, no mess driving me crazy. My house looks perfect when I walk in, and I love that, because *I can't stand mess*. But it's also empty, and that I don't like."

It was obvious that John wanted perfection, and for it, he was paying a high price. As I prompted more answers from him, it became evident that perfectionism had been a real cause for John's divorce, his loneliness, his ulcer, his insomnia, and his occasional abuse of alcohol as a sedative. Due to his need for others to be perfect, John had driven away friends and relatives over the years, including his three sons. Expecting perfection from any potential mate, he had managed to push away a number of women and break off one engagement. John confessed that he suffered as he felt perpetually disappointed at reality for not meeting his standards. But in essence, it was his own perpetual denial of reality that was making him unable to deal with it.

"John, do you ever pray?" I asked him one day.

"In fact, I do," he answered with a smile. "God is the only one I seem to get along with. He's *perfect*, so he knows what I'm going through down here."

"What do you tell God in your prayers about this imperfect world?" I asked.

"To do something about it before I go crazy," he said seriously.

"And has God granted you an answer?" I prompted.

"Obviously not," he admitted, "otherwise, this world would have become perfect a long time ago, and I would be out there being happy and not here, in your office, talking about how messed up everything is."

"Could it be this is exactly God's answer?" I said. "Is it possible that God is telling you that this world is not perfect? If even God knows that reality is not perfect but embraces it as is, why don't you do the same?"

"Then, I would also be part of this world, which means I would be imperfect, too!" he answered emphatically.

"God already knows that you are imperfect like the rest of us, and he would still love you the same way," I said. "Talk to him about it."

John and I worked together for two years. During that time, as he accepted imperfection as part of life, he felt more open to love. Gradually, he began to rebuild his relationship with his sons, visited his mother and sister more often, and started dating. One day he showed me a photograph of himself embracing an attractive, younger woman with two little dogs. His beaming smile at the camera showed newly found happiness.

"I love her," he said calmly. "She means more to me than anything else."

"But she has two dogs," I kidded him. "That means mess!"

"She wants children, too, and that's even messier," he replied. "But I don't mind! No one's perfect!"

John's willingness to embrace an imperfect reality opened his path to love, which is also the path to God. As long as he continued to pray for perfection, God's answer was always the same: "This is an imperfect world, and I want you to be happy living *in* it. Embrace it and love it as I do." When John understood this and responded accordingly, he was rewarded with the happiness the Creator wanted him to have.

Effective prayer requires the willingness to embrace an imperfect world and find our purpose in it. It also requires our willingness to be fully human, which is the willingness to accept our imperfections and learn from mistakes. We then show our faith through actions of love, in which we overcome evil not with evil but with good. Three people who achieved this and whose lives became the subjects of movies are Mother Teresa, Malcolm X, and Mahatma Gandhi: a Christian nun, a Muslim black activist, and a Hindu spiritual and political leader. All three considered prayer central to their lives. For Mother Teresa, prayer was "the bread of the soul." For Malcolm X, prayer was the tool that catalyzed and sustained his transformation from a convict to a world leader. Gandhi prayed every day for the courage to lead India into the peaceful revolution that brought about its independence from England.

The film *Mother Teresa: In the Name of God's Poor* is the account of a nun's service to the poorest of the poor, as she embraces a reality that is far from perfect. While living among the destitute in Calcutta's slums, Mother Teresa does not deny the world she sees. That is the reality that she is called to face, and she handles it as such. By loving the unlovable and touching the untouchable, she instills hope in the desperate and restores their dejected faith that God has not forgotten them. She does not try to escape the world, nor does she judge it for being imperfect. She serves it with compassion, and this is how she changes the world, a person at a time and a day at a time. This is how Mother Teresa brings a perfect God down to an imperfect reality.

Malcolm X is a film about a personality and legend totally different from Mother Teresa's. One of the most influential black activists in American history, who initially attacked white oppressors with religious fanaticism, Malcolm X is also portrayed as an advocate of self-help, self-defense, and education, all of which led to a strong sense of black identity. We are shown that in his life's learning process, he integrates history, religion, and mythology to arrive at his ultimate belief that this imperfect world is, in fact, a world of universal brotherhood in which justice must prevail and the needs of blacks must be recognized by the white race. In his life, faith was a prelude to action. For him, ideas were feckless without policy. The film *Malcolm X* is a visual narrative about a real person whose faith, activism, and fiery speeches inspired oppressed black Americans to first face an imperfect reality and then empower themselves through actions of self-change.

The film *Gandhi* is an epic about Mohandas Karamchand Gandhi, a man whose faith became his strongest political weapon and whose practice of nonviolent protest successfully liberated India from the British. A leader inspiring millions of colonized Indians to regain their cultural identity, Gandhi loved humanity as a whole but was not afraid to fight for India on his own terms. He is portrayed as a visionary whose words and actions, unlike those of many politicians, shine with spiritual and moral clarity. As we watch Gandhi's faith in God expressed as self-confidence in his political meetings with the British, he inspires us to seek and develop a stronger faith as well. As we watch him pray, we witness how the truth he has discovered gives him the comfort, strength, and confidence to face the reality of his nation as he leads his people to change it. Many of us hunger to have such clarity, strength, and ability to fight life's battles without violence. The film *Gandhi* tells the story of a man who proved that this is possible.

Reel Fulfillment in Action

Movie Time! ▶ *Watch a Movie for Fun, Learn a Lesson of Life*

Following are three lists of films about prayer, faith, and wrongdoing in the name of faith. Choose a movie from each list, and watch them alone or with your group. Afterward, think about the questions that follow each list. Write down your thoughts and share them with others.

Movies About Prayer

Amadeus (1984), directed by Milos Forman

Becket (1964), directed by Peter Glenville

Brother Sun, Sister Moon (1972), directed by Franco Zeffirelli

Bruce Almighty (2003), directed by Tom Shadyac

The Color Purple (1985), directed by Steven Spielberg

Francesco (1989), directed by Liliana Cavani

Gandhi (1982), directed by Richard Attenborough

Joan of Arc (1948), directed by Victor Fleming

Kundun (1997), directed by Martin Scorsese

Malcolm X (1992), directed by Spike Lee

The Messenger: The Story of Joan of Arc (1999), directed by Luc
    Besson

Michael (1996), directed by Nora Ephron

Mother Teresa: In the Name of God's Poor (1997), directed by Kevin
    Connor

Nixon (1995), directed by Oliver Stone

Oh, God! (1977), directed by Carl Reiner

Schindler's List (1993), directed by Steven Spielberg

Questions to Answer

1. How does the film portray prayer and meditation, and how are
   they employed by the main character?
2. What are the major effects of prayer on the lives of the story's
   primary and secondary characters?
3. A well-known quote from Mother Teresa is "Prayer is the bread of
   the soul." How can you relate to its meaning?
4. Have you ever had a prayer answered? Write down what happened,
   and share it with your group.
5. In the film's story, what is the relationship between praying and
   developing faith?
6. Do you notice any "right" or "wrong" elements of prayer being
   portrayed in the film? Make a list of them.
7. What did you learn about prayer and faith from the movie you
   watched?

Movies About Faith

Braveheart (1995), directed by Mel Gibson
Chariots of Fire (1981), directed by Hugh Hudson
Crimes and Misdemeanors (1989), directed by Woody Allen
Field of Dreams (1989), directed by Phil Alden Robinson
In the Name of the Father (1993), directed by Jim Sheridan
Joe Versus the Volcano (1990), directed by John Patrick Shanley
The Lord of the Rings trilogy (2001, 2002, and 2003), directed by
    Peter Jackson
Mulan (1998), directed by Tony Bancroft and Barry Cook
Phenomenon (1996), directed by Jon Turteltaub
Powder (1995), directed by Victor Salva
Simon Birch (1998), directed by Mark Steven Johnson
Star Wars (1977), directed by George Lucas
Still Breathing (1997), directed by James F. Robinson
Whale Rider (2002), directed by Niki Caro

Questions to Answer

1. How is faith portrayed in this film? How does the main character develop and show faith?
2. How is faith useful in pursuing the goals the character tries to achieve?
3. What forces, people, or events oppose faith, and what prevails in the end? How does it happen?
4. How do the characters in the story keep their faith strong?
5. How would you describe your faith, and when do you call upon it?
6. What is the film's gift for you, and what insights did you gain from watching it?

Movies About Wrongdoing in the Name of Faith

The Apostle (1997), directed by Robert Duvall
The Crime of Father Amaro (2002), directed by Carlos Carrera
Elmer Gantry (1960), directed by Richard Brooks
Holy Smoke (1999), directed by Jane Campion
Leap of Faith (1992), directed by Richard Pearce

Questions to Answer

1. Which strengths does the main character use to exert power and manipulate innocent people?
2. How can you tell the difference between a spiritual director and a manipulative, self-appointed messiah?
3. Which qualities do you seek in the spiritual directors you choose to trust?
4. What did you learn from this film that you can apply in your life?

Practice Effective Prayer ▸ *Exercises and Activities*

▸ **How Spiritually Fit Are You? An Exercise on Self-Reflection**

Read the following questions, and spend some time thinking about them. Briefly write down your answers. Come back to them in a few weeks. Compare your answers and notice your progress.

1. How do you experience your spiritual nature? Do you have a preferred practice, a ritual, or an ongoing activity that connects you to a sense of inner peace and completeness in spite of the tribulations of your daily life?
2. If you answered no to the second question in the preceding, how do you find the inner peace and energy to carry out your life's duties?
3. Do you use drugs or alcohol trying to find inner peace and energy? How often?

Note: if you regularly use drugs, alcohol, or any other substance in an attempt to find inner peace and energy, you may have an addiction problem that will progressively complicate your life and ultimately hinder you from finding the fulfillment you desire. You must address this issue as soon as possible by seeking professional help and spiritual support as you continue your self-discovery process.

When you apply this exercise consistently over a period of time, you will develop

- The ability to use silence to calm your mind and find your inner focus
- The ability to feel serenity regardless of the turmoil of your external life
- A growing connection with your inner core
- The ability to stay focused on your tasks for longer periods of time
- A growing appreciation for the energizing effects of silence

At the beginning, try to do this exercise once a day, preferably at the same time each day. As time progresses, try to fit in this two-minute meditation several times in your day. Try keeping a timer at work, and practice this meditation every few hours. It takes only two minutes and yields phenomenal results.

Instructions: Choose a time of the day when you can retreat to a quiet space. You must be alert, not exhausted, and determined to put aside all thoughts about your busy life for two minutes.

1. Choose a quiet place where you know you will not be interrupted.
2. Sit comfortably on a chair or a cushion. Lay your arms on your thighs. Rest your back comfortably against the back of the chair or wall. Do not lie down.
3. Set your timer for two minutes. Set it aside and close your eyes.
4. Keeping your eyes closed, breathe normally and focus on your breath as it flows in and out of your body. As time progresses, you will also feel the gentle beating of your heart. Keep your focus on your breath and your heart for the entire two minutes.
5. When you find your mind wandering back to thoughts and concerns of the day, try to return your attention to your breath and heartbeats.
6. Stay silent and keep your eyes closed.
7. When you hear the timer sound, gently open your eyes. Continue with the activities of your day, looking forward to your next silent date with your inner core.

▶ Clarifying Your Intention: Practicing the Serenity Prayer

The Serenity Prayer is a powerful tool to keep your intentions clear as you ask a superior source to help you handle life's challenges.

God grant me the serenity to accept
the things I cannot change,
the courage to change the things I can
and the wisdom to know the difference.

1. Read it several times and memorize it.
2. Make a list of "the things that cannot be changed" in your life. Name those things in your prayer.
3. Make a list of "the things that you can change." Name those things in your prayer.
4. Concentrate on changing the things you can change, one at a time.
5. Let go of the things you cannot change once you have named them.

▶ Fourteen Days of Emotional Healing: Practicing the Prayer of St. Francis

Regardless of the religious doctrine you may follow, I encourage you to consider the following prayer, the eight-hundred-year-old legacy of a great healer who dedicated his life to alleviating human suffering. The prayer is a tool for emotional cleansing and healing. You may want to carry it with you and meditate upon it several times a day. Read it slowly and set your intention on freeing yourself from destructive emotions and harmful actions.

The Prayer of St. Francis
Lord, make me a channel of thy peace,
1. *that where there is hatred, I may bring love;*
2. *that where there is wrong, I may bring the spirit of forgiveness;*
3. *that where there is discord, I may bring harmony;*
4. *that where there is error, I may bring truth;*

5. *that where there is doubt, I may bring faith;*
6. *that where there is despair, I may bring hope;*
7. *that where there are shadows, I may bring light;*
8. *that where there is sadness, I may bring joy.*
9. *Lord, grant that I may seek rather to comfort than to be comforted;*
10. *to understand, than to be understood;*
11. *to love, than to be loved.*
12. *For it is by self-forgetting that one finds.*
13. *It is by forgiving that one is forgiven.*
14. *It is by dying that one awakens to Eternal Life.*

You may also use this powerful prayer over fourteen days to deepen your emotional healing and to transform negative patterns.

Instructions: for the next fourteen days, read and practice *one line* of the prayer as follows:

1. Every day, read the entire prayer once in the morning.
2. Reread the first, unnumbered line and *one line* from lines 1 to 14, corresponding to each day.
3. Set your intention to practice, through your actions, your prayed wish for the entire day.
4. Notice how you act in situations that call you to practice your prayed wish of the day.
5. Several times during the day, repeat in your mind as a mantra the first line and the line of the day, to reinforce your intention.

Things to Remember

- Prayer is an ongoing practice: it is the practice of wishing for the right things and the practice of doing the right things to receive them.
- Use the power of prayer for healing, never for destruction.

Fourth Gain: Joy

▶ JOY IS NOT just a passing feeling but a conscious attitude toward life. When you are joyous with life, you have enormous reserves of acceptance, forgiveness, and kindness for yourself and for others. A truly fulfilled life is a life lived with joy.

As a joyous person, you will have a light heart, appreciation for creativity, and generosity of spirit. You will spread joy through conscious acts of kindness, and you will express gratitude through empowering acts of giving.

The next three chapters will guide you into the joy of being alive. Using movies for inspiration and special activities, you will learn how to:

- Lighten your heart
- Enjoy your creativity
- Create abundance through generosity of spirit

10

Lighten Your Heart

A FEW YEARS AGO, at four o'clock on an unusually warm May afternoon, I was on a theater stage in Austin, Texas, presenting a seminar on the guiding power of dreams to a standing-room-only audience of more than three hundred participants. Suddenly, we heard a loud thunderclap; two seconds later, we heard a torrential downpour outside. Welcoming the unexpected rain, I went on to introduce a movie clip about a man who used the wisdom of his dreams to resolve a life-threatening problem. Just as I said, "And now, let's see how this man's dreams *shed light on*," a second thunderclap struck, the lights went out, and we were all left in the dark. As the startled audience let out a whimper, I thought to myself, "Since we still have sound, I will not stop the seminar. Perhaps it's a fuse; it won't take them long to turn it back on." So I tapped on the microphone to get everyone's attention and went on. "It seems that this movie character is a little shy about making an appearance today; so instead of showing the clip, I will tell you a real-life story. Just follow me with your imagination until the maintenance crew gets the lights back on." The audience laughed kindly and remained seated as I began to relate a real-life scenario to the sound of the rain beating down outside.

Five minutes later, the lights remained dark but we still had sound. Just as I had finished saying, "Sometimes God sends messages through dreams, calling us to *listen*," another clap of heavy thunder struck and killed the electricity feeding the sound system. The coincidence was tragicomic. In the darkened theater, I was the only one who had heard the word *listen*. It sounded like a stifled whisper as I spoke into the dead microphone. Even though I could barely see the audience, I immediately felt their tension rising. There was no time to ponder; I had no other way of dealing with what was happening except to use humor. So I took a deep breath, filled my lungs with air, and, projecting my voice to the far end of the room, shouted, "Listen, oh dear God, please listen! I am giving a seminar about *you* down here! Can you please stop playing with the switches up there and let me go on?"

The effect of my spontaneous prayer was amazing. Three hundred people burst into laughter and started to applaud. Their heartfelt response cheered me through a very awkward moment and changed the energy in the room. Tension gave way to comfort, nervousness gave way to hope, and helplessness gave way to self-empowerment. We all wanted the electricity to be restored immediately for the seminar to be successful, and we were asking for a miracle right then and there.

That "miracle" happened: seconds after my humorous plea, the electricity came back, filling the room with light and sound and prompting a huge applause of relief from the audience. Together, we had made it through a real crisis, and I was still on my feet, having survived a public speaker's deadliest nightmare. But neither the audience nor I could have managed that ordeal as well without lightheartedness.

What Lightheartedness Is

Humor and laughter have always been an essential element of the human culture. The art of comedy can be traced to the ancient Greek theatre, which evolved from religious ceremonies dedicated to the god Dionysus, dating back to at least 1200 B.C. Throughout history, jesters and comedians became essential members of royal courts as they provided a source of levity for emperors and kings around the world. Today comedy flourishes as an industry that everyone can enjoy. In America alone, billions of dollars are spent each year on comedians, venues, movies, plays, video games, television programs, public and private extravaganzas, software, websites, books, magazines, postcards, toys, and other objects that bring humor into our lives. Laughter is in as high demand as are food and water. Yet in spite of the seemingly infinite sources of comic relief available in our culture, at least $12 billion was spent in 2003 for drugs treating anxiety and depression; according to consumer reports, that is almost 75 percent more than the amount spent in 2000. Apparently laughter, despite its abundance, has not proven sufficient to lighten our hearts. When our mood becomes so heavy that it feels unbearable, we still resort to drugs.

These statistics reveal our enormous need for lightheartedness not as entertainment but as a way to maintain our psychic and emotional health as we deal with increasingly complex and demanding realities of day-to-day life. We need to become lighthearted, period. As our society has evolved, we have managed to become proficient in competing, juggling multiple tasks, excelling, adapting to fast change, thriving through adversity, and, recently, dealing with the threat of terror. We can now become proficient in keeping a light heart.

Lightheartedness is commonly considered the cheerful feeling we have when nothing is troubling us. A lighthearted person is generally thought of as someone who is free from anxiety because he or she does not take things too seriously. However, lightheartedness should never be mistaken as insensitivity, irresponsibility, or superficiality in dealing with the complexities of life. Rather, it should be seen as a spiritual quality associated with inner strength, faith, and the ability to face life's adversities with a positive mental attitude and good humor that encourage and inspire others as well.

A modern parable about how a lighthearted man defied the atrocities of war and saved what was most valuable to him is the film *Life Is Beautiful*. This film celebrates the spirit of all holocaust survivors, who have proven that no crime against humanity—no matter how horrible and sadistic—can ever kill the will to survive, the desire to preserve what we love, or the courage to forgive and celebrate life.

The story unfolds in Italy in the late 1930s. Guido Orefice, the main hero, is an Italian Jew and a genuinely happy man who has all he needs:

Dora, his beloved wife, and Giosué, their only son, the apple of his eye. Then the outbreak of the Second World War threatens this happiness. One day, as the family is about to celebrate Giosué's fifth birthday, the Nazis arrest Guido and his son and send them to a concentration camp with thousands of other Jews. Dora, who is not Jewish, demands to be taken away with them and gets relegated to a women's camp, not knowing if she will ever see her husband and son again.

As soon as Guido absorbs the gravity of what has happened, he summons his spirit to face reality. For Guido, it is imperative that fear not touch the boy, and he knows this can happen only if the boy does not learn the truth about the camp. So to keep the boy calm and safe, he explains war as an elaborate game in which the rules change every day but that always involves playing a lot of hide-and-seek, plenty of make-believe, and something called silence. One by one, he filters through lightheartedness all the inhumane crimes taking place in the camp and explains them to the innocent boy as intricate games that adults are playing to earn points and win a real tank. The thought of winning a real tank keeps the boy motivated to "play" by the rules Guido invents every day to keep him safe, even as his own death approaches. But even the prospect of dying cannot stifle Guido's spirit. Keeping a light heart to the very end, he never loses his courage, his love for life, or his smile. It is his spirit that triumphs after all. Thanks to his inventive games, Giosué is saved and wins a real tank, just as his father had promised. Victorious, the boy reunites with his mother, and they both celebrate freedom and life that begins anew after the war is over.

Life Is Beautiful was inspired by the experiences of the director's father during his two-year imprisonment in a Nazi labor camp. Using the horror of the Jewish Holocaust as the backdrop, this film is a metaphor about the courage to celebrate the beauty of life amidst the most brutal circumstances. Life is beautiful when we act beautifully, and beautiful actions are the actions of a loving heart. The film shows how Guido saved his son from the Nazis, thanks not to a scheming ploy but to his beautiful actions inspired by a light heart. The lies he tells to his son about their deadly reality were not manipulative stories distorting the truth but love-inspired tales of hope. Guido's lightheartedness was consistent. In times of peace, it was his way to celebrate the beauty of life. In times of war, it was his only means to preserve his spirit and save his son's life.

Lightheartedness Requires the Courage to Hope

Life is a series of ongoing tests that we are called to pass. As children, we are faced with a challenging adult world where we are tested for our adaptability, stamina, and resilience. As adolescents, we are tested for our ability to make wise choices about our future and follow a path that will lead us to the life we dream. As young adults, we are tested for our ability to fulfill our dreams and provide for ourselves the life we love, in spite of the difficulties we encounter in the real world. As mature adults, we are tested for our courage to face old age and our ability to create material and spiritual resources to support ourselves through our golden years. As parents, we are tested for our abilities to provide our children with a safe home, a nurturing environment, and the material means for good education and a future with possibilities. As spouses or partners, we are tested for our ability to communicate our love effectively through words and actions. As members of society, we are tested for our abilities to create community and safeguard its freedom, respect human rights, create just economic and health policies, and protect the environment.

Passing life's tests requires preparation. We may be prepared for some of these tests, but sometimes life puts us through trials when we least expect them. Unanticipated challenges might include an accident that causes us to lose our health or our job, a layoff due to an economic downturn, the sudden loss of a loved one, or a terminal diagnosis. Others might be a friend's betrayal, a "perfect" marriage that ends in divorce, a fire that burns down our home, or a hurricane that destroys everything we own. In such cases, we must summon all resources available to us to show courage, have hope, and face the crisis. Keeping a light heart is essential in giving us hope to live through these hardships.

Hope cancels the sense of powerlessness over our destiny and motivates us to take action and conquer the menacing crisis, as opposed to giving in to despair. When we keep a light heart, life's hardships can never rob us of our spirit. As we go through our ordeal, hope inspires us to see the light at the end of the tunnel and stay the course until it is over. To achieve this, we may give ourselves license to do things that might otherwise be considered outrageous. Like Guido, we may invent an "as if" reality and pretend to live in that reality in order to handle the crisis we face in the real world. This is the power of lightheartedness; it dignifies our seemingly out-rageous actions and gives us authority over life's unfair attacks. When we celebrate life's worst moments with lightheartedness, we prove that we are the Creator's strongest, most magnificent spirit-filled beings: amazing humans, full of grace.

The story of Gaz and his friends in *The Full Monty* illustrates how lightheartedness dignifies even our most outrageous actions when we are called to overcome a real hardship without losing hope. Gaz, a steel factory worker, lives in Sheffield, England, an industrial city that used to enjoy a healthy economy until an economic depression closed down all the facto-ries and forced the city's male population into unemployment. Gaz, hav-ing been unemployed for months, cannot make ends meet. After days spent at job fairs with no results, he wanders home to his bleak housing project to face another crisis: a threat from his ex-wife to remove his visiting rights because he has not kept current with child support.

Fearing that he may never be allowed to see his son again, Gaz won-ders how he can find employment and earn money in a city where employ-ment for men is nonexistent. Women now dominate the job market and are the ones who can afford shopping and entertainment. Looking closer at his existing reality, Gaz finds the solution in an advertisement for the upcoming performance of a touring Chippendale troupe in a local pub. An idea strikes, filling him with hope: he will create a group of male dancers who will give a night of entertainment to the women of Sheffield and that way raise money to pay his child support. But his group will do onstage what no other show has ever dared: they will go "the full Monty," which means they will perform completely nude.

Gaz's challenge is now to convince his unemployed friends that his idea has merit and can be realized if they create a group and learn to dance like professional strippers. A few days later, a diverse group is formed. The five men gather in an abandoned factory and begin rehearsals immediately, moving to the sound of Donna Summer from an old tape recorder. But the road to success is not easy; soon after they begin rehearsals, the men are all struck with the reality of their decision as they find themselves challenged to confront their limitations, fears, and self-doubts. They soon discover that they are too clumsy, too old, too unattractive, too inhibited, and too unprepared to appear naked for money before all the women of Sheffield. On the other hand, the dreadful economic reality gives them no alternative other than to stay committed to their outrageous plan.

This is how all the group members are called to lighten their hearts, show courage, and overcome self-pity, self-doubt, and self-criticism. Honoring their decision to go the full Monty as a dignified way to earn money in a cruel job market, they give the best show Sheffield has ever seen, in a pub packed with cheering fans. Their show, highlighted with humor and genuine charm, is not an exhibition of commercialized sensuality but is a celebration of the courage to choose unconventional ways to stay hopeful and prevail through life's toughest tests.

Another unemployed father who will do anything to be close to his children after losing their custody is Daniel Hillard, the hero of the touching comedy *Mrs. Doubtfire*. A comedian who works as a cartoon voice-over, the devastated Daniel will not allow this defeat to lead him to despair. Moved by his love for his children and a desire to spend more time with them, he decides to follow an outrageous plan to be close to his children *and* keep a light heart about the actions he is about to commit. Answering his ex-wife's ad for a housekeeper, he goes to the interview dressed up as Mrs. Euphegenia Doubtfire, a middle-aged woman from England, and gets hired by his wife as the nanny of his three children. A man in women's clothes, Daniel spends every day with his own children, who grow attached to their "nanny" as "she" fills their home with love, laughter, and warmth. Mrs. Doubtfire's magic touch transforms even Daniel's wife, who, after long days at work, comes home to a clean, calm house to eat Mrs. Doubtfire's delicious food, never knowing that it was ordered from a French restaurant with Daniel's own money.

Mrs. Doubtfire is a tale about the power of lightheartedness to transform an entire family in crisis. We see how Daniel, by creating the "as if" reality of Mrs. Doubtfire, is healing himself, his children, and his wife from the wounds of the painful divorce. His humor not only lightens up the heavy reality but gives everyone courage, comfort, and hope. Even when Daniel's lie is exposed and Mrs. Doubtfire can no longer exist, her lightheartedness has touched everyone. No one can resent Daniel for his out-rageous act. His fraud is forgiven as an act of courage powered by his love for his children and his determination to do anything to be near them.

Can you think of a difficult moment in your life that you overcame with lightheartedness? Did you also give yourself permission to be outra-geous and pretend you lived in an "as if" reality, as the heroes of these movies did? If your answer is yes, I invite you to celebrate yourself for showing courage and staying hopeful throughout your ordeal. You are a winner!

Lightheartedness Requires the Use of Play in Order to Handle Fear

When Christine first walked into my office, I thought my heart stopped beating for a second; the sight of that young woman had startled me. She had been referred for depression, but one look at that twenty-two-year-old woman revealed other severe health problems. At five feet five inches tall, Christine weighed less than eighty pounds and had a tremor that she did not seem able to control. Greeting me with a hoarse, barely audible whis-per, she walked slowly toward the couch and sat down, exhausted. I knew immediately that she needed hospitalization and there was very little I could do to help her.

"I am sick," she said slowly, looking at me with hollow, sad eyes. "I have a blood disease and I may die. I am here because I feel dead already. I am so depressed that I can't go on. Nothing helps. Nothing."

I sat there, looking at her, unable to speak for a few moments. Very rarely had a client's state affected me in that way: this woman was too young to be dying, and I could understand her resignation. She was fifteen when she first fell ill. Spending seven years in and out of hospitals with no hope of improvement had exhausted her. I knew that she had heard it all: words of encouragement from doctors and nurses, prayers of hope from priests and relatives, and other therapists' advice to stay strong and not give up. But there is a point at which all words of encouragement lose their power to the ears of a chronically ill person and become empty sounds, just nuisances of no intent. That was the point Christine had reached on that day; feeling death approaching, she had given up.

"What do you miss?" I asked her as soon as I was able to speak. "What do you miss that you'd like to be able to do?"

"Feeling happy, even for a minute," she answered. "I miss laughing. I don't remember how it feels to laugh anymore."

As soon as I heard her answer, I stood up. "Excuse me for a minute," I said. "I'll be right back."

I left my office immediately and went straight to the kitchen. There, in a newly purchased kennel filled with toys and soft cushions, was Nicco, an adorable black-and-white three-month-old puppy, with big brown eyes and a happy face, that I had taken home after falling in love at first sight. I opened the kennel, picked him up, and, holding him gently, brought him into my office. I walked up to Christine and offered her the puppy.

"This is Nicco," I said. "He's been all by himself in a kennel, and I thought the two of you might want to meet."

Christine took the puppy and lifted him like a baby. Bringing him close to her cheek, she kissed him lightly on the nose. "Hello, puppy!" she said softly. Nicco responded immediately. Wiggling his tiny tail with zeal, he extended his little pink tongue and returned the kiss ten times more rigorously, slurping Christine's cheek with the playful affection only a happy puppy can show. Christine's face lit up; letting Nicco kiss her entire face, she began to talk to him, prompting more affectionate, playful responses. A few seconds later, Christine was smiling at her new friend. I let her continue to play with Nicco, watching her smile for the entire time. In that session, we did not talk much about her depression, her fear of dying, or her suffering through the years of being ill. Giving her the opportunity to play with Nicco and savor his love was much more therapeutic than filling out routine questionnaires.

"Thank you very much," she said when our time was up. "I have not felt like that in a long time. Nicco gave me hope. For a while, I stopped thinking of how scared I was."

We can learn a great deal about lightheartedness by watching children at play. Playing is their way of interacting, learning, showing emotions, and communicating their thoughts with the reality surrounding them. Play allows children to create an "as if" world in which they relive and process their experiences in order to assimilate reality and learn to cope with it.

As adults, relearning to play helps us return to that flexible state of childhood in which the "as if" reality of our games actually became the real world and reality itself momentarily reverted to a foreign dimension. Playing helps us to enter that "as if" reality and gain distance from our real fears and worries. Being in an "as if" reality helps us recover the lighthearted-ness we naturally had as children and use it as a lens to view the real world from a distance, thus gaining a fresh perspective and new strength with which to approach our lives.

A film about how playing helps us, as adults, to handle a complex and often dangerous reality is *Kindergarten Cop*. An action comedy, this movie could be a real story about discovering what is truly important in life, thanks to children's play. The main character is Detective John Kimble, a man whose size and muscles are big enough to intimidate all the bad guys of the underworld. For years, Detective Kimble has been on a mission to catch and incarcerate a dangerous criminal named Cullen Crisp. His pursuit of Crisp eventually leads him to the toughest assignment of his career: he assumes an undercover identity as a kindergarten teacher in Astoria in order to find Crisp's wife and force her to testify against her husband.

When Detective Kimble begins to work as a kindergarten teacher, he does not expect to be completely outmatched by the children. His police methods are obsolete, and the children teach him more than he is able to teach them. Soon he discovers that the only way to enter the children's world and earn their cooperation for his mission is through play. As he learns to play, he enters the "as if" world of children, and from there, he sees how lonely and unfulfilled his real life is. The tough Detective Kimble is, in fact, a divorced father who has not seen his son in years. As he watches the children's lighthearted way of dealing with their own difficulties, he begins to see the world of adults through their eyes and is able to get in touch with emotions that being a cop never allowed him to have.

"You aren't getting mellow on me, are ya?" asks his partner, Detective Phoebe O'Hara, who is noticing Detective Kimble's change. Indeed, this big, tough man is softening up. Being with children has lightened his heart and opened it to emotions that previously used to scare him. As a result, our hero begins to fall in love with Joyce, a young schoolteacher and the mother of a little boy in Detective Kimble's class.

Kindergarten Cop shows that lighthearted play can be much more powerful than strong muscles in changing our world. While Detective Kimble used guns and violence to keep the world safe, the kindergarten children used play to teach him about emotional safety and the beauty of loving. At the end, the lightheartedness of kindergarten triumphs over the wrath of the streets. After destroying Cullen Crisp, Detective Kimble resigns from the police force and commits to a career teaching kindergarten and being a husband to the woman he loves and a father to Dominic, who, along with all the other children, had shown him the path to his own true happiness.

Lightheartedness Requires the Will to Love Life and Be Unconditionally Happy

Most of us dream that someday, when all our troubles melt away, we will feel the happiness advertised in commercials. When that problem-free day comes, our hearts will lighten. We will no longer need sleeping pills, our ulcer will disappear, and we will never again feel the sting of anxiety in our chest. Of course, we expect that we will become lighthearted on the conditions that we can be debt free, buy our dream house, lose the extra weight, get that promotion, win the lottery, make our children behave themselves, or make our spouse give up the bad habit that drives us crazy. So, as life gets shorter every day, we continue to postpone feeling happy and promise to do it one day, when everything in our world is perfect. Until then, we suffer under the weight of our own attitudes toward life that cause us to be disgruntled, restless, and miserable.

An example of a person who manages to keep not only himself in a state of misery but everyone around him as well is Melvin Udall, a main character in *As Good as It Gets*. Melvin is a brilliant, witty New York author suffering from an obsessive-compulsive disorder that he refuses to treat, thus making human relations impossible. In addition to his strange rituals, assorted irrational fears, and an obsessive need for control, Melvin has no social graces whatsoever. He treats men, women, children, and animals with the same sarcasm, driving them away and making sure he is despised and avoided by everyone. Everyone, that is, except Carol, who is the only person in the world who talks to Melvin. A thirty-year-old waitress and the single mother of a sick boy, Carol is an unappreciated woman who works very hard but receives very little from life for her efforts. She is the only link Melvin has to society, and when she suddenly disappears from the restaurant, she becomes the reason for Melvin's life-changing adventure that will transform him into a new person. In this adventure, Melvin takes a journey from being a misanthrope to becoming a man who accepts life with all its imperfections, thanks to his willingness to change and open his heart. The same Melvin who, at the beginning of the movie, insulted Carol with abusive remarks about her and her son is now asking her to accept him as an imperfect, vulnerable, and well-meaning man who needs her in his life more than anything else.

"I might be the only person on the face of the earth who knows you're the greatest woman on earth," he tells her with a tender voice, having knocked at her door at four o'clock in the morning to beg her forgiveness. "I think most people miss that about you, and I watch them, wondering how they can see you bring their food and clear their tables, and never get that they have just met the greatest woman alive. And the fact that I get it makes me feel good, about me."

As Good as It Gets uses everyday characters with imperfect lives to teach us how to accept life and surrender to love with a light heart. Thanks to Melvin's transformation, we learn that lightheartedness is unconditional. It is a state of mind that exists in spite of the imperfect, messy reality in which we live. It is an expression of unconditional love for life and the will to be happy regardless of our circumstances.

In more than fifteen years of working as a therapist, I never had a client come in for professional help beaming with happiness and unconditional love for life. Feeling love for oneself and one's life are the goals, not the impetus, for therapy. When a client becomes lighthearted, the therapeutic relationship is over; there is no need for it anymore. But it was outside my office, during my travels around the world, where I met a number of lighthearted, unconditionally happy people. They blessed me with their wisdom, their love for life, and the inner light that shone through their lives' darkest moments. One of them is Mrs. Betty Mae Hardy.

I met Mrs. Betty Mae Hardy in her home in the spring of 2000, while I was doing research about the American civil rights movement in Selma, Alabama. She was a small African-American woman with a calm face radiating dignity and a lucid mind full of clear, wise thoughts. At ninety-four, she was in excellent health and lived alone in a very simple one-room apartment in East Selma, the poorest part of town. Her story is one of a lifetime of hard, hard work without material or social rewards. Her ancestors were slaves. Her parents were plantation workers. She worked in the fields as a child and later worked as a domestic servant, until she was in her late seventies. She buried three of her seven children before they reached the age of five and raised the rest of them without a husband. Her children's father was killed in a mysterious accident that the authorities never resolved.

Life offered no apology for the hardships Betty Mae had endured but gave her every reason to hold anger, resentment, or even hatred for the pain she had suffered. When I asked her how she was able to survive such unfairness, she explained, "Hate is like a cancer. You can't carry that anger with you; you have to let it go. God wants to test our heart and see if we can open it up. God is not bad. Only people are bad because of ignorance. It's so much easier not knowing. It's hard to know that there are kids in the world who suffer and not want to do something about it. It's easier to turn the head away, not wanting to know."

And then she said, "When I need something and people don't help me, I talk to the Lord, and he always sends it to me. I don't ask for what I want, but for what I need. Sometimes my life was so hard, I lay down, I was like dead. God came and woke me up. He touched me, he blessed me, he raised me from the bed, he put food on my table, he gave me health and strength, he gave me wisdom to do what I needed to do. Every mornin' I wake up and go to my kitchen and start fixin' my breakfast and start praisin' the Lord because he blessed me to see another day."

When I asked her what life had taught her, she answered, "You must live your life today. You don't know when God will terminate your days. Don't spend your days doin' things that won't benefit you, causin' you grief. If you want to feel good and if you want good to happen in your life, you must do only good."

Betty Mae lived through one of the darkest periods of American history, which ended only thanks to the long struggle of African-Americans for freedom and civil rights. Growing up in a racist and segregated society, she was robbed of opportunities for education and social advancement. But in spite of all the human cruelties against her, her inner source of wisdom, clarity of thought, and love for life remained untouched. Betty Mae was an enlightened woman, a truly blessed one. She never became a high-status guru enjoying the adoration of the masses. But in my eyes, Betty Mae became one of the very few true-life teachers and self-dignified human beings that I have ever had the honor to meet.

How to Be Lighthearted

Laughing often is good for you. Research has shown that humor and laughter reinforce the effects of therapies treating cancer, chronic illness, clinical depression, respiratory disease, heart disease, chronic pain, skin allergies, and diabetes. Humor has been shown to reinforce teaching methods, facilitate learning and problem solving, improve team performance, and increase productivity. People with a sense of humor receive higher rates of social appeal and are perceived as more intelligent than people who are humorless.

You can become lighthearted. As you work with this method, keep in mind the points that follow. They are also helpful in completing the exercises that appear after this section.

In order to be lighthearted, you must be willing to

- Be spontaneous
- Enter an "as if" reality to gain distance from the reality you are facing
- Suspend judgment and laugh
- Think of yourself as having overcome the problem you are facing instead of thinking of yourself as being burdened by it
- Enrich your life with objects, activities, animals, and people who inspire and encourage you to act with lightheartedness

Reel Fulfillment in Action

Movie Time! ▶ *Watch a Movie for Fun, Learn a Lesson of Life*

Following is a list of films, mostly comedies. They all address human issues and portray different aspects of humor and lightheartedness, as well as the human will to embrace life and overcome its hurdles. Choose a movie, and watch it alone or with your group. Afterward, think about the questions that follow each list. Write down your thoughts and share them with others. Repeat the activity with as many movies on the list as your time permits.

Movies About Lightening Your Heart
As Good as It Gets (1997), directed by James L. Brooks
Being There (1979), directed by Hal Ashby
Big Fish (2003), directed by Tim Burton
The Color Purple (1985), directed by Steven Spielberg
Finding Nemo (2003), directed by Andrew Stanton and
   Lee Unkrich
The Full Monty (1997), directed by Peter Cattaneo
The Great Dictator (1940), directed by Charles Chaplin
Kindergarten Cop (1990), directed by Ivan Reitman
Life Is Beautiful (1997), directed by Roberto Benigni
Man on the Moon (1999), directed by Milos Forman
Mrs. Doubtfire (19993), directed by Chris Columbus
Shrek (2001), directed by Andrew Adamson and Vicky Jenson
Some Like It Hot (1959), directed by Billy Wilder
Tootsie (1982), directed by Sydney Pollack
Wit (2001), directed by Mike Nichols

Questions to Answer
1. Which scenes in the film did you enjoy the most?
2. What did you like about them?

3. How did the humor in this film touch you? What messages did it give you?

4. How did this film inspire you to handle a difficulty in your own life?

5. Which character did you like the most? What did you like about him or her?

6. Can you summarize a hopeful message from the film in one sentence? Place this message in a visible spot, where you can read it often.

7. Can you recall a time of difficulty in your life when you used humor to stay hopeful and keep your spirits high? How did you overcome your difficulty?

Lightening Your Heart ▸ *Exercises and Activities*

The essence of humor and lightheartedness is spontaneity. In my opinion, laughter is like love: it cannot happen by force or prescription. But just as you can learn to create an environment in which love may flourish, you can also learn to create a lighthearted environment in which you feel free to be spontaneous and laugh.

The following activities are recommended for creating environments conducive to laughter. You will notice that they all give you permission to enter an "as if" reality, which in turn provides distance from the reality of your life. Ensconced in that "as if" reality, you can then better appreciate your own humor and that of others and live unforgettable moments with a group of friends or family.

Most of the activities that follow are designed as group activities. You may use one or more of them with your group as part of your weekly assignment.

- **Host a poetry jam.** It may be theme free, or it may have a theme. Everyone is invited to write a poem, free from rules, but with a lighthearted tone. Unleash your imagination and create a poem that you like. Then present it to the group. You might add more drama and fun if you dress the part.

- **Have a game night.** Choose a game that gives opportunities for laughs and have a game night, playing charades, Twister, or board games, for example.

Prepare a relaxed, fun environment in which you can feel free to laugh. Dress comfortably and adopt a playful attitude. Remember, this is not a contest. The one who laughs the most is the real winner.

- **Have a comedy fest.** Remember and describe the funniest thing that has ever happened to you, or tell a story that makes *you* laugh. Then ask the members in your group to describe what makes them laugh. Or you can do impersonations of people who inspire you to impersonate them. You can make this even more entertaining if you dress up like the people you impersonate and stage a skit or miniplay. It becomes even funnier if the people you impersonate are completely irrelevant in real life.

- **Share your funniest videos or movies.** Create a comedy video library with your group, and start a regular comedy night, alternating homes. Dress comfortably, bring food, relax, and laugh. Remember, at no point must an activity about humor become work.

- **Write a funny story as a collective effort.** Have one member write a sentence on a piece of paper and then fold the paper so that the sentence cannot be seen. The author tells the group only the last word of the sentence. This word is to be used by the next person, who writes a new sentence, folds the paper so the sentence cannot be seen, tells what the last word is, and so on. The group can decide how many times to go around. At the end, the papers are unfolded and the story is read.

- **Create funny headlines.** Cut words from tabloid headlines and fill a basket with the words. Choose up to ten words from the basket, and create your own headline using those words. You may write a short article elaborating on the headline. Unleash your imagination. Read your headlines and articles to the group. Keep in mind the points about humor explained in this chapter, and enjoy yourself.

- **Perform a skit in a foreign language.** Create ten cards describing simple life situations (for example, wanting to go to the bathroom, asking directions to the pharmacy, ordering a tuna sandwich in a restaurant, or trying to buy a gift for a relative in a department store). Pick one card, and choose one or two other people with whom you will perform the skit—but do not let them read your card. Let the rest of the group read the card. Then begin acting out the scenario with your partners. In the skit, pretend that you are a tourist visiting a foreign country, and the other actors are natives of that country. All actors must pretend to speak a "foreign" language. (You do not have to know a foreign language, only pretend that you speak one.) Using pantomime, body language, and sign language, try to explain to your partners what your situation is. The more spontaneous and inventive you are, the funnier your interactions may be.

Things to Remember

- Lightheartedness is a sign of strength.
- It is easier to love when you have a light heart.
- Attitudes are contagious. Spreading a lighthearted attitude makes you attractive.

11

Practice Creativity

IMAGINE SOMEONE asking you, "How many hours a week do you spend working?" or "What do you do?" You are likely to answer something like, "I am a full-time student, and I work part-time at a department store," "I am a full-time mom of three boys," "I am a professor," or "I am a computer analyst." Your answer describes the daily routine of what you do for a living, which is a job that gives you income, a social identity, a certain professional status, and, sometimes, public recognition. However rewarding, a job very often includes duties, tasks, and requirements that we are obliged to perform, whether we like them or not. Our freedom to do only what we like in our job is almost always limited. This is a main reason why so many people suffer from job-related dissatisfaction and see their work as the necessary evil they must endure in exchange for a monthly paycheck.

Now imagine someone asking you, "How many hours a week do you spend creating something that gives you joy?" or "Do you have a creative habit that helps you handle stress?" Think of your answer. You may take a little longer to give a reply, and when you do, you may say something like, "Hmm, you know, *I'd like* to be creative, but, truth is, I'm too tired," "Well, *I'd love* to have some time for creativity, but I'm too busy with other things," "*It would be awesome* to have a creative habit, but that's a luxury for the rich, and I have bills to pay," or "*Me*, creative? But I'm not an artist—I'm an office manager!"

If your answer to the question about creativity resembles any of the answers just given, it is high time you changed your attitude toward your ability to be creative. In this chapter, you will be introduced to a number of mythical characters and real people who consider creativity not as a luxury but as their birthright. The truth is that we are all born with the ability to be creative, just as we are born with the ability to think, dream, and imagine. But while some of us continue to honor creativity throughout our lives and enjoy the benefits of a creative habit, many others betray their creativity as they seek joy in habits that are not only noncreative but, oftentimes, self-destructive.

The prices we pay when we stifle our right to be creative are as high as those we pay when we stifle our dreams. In my practice as a psychotherapist and coach, the majority of clients complaining about feelings of depression, insomnia, panic attacks, low self-esteem, or a sense of meaninglessness are the ones who ignore their dreams and their own creative impulses. Over the years, I have helped a number of people reconnect with their natural ability to create, watching them enjoy the benefits of their creativity: a recovered self-confidence, an improved ability to handle life's daily stress, freedom from depression, and a sense of fulfillment that no medical treatment alone can ever catalyze.

As you are working through the fourth part of this method, it is essential that you experience the joy of developing and maintaining creative habits. Reconnecting with your creativity will allow you to be spontaneous and daring as you suspend judgment about the outcomes of your creative efforts. Your benefits from becoming creative will be a sense of sustained pleasure, inner freedom, and independence from other people's approval. The more you allow yourself to be creative, the more self-confident you will be and the better you will like yourself.

Creativity 101

To create means "to cause to exist" or "to bring into being something that has never existed before." Everything created is first imagined. Therefore, creativity is the human activity in which we constructively use our imagination by giving material form to our creative ideas. In this context, a creative person is not only prolific in ideas but also active in materializing creative ideas in the real world. This creative input enriches not only the individual life of the creator but also the world at large.

Creative people are not necessarily professional artists. They come from all walks of life, and their creativity applies to all aspects of our civilization. They may be scientists discovering the hidden laws of the universe or new cures for terminal diseases; businesspeople creating breakthrough opportunities in national economies; lawyers excelling in their field, thanks to their creative problem-solving ideas; visionary politicians leading nations to freedom and prosperity; teachers creating innovative methods for the classroom; farmers creating breakthrough methods of farming or breeding; cooks creating culinary masterpieces or revolutionary cooking methods; administrators guiding organizations into success through creative leadership; police detectives solving mysteries and incarcerating criminals, thanks to creative thinking. Age, level of education, and socioeconomic status do not matter: a creative person can be a child, an adolescent, an adult, or a senior. He or she can be single or married, divorced or widowed, childless or with children. Individual differences may be unlimited. But there are three characteristics, described in the following sections, that all creative people share in common, which you must also develop as you work with this method.

Creative People Honor Their Creative Impulses

Creative people know the relationship between creativity and productivity, and they are careful to keep them in balance. They nurture their creative needs by taking the necessary time and space to access imagination and stimulate creative thinking. And they bring their creative ideas into fruition by being productive. They also honor their creativity by protecting and nurturing their ideas and by following a discipline that involves hard work, concentration, isolation, unusual decisions, sacrifices, dedication to the creative purpose, and trust in their inner voice. Nevertheless, in spite of the demands of the creative process, staying loyal to their creative pursuit is never a burden for creative people. The joy from seeing their completed creation is so pure that it redeems all the strenuous efforts exerted during the process.

Examples of movie characters portraying creative individuals abound. Some of them are introduced in this chapter. I encourage you to see the respective films and notice how different those characters are, yet how similar in the way they honor their creative impulses. These characters represent simple people yearning for the joy of creating, much as we all do. As you watch the films, let them inspire you to reconnect with your own creativity and feel the joy that you see the characters experience in the films.

Working Girl is the story of a young woman's determination to bring her creative ideas into fruition, having to protect them from being appropriated by her boss. Tess McGill, the main character, is a thirty-year-old administrative assistant who lives in Staten Island and commutes every day to work in the Manhattan financial district. On the ferry, she reads, and in the evenings, she takes classes. Tess wants to become something more than a secretary. She is bright, talented, and informed, and, most important, she has creative ideas about mergers and acquisitions that she presents to her new boss, Katharine Parker, hoping to be appreciated and offered a better position in the company. But Katharine has different intentions: when Tess offers her a brilliant idea that will save a large company from a foreign takeover, Katharine steals it and presents it to her clients as her own, advising Tess not to mention it anywhere else.

It is not too long before Tess finds out that her creativity is being exploited. She vows to protect her idea and use all means available to make it happen, even if this means that she will pretend to be Katharine. While Katharine is away recovering from a skiing accident, Tess assumes Katharine's identity and follows through with her plan, fighting to see her idea become reality until the very end, even after her true identity is discovered and she is exposed as an imposter. But thanks to her persistence and willingness to take risks for her own creative idea, Tess does not give up. Exposing Katharine minutes before she signs the deal with the clients, she proves that the idea was originally hers and wins. When Oren Trask, the client, asks Tess why she had to do this and risk her reputation, she answers, "You can bend the rules plenty once you get to the top, but not while you're trying to get there. And if you're someone like me, you can't get there without bending the rules."

Oren, admiring her courage to fight for her idea, responds, "You've got a real fire in your belly, Ms. McGill."

Tess's answer to this compliment only means that fighting to protect one's creativity is never easy. "I'm not quite sure what you mean, sir. I've got something in my belly, but I think it's nervous knots."

Tess McGill is not an artist. Her creativity is not expressed through poetry, writing, or painting but through ideas creating multimillion-dollar breakthroughs in the financial world. But just as an artist who fights to protect her work from being appropriated, she fights to have her idea recognized as being her own. She is diligent, thorough, and brave, and she loves what she does. She does not rest until she sees it take form in reality. And considering her limited means, she thinks and acts creatively throughout her ordeal against all odds, until the truth surfaces and she fulfills her dream.

Another tribute to creative people is the epic *Titanic*, which is filled with characters honoring their creativity until their last moments, even as they are drowning with the "unsinkable ship" into the abysmal depths of the North Atlantic. The story is told eighty-four years later through flashbacks by Rose DeWitt Bukater, a survivor, as she is sitting in her pottery studio. Rose is 101 years old, and she is still creating pottery. Surrounded by her works, she recalls her fateful trip and introduces Jack Dawson, a young artist and the love of her life, who died during the tragic voyage. She spent only a matter of hours with him, but their love became immortal.

As she recalls their moments together, Rose brings us eighty-four years back to what she considers the most erotic moment of her life, which she lets us witness: hours before his death, Jack is drawing a nude of her wearing only a necklace with a big, blue diamond. The beauty of a seventeen-year-old Rose in love is immortalized in the drawing, seen through the eyes of the artist. "I couldn't stop shaking," Rose confesses, alluding to the erotic intensity of the experience that has stayed with her ever since. Jack's art captured a lifetime of love that survived his death. For Rose, his art did not only create her drawing—it created Jack's immortality.

As Rose remembers, we live with her the tragic scenes that unfold as the ship is about to sink. We are shown five musicians of the ship's orchestra completing their last piece of music. We watch the unknown musicians bid their last farewell and walk away, except for the violinist, who stays in the same place and starts playing solo. As the other orchestra members hear him play, they stop, return, and join him in the piece. Amidst a crowd of screaming passengers running in vain to save their lives, these musicians peacefully accept their imminent death and choose to celebrate life with their music, until the dark ocean swallows them playing their last note. Defying death by remaining creative until one's last breath is one of the most powerful messages in this epic, which is also a tribute to inner freedom, immortal love, and the inexorable right to honor one's truth.

Creative People Regard Creating as Healing

Creative people are healers. They create to bring wholeness to the inevitable wounds inflicted by life. Their creative output is their answer to aggression, deprivation, unfairness, and injustice that, unfortunately, abound in reality. Through creating, they contribute toward increasing beauty, harmony, and love, without which life cannot exist. Creativity is their only weapon against the afflictions of depression, boredom, or loneliness and the source of strength, courage, and hope. Creative people do not allow the burdens of life to discourage them. They create in spite of the daily pressures and dramas to conquer pain, fear, poverty, illness, and even death.

"When I dance, something happens and I sort of disappear," says the title character of *Billy Elliot* during his interview with the Committee of the Royal Ballet School. "It's hard at the beginning, but then something happens and I start flying. I feel free. I disappear into the air like a bird, like electricity. Yeah, like electricity."

Billy calls electricity the divine light that sparks in him when he is immersed in the creative process, enlightening his existence and the world around him. Through dancing, his essence becomes one with the Creator, as he, little Billy, disappears. The joy of dancing heals his grief for his desceased mother, his worry for his ill grandmother, his sadness for being mistreated by his brother, and his sorrow for being rejected by his father. Billy's wholeness is in his dance. That is when his daily life becomes secondary and he feels truly alive.

There is no process livelier than the creative process. Its essence is the very stuff of life, which is nature's will to push beyond limitations in order to accomplish creation. And once the creation is accomplished, there is no joy deeper for the creator than the joy of sharing it with the world. A modern myth describing how the creative process brings wholeness not only to the creative agent but also to those who commune with the creative outcome is *Babette's Feast*.

Based on a short story by Isak Dinesen, *Babette's Feast* is set in remote Frederikshavn, a small Lutheran community on the Jutland peninsula in Denmark, in the second half of the nineteenth century. The villagers are fundamentalists adhering to a rigid puritanical dogma. Their life is dedicated to religious observance, reciting of the scripture, material poverty, and avoidance of all temptations of spirit and body. Their spartan homes and churches are devoid of embellishments or furniture that might provide the slightest comfort. Their manners are restrained; wordy interactions are restricted, as silence is enforced to maintain the spiritual tone of relationships; indulging in simple pleasures, such as food or other, more complex, physical desires, is simply unfathomable. For this community, joy is a sin.

One day, a French woman named Babette arrives at the village and knocks at the door of Martina and Philippa, the two unmarried daughters of Pouel Kern, the desceased spiritual leader and founder of this community. While he was alive, father Kern had managed to keep his daughters from having any relationship with the outside world, forcing them to abandon all prospects of marriage or career. Due to his intervention, Martina ended her relationship with a young officer wanting to marry her, while Philippa ended, on her own accord, her friendship with a Parisian opera singer, afraid of the joy she felt during their singing lessons. The opera singer, always remembering Philippa, sends Babette to Frederikshavn to be a loyal servant and housekeeper to the two orphaned sisters. Babette agrees to work without wages, which she does for fourteen years, diligently following the community's rules, cooking simple meals, observing the silence, and helping the two sisters with their community service.

No one knows that Babette has been a gourmet chef in Café Anglais, a famous French restaurant, until, one day, she asks the two sisters if she can prepare a lavish French dinner for the entire village, to celebrate their father's one hundredth birthday. Babette offers to pay for the entire feast with the money she won in the Paris lottery. The sisters hesitate but finally agree, on the condition that the guests observe the vow of silence through-out the meal, so as not to indulge in pleasure. Babette orders the food from France and sets out to prepare the feast. Soon the ingredients arrive—live turtles for soup, game and meats for the main courses, a wheelbarrow full of offal, bottles of champagne and fine wine—along with trunks full of fine china, silver, crystal glasses, lace linen, and fancy candles. For days Babette works in the kitchen, creating a feast of love, a true art masterpiece that will forever change the life of the community.

As the evening of the feast arrives, the villagers congregate around a table where they taste caviar with mussels in vodka sauce, turtle soup, quail filled with foie gras and truffles, fine meats, expensive cheeses, and exquisite desserts. As they raise their glasses to drink Veuve Clicquot, a superb champagne, they cannot help it: moved by the spirit of the food and enveloped in the delight of its taste, they break the vow of silence and begin interacting. For the first time, they realize that spiritual prosperity can be enjoyed through material abundance. As the joy of tasting Babette's food is lifting everyone off the ground into higher spheres, the retired general, Martina's discouraged suitor from the past, suddenly raises a glass to declare that nothing is impossible. Babette's abundance has brought joy beyond words to everyone, empowering their spirit with the hope that no opportunity in life is truly missed as long as one wants to achieve a dream wholeheartedly. Her feast, creating such spiritual and emotional abundance for that deprived community, also proved that the one who creates is never poor.

While the villagers delight in the majesty of the senses, Babette, alone in the kitchen, delights in the fulfillment of her dream: her culinary art has healed an entire village, banishing everyone's fear of joy. Looking at us, she reaches out with a plea that speaks for the desire of all creative people to create wholeness: "From across the world there goes one long cry from the heart of the artist: give me leave to do my utmost."

Creative People Pursue Their Projects to Completion

Out of the creative projects you have begun over the years, how many have you actually finished? Remember, *to create* means "to bring something into *full* existence." If your creative projects are begun ideas that have never found completion, they do not count as creative endeavors. Sorry, but these are only abandoned efforts patiently awaiting your honest attention.

We all have "abandoned efforts" hiding somewhere at home, in our drawers, in our computer's hard drive, even in our mind: a screenplay that is only twenty-five pages along and has no conclusion; an incomplete needlecraft, quilt, or knitting project; a bookcase we built in the garage but never varnished or placed in our son's bedroom; an antique car that we have been rebuilding for the last ten years; a foreign language that we never learned to speak fluently; a dance that we never learned to dance without stepping on our partner or causing public embarrassment; a recipe for the special cookware we purchased but never removed from its box; an idea to expand our business that we never pursued beyond writing it in our notepad; and so on.

What causes us to abandon our creative projects and betray the joy of creating? A usual explanation is that we stop the creative process because we give in to fear of criticism or fear of failure. This is only partially true considering that, in reality, we engage in many self-destructive endeavors, ignoring criticism *and* inviting failure in our health and finances, as well as our personal and professional life: we indulge in junk food, knowing that our cholesterol count will go up; we watch countless hours of television, neglecting to communicate with friends, family, and loved ones; we spend money compulsively, knowing that we are damaging our credit; we cut corners at work, knowing that we will eventually be discovered and called accountable; and so on. The truth is that the reason for abandoning creative projects is not our fear of criticism but our fear of commitment to a challenging process, period. It is in our nature to abandon a creative habit when arising difficulties cause discomfort and to indulge in destructive habits just because they are easy and immediately gratifying.

One of the most deceptive beliefs about the creative process is that it is a constant source of joy, freedom, and success. Nothing could be further from the truth: the creative process is as challenging as any other endeavor, and it requires heartfelt commitment from the beginning to the end. Every creative project presents challenges, obstacles, difficulties, and problems that suspend pleasure until we resolve them. This is why the joy of creativity is 10 percent in starting a project, 0 percent in persevering through its challenges, and 90 percent in accomplishing it. But once the creation is completed, the experience of the creator from sharing it with the world is filled with pure delight. In Western religious teachings, the Creator's profound, restful enjoyment from having completed the universe is described as the seventh day of creation. Creative people seek this joy and, therefore, do not abandon their efforts as unwanted children; instead, they treat their creative projects as children needing to be parented until they become self-sufficient through consistent love and dedication despite challenges and rough spots.

An example of a creative person who accomplished her project with amazing determination, overcoming criticism and personal attacks of national proportions, is Maya Lin. Her story is the theme of the documentary *Maya Lin: A Strong, Clear Vision*, a tribute to her creative work with a special focus on her remarkable achievement, the Vietnam Veterans Memorial Wall. In 1981, as a twenty-one-year-old senior architecture major at Yale University, Lin won first prize in the contest to design the Vietnam Veterans Memorial in the northwest corner of the Mall in Washington, D.C. She had proposed a simple, graceful, and abstract design of two 247-foot-long walls of polished black granite, set below grade and connected at a 125-degree angle, on which the names of all of the more than 58,000 American dead and missing from the war would be carved in letters a little over half an inch high and arranged chronologically, according to the year of death or disappearance.

Lin's winning design did not enjoy the public acceptance one would have expected. As soon as it was publicized, it triggered the bitter criticism of a small but powerful group of Vietnam veterans about its color, proposed placement below ground level, and lack of heroic quality. The design was characterized as a "black ditch" or "black gash of shame." A few conservative politicians supported the opposition until a compromise was reached. Following a number of highly publicized meetings, in which Lin was personally attacked and repeatedly forced to defend her project, it was finally agreed to add to the monument an American flag on a 60-foot pole and a group of three realistically modeled, seven-foot bronze figures of Vietnam-era American soldiers by another artist. Fortunately, these additions were placed far enough away from the wall so that its artistic integrity was not seriously affected.

Lin withstood unfair, chauvinistic, and occasionally racist attacks with admirable strength and inner composure. She never compromised the integrity of her vision or negotiated the principles of her conception: the Memorial Wall was a healing monument, offering visitors an intimate and contemplative experience as it allowed them to feel the deep sense of loss it conveyed. Lin's perseverance resulted in the phenomenal success of her project, once it was completed. The monument was dedicated and officially opened to the public on Veterans Day, 1982. Since that day, more than ten thousand people visit the Wall per day; among them are Vietnam veterans, families of the fallen, and the public at large, who experience profound healing as the names of the dead or missing, which seem to float on a transparent black plane, exert their power evoking strong emotion. Additionally, as the visitors can see their own faces dimly reflected on the polished black granite, they are invited to enter a dimension in which life and death are two facets of one continuous experience. The monument, in silence, speaks to each visitor in a very personal yet universal way about life and death, grief and loss, and embracing what one cannot change.

Another remarkable woman who left a legacy of overcoming difficulties in order to bring a creative project to completion is Roberta Guaspari, the heroine of *Music of the Heart*. Based on Roberta's real life, the film tells the story of a schoolteacher's struggle to teach violin to underprivileged children in East Harlem. After her devastating divorce, Roberta finds herself with two children and in need of work. A music teacher facing few opportunities for work, she becomes aware of an opening at an East Harlem public school. After convincing the school principal about the value of teaching music in her school, she is hired. Roberta begins her work in a problem-ridden environment, filled with burned-out, underpaid teachers accustomed to expecting very little of themselves and the school system. In addition, the children, most from troubled families, have little support at home for academic achievement, let alone learning the violin.

Roberta begins working with the zeal and stubbornness of a neophyte, as the children challenge her authority and question the value of her work. But she does not get intimidated. Showing determination, amazing inner strength, and genuine interest in the children, she eventually wins their trust and connects them to the violin. As her students learn to play, their improving self-confidence has a positive influence on other aspects of their lives. Their parents, formerly skeptical about Roberta's function in their school, notice their children blossom and begin to respect and admire Roberta. She has earned everyone's trust.

For ten years, Roberta's program flourishes, earning a great reputation in the city until, in 1991, the school board seizes the funding. Roberta will not allow this to happen. Determined to give the biggest fight of her life, she summons the help of the parents, a journalist, and a number of the world's best violinists and organizes an amazing concert at Carnegie Hall to raise funds and save her program. The concert, in which she and her students share the stage with artists such as Isaac Stern, Arnold Steinhardt, Itzhak Perlman, and Sandra Park, is a phenomenal success and raises funds that ensure the survival of her program for several more years.

Roberta Guaspari is a living legend. An Italian-American woman who made Harlem her home, she had been playing the violin since nine years of age. Music gave her peace, sanity, and inner strength when her divorce shattered her life. She brought her gift to inner-city schools and shared it generously with the children, empowering them to honor their creativity and always pursue their dreams.

The Characteristics of a Creative Habit

In the next section, you will be encouraged to develop a creative habit following recommended activities and exercises. As you discover and nurture your own creative habit, keep in mind its main characteristics. A creative habit

- gives you energy
- holds your interest
- gives you the freedom to make mistakes and see them as learning experiences
- challenges your thoughts, stretches your imagination, and generates new discoveries and problem-solving ideas
- increases your self-confidence and self-acceptance

Reel Fulfillment in Action

Movie Time! ▸ *Watch a Movie for Fun, Learn a Lesson of Life*

The following films portray different characters with one thing in common: their lives are determined by their willingness to be creative. Choose a movie, and watch it alone or with your group. Answer the questions at the end of the list in writing, and discuss your answers with your group. Repeat the same with more films on the list, as your time permits.

Movies About Creativity
The Agony and the Ecstasy (1965), directed by Carol Reed
Amadeus (1984), directed by Milos Forman
Artemisia (1997), directed by Agnès Merlet
Babette's Feast (1987), directed by Gabriel Axel
Big Night (1996), directed by Campbell Scott and Stanley Tucci
Billy Elliot (2000), directed by Stephen Daldry
Camille Claudel (1988), directed by Bruno Nuytten
A Chef in Love (1997), directed by Nana Dzhordzhadze
Chocolat (2000), directed by Lasse Hallström
Finding Neverland (2004), directed by Marc Forster
Frida (1988), directed by Paul Leduc
Frida (2002), directed by Julie Taymor
The Ghost and Mrs. Muir (1947), directed by Joseph L. Mankiewicz
Immortal Beloved (1994), directed by Bernard Rose
Like Water for Chocolate (1992), directed by Alfonso Arau
Maya Lin: A Strong, Clear Vision (1994), directed by Freida Lee
   Mock
Music of the Heart (1999), directed by Wes Craven
Pleasantville (1998), directed by Gary Ross
Pollock (2000), directed by Ed Harris
Shall We Dance? (1996), directed by Masayuki Suo
Shall We Dance? (2004), directed by Peter Chelsom

Surviving Picasso (1996), directed by James Ivory
Titanic (1997), directed by James Cameron
Working Girl (1988), directed by Mike Nichols

Questions to Answer

1. What role does creativity play in the life of the main character of the story?
2. How does the environment respond to the main character's creativity?
3. What other forces in the life of the character oppose his or her creativity? Notice that these forces may be not only external but also internal.
4. How does the character stand up for his or her need to stay creative? How does he or she defend his or her creativity? List his or her actions and evaluate them.
5. How does the story reach you, and what lessons did you learn about your own creativity?
6. What are you prepared to do to be more creative?

Practice Creativity ▶ *Exercises and Activities*

▶ **Developing a Creative Habit**

1. Think of something you have long wanted to do or something you used to like doing as a child but later abandoned because you got on with life obligations. It must be something that used to give you pleasure.
2. Set time aside and begin the process of developing a creative habit. At the beginning, you may feel awkward, as though you were out on a first date. Do not give up; in time, awkwardness will dissipate and will be replaced by delight.
3. From time to time, check your progress of becoming creative by running through the five characteristics of the creative habit

mentioned earlier. Remember, you will know that you are becoming creative because you will feel inner joy and trust in your ability to resolve problems in unusual, new, surprisingly intelligent ways!

▶ **How Much Do You Avoid Being Creative? A Check-In**

1. Use a daily schedule to count the number of hours you spend watching television in a week.
2. Also, count the number of hours you spend every day surfing the Web, chatting on the Internet, or reading and writing e-mails.
3. Promise yourself to spend half of this time on television and the Internet and the other half doing something creative. Challenge yourself.

▶ **Dare to Be Creative: Some Ideas**

1. Do something you have wanted to do but have been postponing for a long time—for example, learn how to cook, work on your car, decorate a room in your house, develop a business idea, learn how to dance, begin a collection, learn how to make jewelry, or learn a foreign language. Follow your desire and listen to your heart.
2. Make it your habit to do something constructive or creative when you are in the grips of an unhelpful emotion, such as anger or sadness. Keep a log of your activities and progress. You will be amazed with the results in your life in a very short time. (*Hint:* watch Billy Elliot dance his anger off in the film by the same name.)
3. Join a group or a class and learn to do something with your hands— for example, pottery, gardening, baking, making jewelry, welding, making furniture, or knitting. Engage your body in the creative process, especially if you spend hours in an office.
4. If you like music, join a choir or learn an instrument. Organize music nights at your home. (A client of mine organized opera nights in her

home; her guests dressed up as famous opera characters and each performed his or her favorite aria. Then they had champagne and a lavish, home-cooked dinner.)

5. Finish a project that you began and abandoned some time ago. When you finish it, have a party to celebrate your completed creation.

6. There are hundreds of books and videotapes on crafts. Borrow a few from your public library and read through them. Find a craft or an activity that interests you and emerge yourself in it. Allow yourself to have fun in the process.

7. For Christmas, a birthday, or a special holiday, make your gifts for your family, friends, or other loved ones instead of buying them. They can be handmade cards, homemade cakes, a knitted sweater, a carved toy, a framed sketch, a collage—anything that excites your fantasy and gives you pleasure to create. Invite your family to do the same. Handmade gifts are special and very meaningful not only for those who receive them but also for those who make them. They are less likely to be thrown or put away, and they gain value as time goes by.

8. Take a cooking class or host a party of chefs, in which you invite friends to participate in a collaboratively cooked dinner. Rent a cooking video, open your recipe books, and have a lot of fun creating in the kitchen!

9. Interview three people whom you consider creative in any domain. Ask them about their creative habits and their relationship to their creativity. Ask them about the gifts they receive from their creative habits. Ask for advice on how to develop and maintain a creative habit.

10. Write the names of three people who drain your creative energy due to their actions, words, or attitudes. Resolve to limit your contact with these people to a minimum, and use your time to develop a creative habit.

11. List three activities that drain your creative energy or consume your time from having a creative habit. Resolve to stop engaging in those activities immediately and save your creative energy.

Things to Remember

- Creativity needs practice to grow into a habit.
- When you are creative, you feel free. When you feel free, you have an open mind that allows others the freedom of being creative. This makes you attractive and, very often, irresistible.
- Creativity is the fountain of joy.

12

Create Abundance

MOST OF US associate the concept of abundance with wealth and expendable material resources. This is why so many people understand abundance as the accumulation of excessive stuff. Those people are likely to have closets so cluttered that their stuff overflows into their garage, attic, basement, or shed or even their car. Some others need to experience abundance through inexhaustible availability of money and material goods that must flow like a waterfall and not be economized. Such people are very likely to waste not only their own but also others' financial and material resources. They are almost always in debt and almost always in the process of borrowing or asking for more. Finally, there are people with plenty of money and material resources who see abundance as an abstract concept, very hard to define let alone experience. One of them is Stephen, a client of mine, who asked for my help with a number of issues, including relationships and his finances.

Stephen was in his late forties, single, handsome, and very intelligent. He dressed impeccably and wore fine cologne. The first time we met, he shook my hand with confidence and smiled with great charm. Then he sat down and spoke about himself: he was the owner of several luxury car dealerships that he had opened after dropping out of a graduate program in

English literature. He lived alone in a three-story restored Victorian home that he had purchased outright. In addition, he owned a number of rental units around town, a boat that he docked in a private marina, two vintage cars, a sports convertible, a jeep that he used for hunting trips, and a first-class motorcycle. He liked jazz and fine restaurants. He read literature, poetry, and the *Financial Times*. He worked out in the town's most exclusive club. And he liked having big parties in his home, complete with live music and valet service. Theoretically, Stephen was a man out of a fairy tale. But in reality, Stephen was an impossible person to be with.

"I'm always worried about money," he told me during our first appointment. "I don't have enough. This is why I don't get married. I'm afraid that the moment I let a woman into my life, I'll go broke."

It was obvious that Stephen's fear of not having enough money was not based on reality. He was definitely a wealthy man who suffered from lack of abundance. To help him see that, I assigned him a reality check: I asked him to review his assets and liabilities and read his last three years' income tax reports. In our next appointment, Stephen looked embarrassed.

"I'm a lot richer than I thought," he said. "My personal account that I use just for petty cash has an average balance of twenty-seven thousand dollars. I won't get into my other accounts: the balances, there, are six- and seven-digit. For the last several years, I have been declaring an income of half a million dollars. Seriously, I don't know what my problem is."

"Do you declare your entire income?" I asked him.

"To tell you the truth, no, I don't," he answered.

"Do you give any money to charities, scholarships, or tithing?" I asked.

"Tithing?" he asked, surprised. "That's a church thing, and I work on Sundays!"

"Are you helping anyone through a no-interest loan?" I modified my question.

"Well, my accountant tells me it would lower my taxes, but I haven't done it yet," he responded bluntly.

"Tell me, Stephen," I asked seriously, "if you did not have this fear of being broke, what would you feel free to do that you cannot do now?"

He thought for a moment and then he answered, "I would feel safe enough to share myself and my life. I would be married with children. My house would be filled with my family, and I would be sharing what I own with them. I would not be alone, and I would have people to love and share my life with. I would feel secure in myself and free to give without being afraid of losing everything."

"*That* is abundance!" I said. "Did you notice how many times you said 'share'? Sharing creates abundance. Loving creates abundance. Stephen, *you* can create abundance in your life, if you acknowledge that you have enough to share and feel safe to do so through genuine acts of love!"

Stephen saw my point, and he did not resist it; he was a bright man who truly wanted to be happy. For the following few months, he worked diligently on breaking free from his fear of sharing and creating abundance in his life. He saw that abundance was not simply the possession of big sums of money but the joy of knowing that he had plenty to share with others through acts of love and kindness.

Feeling Safe to Give Love Creates Abundance

Stephen's problem was not that he did not have enough money but that he lacked the inner safety to show love through acts of giving. In order to find that inner safety, he had to let go of the wrong idea that accumulating money and being alone would give him the emotional fulfillment he yearned for. So he began practicing acts of generosity and kindness while he observed his and others' emotional reactions to his new behaviors. Gradually, he discovered that there was much joy in giving and that his money was not disappearing but was, in fact, multiplying: he was accepting new orders, getting new clients, and receiving new, more lucrative business propositions. Over time, Stephen felt that he was not alone. The spirit of generosity and love that he consciously expressed through his actions had replenished his inner emptiness and diminished his insecurity. The more Stephen felt safe within himself, the healthier his relationship with money became.

Stephen's case is somewhat similar to that of the mythical character Ebenezer Scrooge in Charles Dickens's classic *A Christmas Carol*. This short story is known worldwide, thanks to the numerous films it has inspired, dating as far back as 1908. As children, we all saw Scrooge in Christmas plays, on the big screen, and in television shows. His character also became the famous Scrooge McDuck, a favorite Walt Disney cartoon. Scrooge represents the person who is afraid of love. He creates his source of security by hoarding money, in the hopes that money will replenish the lack of love caused by his fear. But the more money he amasses, the more fearful he grows of love. Trapped in a vicious cycle of fearing love and hoarding money to feel secure, Scrooge lives isolated and despised by others, until, on one Christmas Eve, he has an experience that forces him to see that the essence of life hides not in amassed wealth but in the ability to give and receive love. Scrooge heals his fear of love by opening his heart *and* his wallet and giving of his wealth to those in need. This is how, for the first time this Christmas, he creates true abundance.

Citizen Kane is a story of another, modern Scrooge who used riches to fill an inner void. After a life of huge financial success, media magnate Charles Foster Kane is dying alone in his extravagant castle. With his last breath, he utters one word: "Rosebud." Its mysterious meaning becomes the theme of a reporter's investigation, since Mr. Kane had never mentioned it while alive. Gradually, through flashbacks into the life of a man with enormous ambition, power, and wealth, we arrive at his deep secret: *Rosebud* is a word associated with his deepest trauma, his sudden abandonment as a little boy by his mother, which left him forever wounded, afraid, and suspicious of love. Kane's fear of being abandoned was never healed, in spite of his amassed possessions that cluttered his entire mansion. The word *Rosebud* symbolizes his lost safety, his perished wholeness, and the love that he was never able to feel again. Kane spent his life amassing wealth, but he never experienced abundance. He died empty, alone, and longing for the only thing he could never possess: the joy of sharing love.

Abundance as a concept means nothing. In order for it to have meaning, it must be experienced as the joy of sharing love through giving actions. For us to create abundance, we must have the inner safety that showing love through giving actions will not destroy us. The key words here are *inner safety*: when we feel secure about our ability to love, we do not use our possessions as a source of emotional safety but as commodities that we enjoy sharing as we express love. Our joy then catalyzes a deep sense of fulfillment as we are able to experience everlasting wealth that transcends matter and fills our lives with spirit.

Practicing Truth Creates Abundance

Besides feeling safe to love, feeling safe to tell the truth also creates abundance. When we conceal the truth, the emotional and spiritual energy meant to create abundance is instead consumed in lying, reflecting a sense of poverty or the experience of material lack. For example, most people who consistently lie about their finances are either consumed by the fear of not having enough or are in serious debt that eventually catches up with them. In either case, they suffer from a sense of poverty. My client Stephen, mentioned earlier, systematically concealed the truth about his income from his tax reports. As a result, he was always worried about being audited and losing all his money to high penalties. His constant worry not only magnified his already distorted view of his financial situation, but it also burdened him with an ongoing sense of poverty that made it impossible for him to experience abundance.

Deliberate lying is the act of presenting an invented reality by distorting real facts. Usually, a person deliberately lies in order to achieve a hidden agenda. This hidden agenda represents the liar's deep desires that he or she denies, being afraid to pursue them following the rules of reality. For example, I once knew a young woman who had inherited millions, yet she always complained that she had no money. To make her condition more believable, she lived a substandard life and often asked for loans from friends, keeping them concerned about her financial situation. Her hidden needs were to be accepted by her peers, have their attention, and not face up to the responsibilities of being visibly wealthy while cultivating real friendships. But once the truth about her real financial situation was revealed, the results were devastating for her need for acceptance: her friends, angry that she had lied to them all along, withdrew from her, feeling betrayed and toyed with.

On another occasion, I worked with a newly wedded client who went into a profound depression, having discovered that her husband was not the person he had initially claimed to be. Prior to their wedding, he had presented himself as a wealthy businessman raising capital for a business expansion, but in reality, he was a white-collar criminal who embezzled from her own bank accounts and credit cards. When I asked her why she never checked her husband's background before they married, she said that she had also lied to him *a little* about her past, so she needed to let the sleeping dogs lie. Her need was to be happily married. She thought that she could fulfill it through lies. She paid a very high price for it.

When we try to fulfill a desire by manufacturing facts about a nonexistent reality, we violate the basic law of fulfillment: happiness can never be achieved through lies that reflect an invented reality but only through truthful intentions and actions that reflect the existing reality. Every time we violate this law, we are bound to create a real catastrophe, the magnitude of which varies depending on the severity of our lies. Usually, the more complex and prolonged our lying is, the bigger and more devastating the resulting catastrophe will be.

Two popular films illustrating how systematic lying not only cannot fulfill the need for abundance but eventually destroys personal and family lives are *Wall Street* and *Boiler Room*.

Wall Street's main character is Bud Fox, a young, ambitious Wall Street stockbroker who will stop at nothing to become rich. Looking for an opportunity to prove his talents, he approaches the extremely successful but ruthless broker Gordon Gekko, whose philosophy is that greed is good and who initiates Bud into a lifestyle that is suffused with wealth but that makes no room for honesty, truthfulness, or morality. Seduced by Gekko's methods of making fast and easy money, Bud espouses his belief that ambition for money can justify any means of acquiring it.

Hungry for money and too weak to stand by any moral principles, Bud gets involved in an illegal transaction for which he tries to use his own father, Carl Fox, a blue-collar worker, as his cover. Carl realizes his son's intentions and lets him know that his involvement with Gekko will destroy him. When Bud flaunts his illicit actions as necessary steps to success, his father sternly reminds him that he "does not measure a man's success by the size of his wallet" but by his ability to create something of himself and contribute positively to the lives of others. Sure enough, Carl's prophecy becomes true: Bud's illegal transactions are discovered, and, to his father's relief, he is arrested, tried, and sentenced to prison. This is how Bud is forced to see that certain things in life must be valued more than money: integrity is number one.

In *Boiler Room*, Seth Davis is a young, talented man seeking his father's recognition for his ability to become wealthy in a short period of time and without having to work hard. He sets out to achieve his goal by running an illegal casino in his Brooklyn apartment. Soon his skills in generating illicit income are noticed by the recruiters of a small brokerage firm that operates like a boiler room. Its brokers are under extreme pressure to make an unusually high number of sales per day, in exchange for enormous amounts of money. The company dangles an extremely lavish lifestyle in front of the young brokers to motivate them into excessive spending. Seth joins this environment eager to prove his skills, and soon he excels. It is not long before he discovers that he is participating in a large-scale fraud that will cost him his freedom. Like Bud Fox in *Wall Street*, Seth will also end up in jail. His experiment of creating a fortune by bending universal laws obviously failed. Not only did he not receive his father's acknowledgment, but he had to face his father as the judge involved in the investigation proceedings.

Lying can have far-reaching financial and social implications. For example, when companies deliberately lie about their finances, they invite a collapse with enormous ripple effects on the lives of their employees, and shareholders and on the financial community at large. Unfortunately, during the early years of the twenty-first century, the world witnessed a number of financial scandals due to the systematic distortion of economic facts practiced by a number of publicly held companies in order to create a short-lived illusion of wealth. The ensuing breakdowns and their devastating financial, emotional, and spiritual consequences for thousands of innocent individuals prove that intentional lying can never create or sustain true abundance.

When we practice truth, we feel—and become—safe. We have nothing to fear, and, therefore, we are free to enjoy and share our possessions. Knowing our net worth, having a clear picture of our assets and liabilities, and handling them with truthfulness and responsibility give us peace of mind. Practicing truth safeguards our integrity and assures us that we do not compromise our innate sense of doing what is right.

Practicing Gratitude Creates Abundance

You do not need to be a millionaire to experience abundance. All you need is to feel grateful for the life you have. When you feel gratitude for your life, you feel a natural need to share your gifts, whether material or spiritual, with those in need. The more grateful you are for your life, the freer you are to give. You can love more easily and laugh more spontaneously. You can comfort others without being afraid of losing your own serenity. When you share your material and spiritual gifts with others, you improve their lives. This creates a flow of abundance that transforms the world around you and comes back to you in manifold. When you give in abundance, you receive in abundance.

An epic about how gratitude generates abundance is the classic *It's a Wonderful Life*. Considered mainly a Christmas story, this film is, indeed, a metaphor about the true meaning of Christmas, which is the celebration of our God-given ability to share our spirit with our fellow humans and touch their lives in magnificent ways. The main hero is George Bailey, a man born and raised in Bedford Falls, a small town almost entirely owned and controlled by a ruthless real estate magnate, Mr. Potter. As a boy, George saves lives, prevents disasters, and helps everyone in need. Everyone loves George, but George's dream is always to leave Bedford Falls. On the day of his brother's high school graduation party, he meets Mary, a beautiful young woman he has known since they were both kids. Trying to impress her with his ambitions and confidence about the future, George tells her his grand plan:

I'm shakin' the dust of this crummy little town off my feet and I'm gonna see the world. Italy, Greece, the Parthenon, the Colosseum. Then, I'm comin' back here to go to college and see what they know. And then I'm gonna build things. I'm gonna build airfields, I'm gonna build skyscrapers a hundred stories high, I'm gonna build bridges a mile long.

But life has other plans for George. Not only is he destined to never leave his hometown, but fate has it that he will become his father's successor at Bailey Building and Loan, a small company that enables low-income families to become homeowners and stop renting from Mr. Potter. George will never build mile-long bridges, but he will become Mary's husband and the father of their four children, and he will create Bailey Park to give low-income families the opportunity to own their own homes and leave Potter's rundown rentals. George gives poor people the dignity and pride of home ownership. And while his clients bless him for all the abundance he creates in their lives, ruthless Potter is trying to find a way to destroy the Building and Loan.

Potter's opportunity to harm George finally arrives one Christmas Eve. A large sum of money that belongs to George is accidentally lost and then found by Potter, who keeps it, knowing that this will hurt George. Indeed, George is suddenly faced with a financial crisis that sends him into a downward spiral in which he sees suicide as the only way out.

Desperate and abandoned by luck, George walks to a bridge, ready to throw himself in the river. But he is not allowed to end his life: God has assigned to Clarence, a second-class angel with no wings, the mission of saving George's life. This is the final test the angel must pass in order to earn his wings and be promoted to first class. So as George is about to jump, Clarence suddenly falls from the sky into the river and appears as a drowning man shouting for help, interrupting George's fatal move. Forgetting about his own suicide, George jumps into the river to save Clarence—just as he did when he saved his little brother from drowning when he fell through the ice when they were kids.

Back on the shore, as they are getting dry, Clarence reveals his identity and his mission: he has been sent by God to save George's life in order to be promoted to a winged angel. Disappointed that he did not die, George wishes he had never existed—he sees no point to his life. This gives Clarence a great idea: he will show George how the world would have been if he had never been born. So he takes him on a tour through Bedford Falls as the town would have been if George had never existed.

That town is called Pottersville, and it reflects the nature of Mr. Potter, who controls everything now. Pottersville is a miserable, dangerous, money-driven place, filled with bars, casinos, and nightclubs. No one smiles, and everyone is suspicious and defensive. The streets, filled with angry drunks, are patrolled by the police, who maintain order through violence and arrests. There are no children playing in backyards because there are no houses built by George. In the place of Bailey Park there is a dark cemetery, where George's brother is buried. He drowned in his ice-slipping accident because George had never been born to save him.

Shocked at what he sees, George gets the point: he was never born to touch the lives of his townspeople with his beautiful spirit.

"You've been given a great gift, George," Clarence tells him. "A chance to see what the world would be like without you. You see, George," he adds, "you really had a wonderful life. Don't you see what a mistake it would be to just throw it away?"

Regretting that he had ever thought of ending his life, George begs God to bring him back to *his* life. His prayer is answered, and George returns home to the biggest surprise of his life: the whole town, having heard about the lost money, is bringing their savings to help him with his crisis. Donations are pouring in, as every person George has ever helped is giving generously, returning the abundance George created through his actions. Grateful to have such loving friends, George realizes that his life is, indeed, wonderful. Amidst the merry crowd, his brother, Harry, raises a glass and toasts to his brother's gift for creating abundance: "To my brother, George, the richest man in town."

At that moment, a bell rings. Clarence had told George, "Every time a bell rings on earth, an angel gets his wings in heaven."

It's a Wonderful Life was director Frank Capra's favorite movie. He always wanted to tell a story about the true meaning of life. Interestingly enough, the director never made money from this movie; the public did not like it when it first came out, and the film soon drifted into oblivion.

Several years later, due to the producers' negligence, the film became public domain, and suddenly, all television stations began showing it during the Christmas season. It was not too long before hundreds of millions of people embraced it as a classic that becomes even more popular as the years go by. It is a strange coincidence that the fate of the film is identical with the story it tells: that we create true abundance through sharing acts of love—that money is not the end but a means of achieving it.

It's a Wonderful Life's message also goes beyond inspiring gratitude for the life we are given; it shows that good depends solely on our conscious acts of kindness in order to prevail over evil in the world. We are the only creatures capable of seeing the greatness of our life and practicing our gratitude through conscious actions. That is how we bring goodness to earth—or, to use the film's analogy, we help an angel get a promotion in heaven. Clarence got his wings in heaven only when George truly acknowledged the value of his life on earth. Up to that point, he was doing the right thing, in part because he was forced by the circumstances. But once he recognized himself as an agent of good capable of touching the lives of so many people, he also saw the higher purpose in the life he was given to lead. Only then did all the strange accidents and coincidences that marked his path and forced him to take turns against his will make perfect sense. There was a plan for him after all: George was born to practice kindness and create abundance.

Most of us are not famous or rich. We may never see our face on the cover of a popular magazine, we may never receive a national award, and we may never win the lottery. We may feel that our lives are ordinary, and we may occasionally resent the fact that we did not accomplish the great fantasies we had as children. Sometimes we may wonder why life forced us to take turns we did not really want to take, bending our will and making us obey rules that we did not know existed. But if we take a moment and imagine how things would have been if we had never existed, then it will all make sense: we will then see that we are given this life to discover the good in everything that comes our way, even if it is painful; to discover the courage to love, the strength to forgive, the power to create, and the wisdom to remember that we are not alone; and to stay connected to our Great Source, knowing that we are here to express magnificence and generate abundance in a universe created and sustained through the eons, thanks to unceasing, unstoppable, abundant love.

Reel Fulfillment in Action

∙∙∙

Movie Time! ▶ *Watch a Movie for Fun, Learn a Lesson of Life*

The following lists of films are about different aspects of abundance. Choose a movie from each list, and watch them alone or with your group. Think about the questions that follow each list. Write down your answers, and discuss them with your group.

Movies About Scrooge

A Christmas Carol (1951), directed by Brian Desmond-Hurst
A Christmas Carol (1971), directed by Richard Williams
The Muppet Christmas Carol (1992), directed by Brian Henson
Scrooge (1970), directed by Ronald Neame
Scrooged (1988), directed by Richard Donner

Questions to Answer

1. What are your fears of not having enough?
2. How realistic are your fears?
3. In what way did this film inspire you regarding the way you see abundance?

Movies About Truth, Lying, and Abundance

Boiler Room (2000), directed by Ben Younger
The Firm (1993), directed by Sydney Pollack
Glengarry Glen Ross (1992), directed by James Foley
Intolerable Cruelty (2003), directed by Joel Coen
Money for Nothing (1993), directed by Ramón Menéndez
Office Space (1999), directed by Mike Judge
Rogue Trader (1999), directed by James Dearden
Wall Street (1987), directed by Oliver Stone

Questions to Answer

1. Is there an area in your financial life where you need to be truthful? What is that area?

2. What did you learn from this film that can help you practice truth in your financial life?

Movies About Love, Gratitude, and Abundance
Citizen Kane (1941), directed by Orson Welles
The Emperor's New Clothes (2001), directed by Alan Taylor
In America (2002), directed by Jim Sheridan
It's a Wonderful Life (1946), directed by Frank Capra
Magnolia (1999), directed by Paul Thomas Anderson
The Man Without a Face (1993), directed by Mel Gibson
Pay It Forward (2000), directed by Mimi Leder

Questions to Answer
1. In what ways did the film influence your attitude toward abundance?
2. How did the film inspire you to make changes in the ways you practice love and gratitude?
3. What are you most grateful for, and how do you show your gratitude?
4. How do you show kindness? What do you do that makes others happy without asking anything in return?

Creating Abundance ▶ *Exercises and Activities*

▶ **Practicing Truth with Money**

In Chapter 7, you completed an exercise asking you to take stock of your finances as a practice of getting grounded in the now. This exercise builds on that one in order to help you stay on course and create abundance while keeping a truthful relationship with money.

1. **Find out your net worth.** If you do not know your net worth, this is your opportunity to find out. Calculate all your liquid and nonliquid assets (this means

all the cash you have available and the current value of all your material possessions). Now calculate all your liabilities (the total balance of your debts, including all loans, credit cards, and mortgages). Subtract the value of your liabilities from your assets. The balance is your net worth.

Ideally, your net worth should be positive. But if your liabilities are higher than your assets, you may have a negative net worth. What are your reactions to your finding? Are you pleased, somewhat disappointed, or just surprised? What is your net worth telling you about your relationship with money?

2. **Find out where you spend your money.** Go over your checkbook and credit card bills of the last three months. Also, go through all your cash receipts of the last three months. If you do not keep receipts, make it a habit to collect them. Notice the trend in your expenses reflecting purchases made on impulse or without your conscious intent. For example, you may have monthly charges for subscriptions that you no longer use and you must discontinue. Notice how much money you spend on impulse on unintentional purchases. Write down and immediately implement three changes to streamline your expenses.

3. **Balance your checkbooks.** This means all your checkbooks, to the penny. If you need to learn how to balance your checkbook, do not be embarrassed—you are not alone. Call your bank or your accountant and ask for help. They can definitely offer advice or recommend someone who can teach you how to balance your checkbooks. The simplest reward from mastering this practice is that no check of yours will ever bounce again. A more complex reward is that you will feel a sense of self-empowerment and enhance your ability to create abundance.

4. **Find out your FICO score.** To conduct almost any kind of business today, from getting a credit card to borrowing money for your first home, you need good credit. This exercise will teach you a lot about your credit score and will help you implement a discipline of improving it, if it needs improvement. An easy way to do this is to visit myfico.com and follow the directions.

5. **Pay off your debts.** If you have long-standing debts, create a payment plan and make it a priority to pay them off. You can never enjoy abundance if you are in debt. Also, the discipline of paying off your debts helps you stay on top of your finances and builds your confidence in your ability to become debt free.

▶ **Seeing the Good and Being Grateful**

This exercise can bring significant relief to chronically tense relationships in the family or work environment. When you complete it, you will be able to recognize good in people with whom you have strained relationships and see the ways in which their presence has benefited your life.

1. Make a list of three people from your work or family environment with whom you have a love-hate relationship.
2. Mentally, go through each person's character and remember their positive aspects. Write down at least three.
3. Write how their positive qualities influenced your life: what is the good that these people have brought to you in spite of their shortcomings?
4. Acknowledge the goodness of these people, and if possible, let them know how their positive qualities have enriched your life.

▶ **Saying Thanks**

Make a list of all the things you are grateful for in your life:

I am grateful for:

These five personal qualities, which have helped me to fulfill my dreams:

_____

_____

These five people, whose help at first seemed irrelevant but, in hindsight, had a significant influence on my path: _____

_____

_____

These five unexpected experiences or moments, which had a significant influence on my path: _____

_____

_____

▶ Seeing the Best in the Worst

Make a list of the five biggest difficulties or challenges you have faced in your life. What were the biggest gifts in the area of personal or spiritual growth that you experienced as a result of your difficulties? As you list them, examine how they helped you build character and become stronger and more mature. Write down your responses to your observations.

▶ Being Grateful for Being You

Watch the film *It's a Wonderful Life*. Afterward, following George's example, go through an imaginary tour of your life assuming that you had never existed: how would the world be without you? Just as George did in the movie, revisit your childhood and remember every good thing that you did for others and how your actions impacted their lives. Continue revisiting all the years of your life up to today. Write down the names of all the people whose lives you have touched. What did you do for them? How did your presence make their lives better? Write down everything you did for each person, as you remember it. How would those people's lives be today if you had never been there to touch them in the way you did?

This is a very powerful exercise to help you get in touch with your own effectiveness and importance in other people's lives and appreciate yourself for the value you have added to this world. Celebrate your discoveries, and acknowledge your contributions in creating abundance in this world!

▶ Creating Abundance

If the preceding exercise has motivated you to impact more people's lives by sharing your gifts and bringing abundance to their lives, here are some suggestions:

1. Join a program of volunteers in a hospital, a home for the elderly, a soup kitchen, and so on.
2. Become a spiritual mentor to a child and a role model of healthy personal growth.
3. Share without charging money your knowledge or expertise with those who need it but cannot pay for it.
4. Become a mentor to someone who can use your help to improve an area of his or her life.
5. Help a person overcome a difficult condition by being present for him or her.
6. Smile at the people who live or work with you, and mean it. See how your smile affects the way others treat you.

▶ **Keep a Promise**

Fulfill a promise you made to someone a long time ago but did not deliver. Wait to receive the benefits of fulfilling your words with actions.

Things to Remember

- The more you practice gratitude through generosity of spirit, the more abundance you create for yourself and others.
- Gratitude is the action of sharing what you have in abundance with those who truly need it.
- Find something good in everything you do not like, and you create immediate abundance.

Appendix A
Alphabetical List of Emotions

accepted
accepting
accomplished
acknowledged
admired
alive
amused
applauded
appreciated
appreciative
approved of
attracted
attractive
capable
challenged
clear (not confused)
close
competent
confident

connected
content
creative
developed
educated
empowered
excited
focused
forgiven
forgiving
free
fulfilled
grown *or* growing
guided
guilt free
happy
heard
helped
helpful

important

in charge

included

in control

independent

interested

interesting

knowledgeable

lighthearted

listened to

loved

loving

needed

noticed

open

optimistic

pleased

pleasured

powerful

productive

protected

proud

reassured

recognized

relaxed

relieved

respected

responsible

rewarded

safe

satisfied

secure

seen

significant

stimulated

successful

supported

treated fairly

understanding

understood

useful

valued

welcomed

worthy

Appendix B

The Six Life Spheres of Human Needs

Material and Physical Sphere

clothing
financial prosperity
food
material security
physical health
physical security
shelter

Ego and Identity Sphere

achievement
challenge
competence
culture
distinction
ego
freedom of expression
independence

possession
privacy
property
recognition

Social Sphere

acknowledgment
affiliation
citizenship
community
competition
cooperation
family
hierarchy
history
legacy
justice
power

recognition
status
success
work

Sphere of Knowledge and Intellect

communication
ideas
information
intellect
knowledge
language
science
strategy, organization,
   structure
technology

Sphere of Emotions

appreciation
belonging
community
entertainment
family

home
love
mating
parenting
play
pleasure
respect

Spiritual Sphere

art
beauty
creativity
dignity
faith
holiness
ideals
innocence
personal meaning
purity
religion
reverence
ritual
self-awareness
sense of higher purpose

Appendix C
Alphabetical List of Human Needs

acceptance
admiration
adventure
appreciation
art
beauty
belongingness
challenge
change
clarity
collaboration
community
competence
completion
connectedness
control
creativity
distinction
education

emotional and spiritual strength
emotional warmth
empowerment
expansion
expression *or* communication
financial stability
forgiveness (to give or receive)
freedom (emotional, intellectual,
    and spiritual)
growth
help
home
honesty
identity (personal, sexual,
    and social)
initiative
joy
justice or fairness
lightheartedness

love

material stability

nurturance

peace

play

pleasure

power

pride

privacy

prosperity

purity

reassurance

rebellion

recognition

responsibility

rest

security

self-confidence

self-worth

sharing

simplicity

social recognition

social support

stimulation

structure

support

transformation

understanding
   (give or receive)

validation

Appendix D
THE SCAR Grid of a Self-Sabotaging Pattern

TRIGGERING HINTS	EMOTIONS	SENSATIONS	COGNITIONS	ACTIONS	RESULTS
What happened? (Describe an event or a series of events, coincidences, or incidents that activated the self-sabotaging pattern.)	How did you feel? (Use the list of emotions in Appendix A for help.)	What physical reactions did you experience? (Describe what you felt in your body.)	What were your ■ automatic thoughts ■ painful memories ■ other associations	What did you do?	What results did your actions produce? (This is your resulting reality.)

Appendix E

ABCDE Pattern-Correction Steps Grid

ADMIT SOLE RESPONSIBILITY	**B**REATHE BEFORE REACTING TO TRIGGERS	**C**LEANSE YOUR LIFE OF NEGATIVE EMOTIONAL INFLUENCES	**D**EVELOP CONNECTIONS WITH POSITIVE ENERGY SOURCES	**E**XECUTE PLAN OF CONCRETE, CONSISTENT FULFILLMENT-APPROPRIATE ACTIONS
Sabotaging pattern:	List of triggers:	1. People:	1. In your environment:	List of actions:
		2. Places:		
Unfulfilled need:			2. In yourself:	
		3. Activities:		

Index